Constructing Cromwell

Constructing Cromwell traces the complex and shifting popular images of Oliver Cromwell from his first appearance as a public figure in the mid-1640s through the period of his power to his death and eventual disinterment after the restoration of the monarchy. The meaning and impact of this enigmatic figure have long been debated in the context of mid-seventeenth-century crisis but contemporary representations of Cromwell have largely been neglected. Cromwellian print, Laura Knoppers argues, transformed the courtly forms of Caroline ceremony, portraiture, and panegyric and in turn complicated and altered the cultural forms available to Charles II. The book draws on extensive archival research, including manuscript sources, startling print ephemera, and visual artifacts. Placing canonical authors such as Milton, Marvell, Waller, and Dryden alongside such neglected writers as George Wither and Payne Fisher, Knoppers demonstrates how literary texts both respond and contribute to political and cultural change.

LAURA LUNGER KNOPPERS is Associate Professor of English at Pennsylvania State University. She is author of *Historicizing Milton: Spectacle, Power, and Poetry in Restoration England* (1994).

Constructing Cromwell

Ceremony, Portrait, and Print
1645–1661

Laura Lunger
Knoppers

CAMBRIDGE
UNIVERSITY PRESS

PUBLISHED BY THE PRESS SYNDICATE OF THE UNIVERSITY OF CAMBRIDGE
The Pitt Building, Trumpington Street, Cambridge CB2 1RP, United Kingdom

CAMBRIDGE UNIVERSITY PRESS
The Edinburgh Building, Cambridge CB2 2RU, UK http://www.cup.cam.ac.uk
40 West 20th Street, New York, NY 10011–4211, USA http://www.cup.org
10 Stamford Road, Oakleigh, Melbourne 3166, Australia

First published 2000

Printed in the United Kingdom at the University Press, Cambridge

Typeset in Dante (MT) 11.5/14.5pt, in QuarkXPress™ [SE]

A catalogue record for this book is available from the British Library

Library of Congress cataloguing in publication data
Knoppers, Laura Lunger.
Constructing Cromwell: ceremony, portrait, and print, 1645–1661
Laura Lunger Knoppers.
p.   cm.
Includes bibliographical references and index.
ISBN 0 521 66261 3 (hardback)
1. Cromwell, Oliver, 1599–1658 – Public opinion.   2. Great Britain –
History – Commonwealth and Protectorate, 1649–1660 – Historiography.
3. English literature – Early modern, 1500–1700 – History and
criticism.   4. Rites and ceremonies – Great Britain – History – 17th
century.   5. Public opinion – Great Britain – History, 17th century.
6. Political satire, English – History and criticism.   7. Great
Britain – History – Restoration, 1660–1688.   8. Heads of state – Public
opinion – Great Britain.   9. Cromwell, Oliver, 1599–1658 – In
literature.   10. Cromwell, Oliver, 1599–1658 – Portraits.
11. Puritans – Public opinion – Great Britain.   12. Cromwell, Oliver,
1599–1658 – Death.   1. Title.
DA427.K66   2000
941.06′4′092–dc21   [B]   99-16228   CIP

ISBN 0 521 66261 3 hardback

For Gary, Theresa, and David

Contents

Illustrations

ix

Acknowledgments

In researching and writing this book, I have incurred many debts. A timely fellowship from the Pew Foundation, Evangelical Scholars Fund, made it possible for me to spend 1995–96 in Oxford undertaking research at the Bodleian and at a range of other libraries, galleries, and museums in Britain. A sabbatical from Penn State provided the time to complete the initial draft of the manuscript. Research and travel in both the early and late stages of the project were generously funded by the Office of Research and Graduate Studies, College of Liberal Arts, Penn State, and The Institute for the Arts and Humanistic Studies, Penn State; I want especially to thank the Director of the Institute, Robert Edwards, for his consideration and support.

Colleagues and friends on both sides of the Atlantic have offered encouragement and advice. For their interest and hospitality during my year in England, I want to thank Thomas Corns, David Norbrook, Joad Raymond, Nigel Smith, Gerald MacLean, Michael Millard, John Morrill, Kevin Sharpe, and Blair Worden. Closer to home, I have benefited from the insights offered by the fall 1996 Milton seminar, hosted at Yale University by Annabel Patterson. My former dissertation director, Barbara Lewalski, continues to provide a model of exemplary scholarship and to offer clear-sighted and sensible counsel. I have appreciated conversations on the book project with other friends from my Harvard graduate school days, especially Mary Crane, Emily Bartels, Naomi Miller, and John Farrell. My Penn State department head, Don Bialostosky, has consistently and strongly supported my work. My colleagues in the early modern period at Penn State have provided a stimulating and sustaining atmosphere in which to work, and I would like to thank in particular Dan Beaver, Philip Jenkins, Francesca Royster, Garrett Sullivan, and Linda Woodbridge. I owe much to Patrick Cheney, who kindly read the manuscript in its entirety, responding with cogent and judicious advice. As my research assistant in 1997–98, Don-John Dugas did outstanding work investigating the visual materials, and also made careful and thoughtful recommendations on an early version of the manuscript. Chad Hayton's incisive reading of a late version of the manuscript helped me to sharpen and clarify my argument. Other graduate students have been attentive to my ideas about Oliver Cromwell and insightful in their responses and observations; I particularly want to thank Jane Baston, Richard Cunningham, and Anne Fisher.

I also appreciate the librarians and curators in Britain and America whose patience in answering questions and resourcefulness in tracking down out-of-the-way materials facilitated my work on manuscripts and visual artifacts. I am particularly grateful to John Goldsmith, curator of the Cromwell Museum, Huntingdon, for his assistance and generosity in providing access to a wide range of archival materials in the museum's holdings. For their courteous assistance, I would also like to thank the staffs at the Bodleian Library, Oxford; the Ashmolean Museum, Oxford; the British Museum; the British Library; Cambridge University Library; the Museum of London; the University of Aberdeen; Westminster Abbey Library; the National Portrait Gallery Picture Library; the Folger Shakespeare Library; Beinecke Rare Books Library; the Huntington Library; and the Penn State Rare Books Room.

The Latin translations and notes for Payne Fisher's *Irenodia Gratulatoria* and *Inauguratio Olivariana* were meticulously done by Jennifer Ebbeler. My own translations, for the remaining Latin texts, were much aided by the erudition and kind advice of Paul Harvey, my colleague in ancient history and classics.

Two anonymous readers for Cambridge University Press provided trenchant criticism and detailed and valuable direction on the manuscript. It has been a pleasure to work with Josie Dixon, who has been unfailingly helpful, attentive, and kind.

My husband, Gary, read multiple drafts of various chapters with perspicuity and care. He has borne the various prolonged stages of this project with patience and good humor, and I owe much to his emotional and intellectual support. I am dedicating this book to Gary and to our two children, Theresa and David, who for the past five years have heard a great deal about Oliver Cromwell and about this project, warts and all.

Portions of the book appeared earlier in "The Politics of Portraiture: Oliver Cromwell and the Plain Style," *Renaissance Quarterly* 51 (1998), 1283–319 and are reproduced by permission. Also broadly related to this book project are two forthcoming studies: "Noll's Nose: Body Politics in Cromwellian England," in Amy Boesky and Mary Crane, eds., *Form and Reform in Renaissance England: Essays in Honor of Barbara Kiefer Lewalski* (University of Delaware Press), and "'Sing old Noll the brewer': Royalist Satire and Social Inversion in Cromwellian England, 1648–1664." *The Seventeenth Century*.

A note on texts

When quoting from early texts, I have retained the original spelling and punctuation but have modernized u and v, i and j. Dates are given as old style, although the year has been taken to begin on 1 January.

Introduction

In June 1657, James Fraser, a Scots Episcopalian, arrived in London just in time to view the second protectoral inauguration of Oliver Cromwell. Fraser offers a first-hand account of the ceremony in Westminster Hall, "where the Parlement sat in ordere to the solemn Installment of the Protector with the greatest Pomp and Magnificence could be contrived."[1] Having described the ritual administration of the oath and the delivering of the ermine robe, Bible, sword, and scepter to Cromwell, Fraser turns to the public response: "all these Solemn Ceremonies being performed and finished an Herald of arms with 3 Trumpeters one in livery sounding proclaimed him Lord Protector of England, Scotland, Ireland, and ye Dominions thereto Belonging . . . the Trumpets sounded again and the people with several acclamations & lowd shouts crying God Save the Lord Protector."[2] Fraser attests to the popular acclaim, although he himself remains skeptical: "I am not to judge if this was with all their hearts but sure it was not with mine though a wittness and Spectator."[3]

In Fraser's account, printed texts supplemented the public ceremony: "[Cromwell] is now adored, admired, addresses made to him. Panagyricks & encomiums made to him. His Inauguration and instalement printed and sold upon the Exchange set out by a flattering Spectator. Severall bookes and Pamphlets printed in his praise."[4] Fraser recounts the various panegyrics, in his view "their pens palpably fraught with flatteryes," as well as material reproductions of Cromwell's visual image: "his statues set up in severall places," and "his picture in tortishell caskets Issued in Colloures nay in silver and gold meddalls."[5] Asserting that one was not "safe" without a picture of Cromwell, Fraser links representation and power: "and what were his pictures but to paint out his power?"[6]

Yet such "flatteryes" did not stand alone. Fraser points out that although

Cromwell "had his flies and flatterers that fawned on him, so also his Satyrest that rated & flouted him."[7] Such satires apparently evaded the printing restrictions: "these comming out daylie in print although the Print offices were stricklie noticed & adverted too."[8] Such satires attacked Cromwell on topics that ranged from the alleged infidelities of his wife to his own sexual escapades with the wife of John Lambert ("old Noll & young Nell"). Another popular subject of ridicule was the size and color of Cromwell's nose, as in a "bitter invective" from the time of the Dutch war that jeered: "Cromwel Cromwell lend us thy Nose, to fire the Navy that doth us oppose . . . Thy nose it will serve us in sted of a Taper; To light the Shipes back again over the main."[9] Finally, Fraser points to a communal use of writing in a satiric poem "set upon whithall gate" that begins: "If any Stranger do but ask what Cromwell doth here / He's Profitable to the state for he can brewe good beere."[10] Oral account, manuscript, printed text, public ceremony, and portraiture intersect in the dynamic process of representing the Lord Protector.

Fraser's account provides an important window on the political culture of the 1650s, including ceremony, visual image, and multiple uses of print: praise and satire, legitimation and attack, reflection and interpretation. Such an account belies the judgmental view that print under the Protectorate was dull and official, restricted to legitimating the new status quo. Nor, in Fraser's account, is Cromwell simply assimilated to monarchy, a king in all but name. Rather, the intersection of text, display, and material objects reveals a vibrant public opinion and critical discourse.

This book traces how print culture interacts with other forms of culture to construct a shifting and diverse image of Oliver Cromwell.[11] The materiality of print transformed Caroline ceremony and portraiture, breaking down the distinction between elite and popular culture in representations of Oliver Cromwell. Paintings became engravings which reappeared in satiric squib and ballad. Ceremony, appropriated from monarchical forms, was in turn contested, interpreted, and disseminated in newsbook and pamphlet, visual image and printed verse. Moving into the public sphere, the Cromwellian image moved out of the control of the court into a world of popular print.

Scholars have long debated the meaning and impact of Oliver Cromwell in the context of mid-seventeenth-century crisis.[12] Yet literary critics, historians, and art historians alike have largely neglected contemporary representations of Cromwell. Although literary scholars have explored the iconography of a wide range of monarchs, no single study treats representations of Cromwell, unique and controversial as a non-monarchical head of state.[13] Recent literary studies of the once-neglected 1640s and 1650s have begun to address Cromwellian literature, but only under other rubrics and not in relation to different forms of Cromwellian representation.[14] Art historians have dismissed the portraiture as an inept aping of monarchical forms.[15] With some notable exceptions, historians have not attended to the production, circulation, and impact of Cromwell's contemporary image.[16] Drawing upon a wide range of verbal and visual images of Cromwell from 1645 (when John Cleveland offered the first extended satiric sketch) to 1661 (the exhuming and immediate printed reactions), I trace the intersection of print culture and political power in a period of crisis and change.

Unlike the monarchs who preceded and followed him, Cromwell did not tightly control the production of his own image. Civil ceremony and portraiture continued in the Interregnum, but they were dispersed, popularized, and recast in print. Popular print constructed Cromwell's image from the margins, in a commercial and political context. Printed texts were in themselves performative, not simply representing but constructing this new authority, which was not based on heredity or divine right. Print both appealed to and constituted the political subject, not as passive spectator or witness but as participant, authority, and critic. Cromwellian print transformed the courtly and aristocratic forms of Caroline masque, portrait, and ceremony and, in turn, complicated and altered the cultural forms available to Charles II.

Cromwellian ceremony, portraiture, and print are part of the larger picture of mid-seventeenth-century print, politics, and aesthetics much debated by recent scholars. Revisionist questioning of the long-term social, political, and economic causes and effects of civil war has moved recently into questions about constitutional theory and its relation to aesthetics.[17] Were there cultural differences leading up to or emerging from the mid-century crisis? Was Caroline court culture escapist or exemplary; self-regarding or politically engaged?[18] Did republican aesthetics arise belatedly and only in opposition to a monarchical Cromwell, or was there an alternative tradition dating back to the 1620s?[19] There is likewise matter for discussion and debate in the 1640s: did the drama, inherently royalist, disappear, or has literary criticism written out a dynamic tradition that took such forms as dialogue and playlet?[20] Does a new kind of revolutionary readership develop?[21] Was there a revolution in literary forms?[22] The question of aesthetics is even more contested for the 1650s: did the republic "invent" itself culturally through icon, ceremony, and symbol or did monarchical images continue to dominate?[23] Was Cromwell himself a king in all but name, aping monarchical portraiture and ceremony, or did he retain an iconoclastic and reforming impulse to the end?[24]

Early scholarly accounts of a court–country cultural divide and of Caroline court culture as aloof and isolated from politics have given way to more nuanced views of the politics of Stuart court culture.[25] R. Malcolm Smuts, for instance, asserts that "the stereotype of [a] totally isolated and unresponsive regime, living in an atmosphere of unreality, is at best totally exaggerated."[26] But the most massive rehabilitation of Caroline culture has been by an historian, Kevin Sharpe, who argues that Caroline masques and other cultural forms were not escapist, a withdrawal from harsh political reality, but rather "the most powerful and perhaps last manifestation of the Renaissance belief in the didactic power of images."[27]

Such work has challenged the court–country divide and altered the traditional view of Caroline court culture as inward-looking and insular. But breaking down the bipolar model and rigid stereotypes does not mean that there were no significant cultural differences or changes during or after the civil wars. If the Caroline image was more widely circulated than was once thought, that image was nonetheless one of divine-right power and majesty. Charles shaped and directed portraiture and ceremony in church and state, and criticisms of the king in these forms were tempered and oblique.[28] In comparison to the heterogeneous and widely dispersed print images of Oliver Cromwell, Caroline images are strikingly court-based and hierarchical, at least until the 1640s. In my view, Cromwellian print images show not only continuity but genuine transformation and change.

Constructions of Cromwell in the 1650s thus also present a new facet of print culture, more widely considered, in the early modern period. Much of the work on print culture in the sixteenth and early seventeenth centuries has focused on the broad historical shift from manuscript to print, stressing a move toward fixity and totalization.[29] But a study of print in the later seventeenth century must engage very different issues: not the stigma of print, but its potential power of opposition or subversion as well as legitimation.[30]

With the abolition of Star Chamber in July 1641 and the temporary end of licensing, an explosion of print opened up an emergent public sphere of political opinion and debate in England.[31] After the prodigious output of pamphlets and newsbooks in the civil war years, both the parliament and the army tried to bring the press under control. Successive laws became increasingly restrictive, and by the mid-1650s only officially approved newsbooks were permitted. Focusing on restrictions and the reduction of news-books, historians of print have characterized the 1650s as a time of repres-sion. Frederick Siebert writes that "whether or not Cromwell was more tolerant than his supporters is a moot question; the fact remains that the Protector brooked no public discussion or criticism in the form of news-books."[32] John Feather asserts that "the newsbooks of the last five years of the Interregnum are as dull and uninformative as only such newspapers can be."[33] Yet such a view is too negative, as is Feather's conclusion that "[John] Lilburne's fears were now fully justified: Cromwell was indeed more tyran-nical than Charles and Canterbury."[34] Feather himself provides evidence to the contrary when he states that "Thomason's 23,000 pamphlets are a more enduring monument of the Interregnum than any of the political or mili-tary manoeuvrings of those decades; after that experience the book trade could never be the same again."[35] Indeed, a wide range of different kinds of texts, not just newsbooks, reflected the politicization of print in the 1650s.[36]

Legal restrictions, then, belie to some extent the complexity and range of print in the 1650s. Cheap print and intermittent severity with offenders gave writing considerable power. The effectiveness of print also relied, of course, on literacy. David Cressy's important work on signatures concludes that by the 1640s male literacy had reached 30 percent nationally, and about 70 to 80 percent in London; more recent scholars, noting that reading was taught before writing, suggest that the literacy rates may have been even higher.[37] Evidence points, then, to a wide market for the circulation and appropriation of printed texts.

In the print culture of the 1650s in England, we find not fixity but its oppo-site: fierce conflict. Print as an instrument of protectoral authority opened up that authority to public debate: in the very act of representing Cromwell, print made Cromwell vulnerable to misrepresentation and rejection. Print created new roles for readers in the 1650s, contributing to an emergent public sphere of political opinion and debate. Nonetheless, the 1650s also complicate the Habermasian model that charts a linear move from theatrical representation to a bourgeois public sphere focused on writing and rational debate. Print circulated rather than superceded the cer-emonial display and showed both liberalizing and conservative effects.[38]

In tracing the production, circulation, and reception of printed texts, I draw also upon Roger Chartier's extensive work on the history of print culture in early modern France.[39] In particular, Chartier stresses the useful concept of "appropriation" to distinguish between production and recep-tion, between attempts to shape public opinion and those (elusive) popular views in themselves.[40] I extend this concept of appropriation to the Cromwellian borrowing and transformation of monarchical forms. Like Chartier, I wish to look at print culture in its richness and multiplicity, to trace the forms in which power was constituted, contested, and legitimated in times of crisis and change. How were images of Cromwell produced, circulated, and consumed? How was print related to civic ceremony? How did print broadcast and interpret portraiture? To what extent did Cromwell shape his own image? How did Cromwell not only appropriate monarchical precedent from James and Charles I but change the forms of power available to Charles II?

Such questions yield some unexpected and surprising answers. Print culture interacts with manuscript, oral performance, and visual display in constructing a Cromwellian image. Print publicized both portraiture and ceremony, eluding centralization and control. Indeed, Cromwell's own plain style increasingly contrasted with the panegyrics and portraits by which others constructed his image. Many of the images associated with Cromwell were classical, in contrast to his own emphatic biblicism. Cromwell's self-effacement and reluctance to shape his own image paradoxically enabled a wide range of image-makers and image-breakers, including those who wished to remake him in the image of a king.

Although structured chronologically, this book is not so much an all-encompassing survey as an in-depth analysis of particular moments in the semiotics of ceremony, portraiture, and print. I choose the term "constructing" not to deconstruct, or even to imply that the images I explore were conscious fictions, but rather to emphasize aesthetic and rhetorical forms, development and change, and the ways in which the images themselves constitute rather than simply record political reality. My six chapters focus on three crucial moments in mid-seventeenth-century political culture: print and visual image surrounding the regicide, print and the appropriation of monarchical ceremony in protectoral England, and the reappropriation of forms in print and pageantry by Charles II in the early Restoration.

The first section, chapters 1 and 2, examines the representations of Cromwell leading up to and following the regicide. Royalists use popular forms and republicans courtly forms, each destabilizing their own cause in the process of supporting it. Chapter 1 looks at royalist satire on Cromwell during the period of the late civil wars and regicide. The royalist tendency to dramatize the struggle between Charles and parliament in terms of character conflict inadvertently increased the power of Oliver Cromwell by portraying him as a key player in the civil wars when – at least early on – he was not a central figure at all. In the figure of an energetic and scheming Machiavellian Cromwell, royalists created their own worst enemy. Chapter 2 explores republican appropriations of monarchical portraiture and panegyric to represent Cromwell. Drawing directly from Sir Anthony Van Dyck and the Caroline court, Cromwellian portraiture boldly revised monarchical forms in service of the new republic. But the very forms used to legitimate Cromwell reminded viewers of the absent monarch, evoking satire and scorn as much as assent. In the context of these fiercely contested images, Andrew Marvell's *An Horatian Ode* does not avoid the regicide, but shows the martyr-king acceding to an activist Cromwell propelled by fate. Payne Fisher's *Irenodia Gratulatoria* revises courtly verse forms, and John Milton's *To the Lord General Oliver Cromwell* eschews the public triumph to depict an activist, iconoclastic Cromwell. But the dissolution of the Rump Parliament renewed debate and speculation over Cromwell and the crown.

Chapters 3 and 4, on the Protectorate, trace the contradictions and ambiguities of Cromwellian appropriations of monarchical forms, leading up to the second protectoral installation. Chapter 3 shows how Cromwellian ceremony drew upon and revised the royal entry, but the display was at first challenged and resisted, fully celebrated only in print. Payne Fisher's *Inauguratio Olivariana*, John Milton's *Defensio Secunda*, and Andrew Marvell's *The First Anniversary of the Government under O.C.* participate variously in the construction of an anti-formalist, syncretic, and activist protectoral image. If Edmund Waller's *A Panegyric to my Lord Protector* moved toward a more iconic and courtly mode, it again differed from monarchical forms in being sharply contested and challenged. Chapter 4 traces an increasing tension between Cromwell as subject and the objects by which others constructed him as a king. Various printed texts, including James Harrington's *Oceana*, implicitly or explicitly advised Cromwell on the issue of the crown. Examination of contested print images helps to account for the discrepancy between the regal installation and Cromwell's actual refusal of the crown. The second inauguration, rather than confirming Cromwellian kingship, transformed the sacrosanct coronation ritual into a civic celebration of the state. Although the protectoral court has been widely viewed as monarchical, manuscript evidence and a late protectoral portrait indicate that Cromwell's own style remained plain and non-regal.

Chapters 5 and 6 treat print, image, and civic ceremony at the death and funeral of Cromwell and the restoration of the Stuart monarchy. Chapter 5 shows how printed texts both circulated and modified the monarchical spectacle of Cromwell's funeral. Indeed, the collaborative, popular forms that constructed "King" Oliver underscored the assumptions of a republic at the moment of its seeming demise: the people make the king. Chapter 6 investigates the paradoxical effects of popular print in giving a renewed afterlife to the figure of Cromwell. Charles II reappropriated the ceremonial display so fully deployed in the Protectorate, and, like Cromwell, recognized the power of print. But the very forms of popular print that helped to legitimate the returning monarch attested to cultural and political change. Further, royalists not only praised Charles but fiercely and repeatedly attacked Cromwell: in print and in person. Disinterred from the grave, Cromwell was up and about in the public sphere, setting the stage for the eventual sympathetic recuperation of Cromwell himself and of republican ideals.

This study of contemporary representations of Cromwell challenges previous views of mid-seventeenth-century English political culture in a number of ways. Both revisionist work in history and a focus on republicanism in literary studies have tended to assimilate Cromwell to monarchy. Yet a panoramic view of popular print images of Cromwell shows a more complex and shifting picture, including the bold revision of monarchical forms, the persistence of non-monarchical images even in the second Protectorate, and the paradoxical role of royalist print in producing Cromwell as a populist figure before and after the period of his actual political power.

Important differences appear between Cromwellian and monarchical forms. Manuscript sources reveal the fraught reception of Cromwellian display and image, attesting to a politically informed populace and an emerging public opinion. The Latin literary culture of the 1650s, in particular the undervalued work of Cromwell's unofficial poet laureate, Payne Fisher, produces a complex and syncretic image of Cromwell that cannot be simply assimilated to Augustanism, in turn assimilated to monarchy. Authors important in their own time, such as George Wither, write non-courtly verse in a largely biblical mode. A range of often startling print ephemera transmits portraiture and civic ceremony more fully into the public sphere, with complex effects. In the context of a broad spectrum of fiercely contested images, canonical texts by Andrew Marvell, John Milton, and John Dryden participate in the formulation of a new anti-formalist, syncretic, and activist aesthetic that mediates between republicanism and monarchy, challenging and revising both.

Shifting, fraught, and highly contested, constructions of Cromwell replace consensus and continuity with difference, debate, and change.

While the cultural *origins* of civil war and regicide have been much debated, its cultural *effects*, and in particular the material texts and objects that bring Cromwell into the public sphere, are an important but overlooked part of the story of mid-century politics and aesthetics. To that story we now turn.

One

"A Coffin for King Charles, A Crowne for Cromwell": royalist satire and the regicide

During the past decade, scholars have done much to elucidate change and transformation in print, literary genre, and readership in England in the once-neglected 1640s.[1] Yet Cromwell figures only obliquely in these studies. Putting together a broad spectrum of high and low texts – newsbooks, broadsheets, playlets, prose pamphlets, ballads, and engravings – reveals the striking centrality of satire on Cromwell early in the civil wars, before he was in fact a key military or political power. Paradoxically, Cromwell was produced as public figure not by parliamentarians but by royalists, who set out to demonize and personalize opposition to Charles I.

The extent to which royalists created satiric images of Cromwell has been little explored. Scholars have tended to take at face value royalist disavowal of popular forms and attack on print as a subversive force that helped bring down the monarchy. But royalists used popular print as widely and aggressively as did parliamentarians during the period of the civil wars and Interregnum. Indeed, royalists took the initiative in constructing a negative image of the enemies of Charles I, particularly of Oliver Cromwell.

In royalist satire, the antimasque figures of Stuart court drama moved into the world of popular print, no longer expelled by the appearance of the king and queen, but presumably to be run off the public stage by popular derision and laughter. Royalists attempted to mediate the tension between the desacralizing publicity of popular print and the heightened sanctity of majesty under siege by exposing to print not Charles himself, but his enemies. But in so doing royalists paradoxically undermined their own cause by creating Cromwell as a populist figure. Although held up for derision as an iconoclast, Machiavel, mock-king, monster, and big-nosed brewer, an energetic and scheming Cromwell threatened in print – as he later would in real life – to steal the show.

In this chapter, I trace royalist texts that gave life to a populist figure of Cromwell, from John Cleveland's *The Character of a London Diurnal* in 1645 to the post-regicide dramas *New Market Fayre* and *The Second Part of New Market Fayre*. Early texts including Bruno Ryves's account of Cromwellian iconoclasm in *Mercurius Rusticus*, the playlets *Craftie Cromwell* and *The Second Part of Craftie Crumwell*, and *A Case for Nol's Nose* gave Cromwell more prominence in print than he had in political actuality. As royalists increasingly resorted to dramatic forms, they constructed an entertaining and comic character who dominated the stage/page. The literary nature of royalist satire made it paradoxically unstable; comedy failed to contain but rather unleashed Cromwell as an important figure in an emergent public sphere.

"So perfect a hater of images": constructing Cromwell in early royalist satire

With the explosion of print in the 1640s and the proliferation of domestic news, the newsbook became the first important genre to construct an image of Cromwell.[2] At the opening of the Long Parliament in November 1640, Cromwell was an obscure back-bencher, although he was from the gentry class, a country squire.[3] Cromwell became increasingly active in opposition to the king, supporting the Root and Branch Petition, the Triennial Act, and the Grand Remonstrance of November 1641.[4] Yet only with the outbreak of the civil wars did Cromwell, in Bulstrode Whitelocke's later words, "begin to appear in the world."

Parliamentary newsbooks praised the military Cromwell, as he raised a troop of horse from his native Cambridgeshire and served with the Earl of Essex at the battle of Edgehill in October 1642. Skillful at commanding men and winning engagements, by February 1644 Cromwell had been promoted to lieutenant-general of the newly reorganized army of the Eastern Association under the Earl of Manchester.[5] His role in the parliamentary victory at Marston Moor on 2 July 1644 was widely recounted.[6] Newsbooks also reported on Cromwell's public quarrel in December 1644 with the Earl of Manchester, his superior in the Eastern Association, over the ends and means of waging war.[7] But Cromwell was not yet a leading commander, and there was no sustained effort to develop his full portrait.

Nonetheless, royalist texts seized upon the publicly pious Cromwell, giving him a greater role in print than he had in political reality. Cromwell's first extended appearance in print comes not in parliamentary texts, but in a royalist satire, John Cleveland's 1645 *The Character of a London Diurnall*.[8]

Cleveland (1613–58), who had joined the king in Oxford as an active royalist, was popular as a poet of extravagant conceit, wit that carried over into his biting satire on contemporaries. *The Character of a London Diurnall* ridicules both the form and content of the parliamentary newsbooks, including their spurious heroes. Cleveland's Cromwell is an absurd, comic figure. But, significantly, even such derision leaves the king and his royalist supporters in the shadows and puts Cromwell (and other parliamentary figures) center-stage.

The Character of a London Diurnall opens with a frontal attack on the parliamentary newsbook or diurnal: "A *Diurnall* is a puny Chronicle, scarce pin-feather'd with the wings of time: It is an History in *Sippets*, the English *Iliads* in a Nut-shell; the *Apocryphal* Parliaments booke of *Maccabees* in single sheets."[9] Through exaggeration and paradox, Cleveland calls attention to the incongruity between the inflated content and the modest form of the newsbooks. The diurnal, Cleveland asserts, is miscalled "the *Urinall*" by the "Country-Carryer," yet properly enough: "for it casts the water of the State, ever since it staled bloud" (p. 2). Cleveland's vernacular language lampoons the vernacular language of the diurnal; he draws upon domestic affairs to object to the diurnal's doing precisely the same thing. But Cleveland uses his main verbal artillery against the heroes of the newsbooks, including Cromwell.

In his portrait of Cromwell, Cleveland first mocks the sectarian makeup of his army: "But the *Diurnall* is weary of the Arme of flesh, and now begins an *Hosanna* to *Cromwell*, one that hath beate up his Drummes cleane through the Old Testament: you may learne the Genealogy of our Saviour, by the names in his Regiment: The Muster-Master uses no other List, then the first Chapter of *Matthew*" (p. 5). He then counters and attacks Cromwell's public piety by transforming him into a canting Puritan: "This *Cromwell* is never so valorous, as when he is making Speeches for the Association, which neverthelesse he doth somewhat ominously, with his Neck awry, holding up his Eare, as if he expected *Mahomets Pidgeon* to come, and prompt him" (pp. 5–6). Cromwell's incongruous physical stance points to his moral and religious waywardness: associated here with the then archetypal form of irreligion, Islam.

In seeming to report upon Cromwell's speech, Cleveland's text is in fact performative, constructing an image of Cromwell that is important and influential in itself. Cleveland introduces what was perhaps the first in a long-running series of jokes about Cromwell's large, red nose: "He should be a Bird of Prey too, by his bloody Beake: his Nose is able to try a young

Eagle, whether she be lawfully begotten" (p. 6). Aligning his satiric target with a bird of prey – or, more accurately, aligning nose with beak – Cleveland is playful but pointed: Cromwell's oversized and protruding body part emblematizes his predatory, excessive nature.

Heightening the satiric attack, Cleveland goes on to portray Cromwell's alleged military victories as simple and destructive iconoclasm:

> But all is not Gold that glisters: What we wonder at in the rest of them, is naturall to him; to kill without Bloodshed: For most of his Trophees are in a Church-Window: when a Looking Glasse would shew him more superstition: He is so perfect a hater of Images that he hath defaced Gods in his owne Countenance. (p. 6)

Deploying irony and overstatement, Cleveland undercuts the heroic image. With witty exaggeration, he builds up to the ludicrous figure of Cromwell defacing images in his own unsightly countenance. Cleveland goes on to reduce Cromwell's battles to encounters with church memorials: "if he deale with Men, it is when he takes them napping in an old Monument: Then downe goes Dust and Ashes . . . Oh brave *Oliver!*" (p. 6).

Finally, Cleveland satirizes Cromwell as a holy man run amok: "But Holy men (like the *Holy language*) must be read backwards. They rifle Colledges, to promote Learning; and pull down Churches for Edification. But Sacriledge is entailed upon him: There must be a *Cromwell* for Cathedralls, as well as Abbyes" (p. 6). The paradoxes of satire purport to explain and legitimate Cromwell's actions: if Hebrew must be read backwards (from right to left), then all the actions of holy men will seem similarly paradoxical. The knowing reader, however, would recognize the irony.

In the very process of attacking parliamentarians for their use of popular forms and images, Cleveland creates a popular satiric image of the big-nosed canting Cromwell. Cleveland's Cromwell is ridiculous, a kind of Don Quixote tilting at windows rather than windmills. Cleveland's ironic narration maintains a distance between the reader and the object of satire. Nonetheless, the very prominence that he gives to the targets of satire makes them overshadow their royalist counterparts in the text. As we shall see, when produced in dramatic form the figure of Cromwell complicated and to some extent undermined the royalist assumptions it was meant to confirm.

Whereas royalists actively employed print to satirize military and parliamentary figures, parliamentarians tended to be, in contrast, defensive. Several texts answered Cleveland by praising the parliament diurnals and their subjects, including the heroic and devout Cromwell. But they were no verbal match for the nimble Cleveland. *The Oxford Character of the London Diurnall Examined and Answered* indignantly labels Cleveland "a very Jack-sauce, who loves eating better than fighting; and because he hath not a heart fit for his stomach, and dares not fight, knowes that this trade of lying, slandering, and blaspheming, is counted a vertue parallel to valour among the Cavaliers."[10] But the refined detail of its defense of Cromwell comes precariously close to sounding like caricature: "In *Cromwels* Regiments there is no *God-dam-me* named, no *Sink-me*, no *Confound-me*, no *Devil nip me by the back*, no *Rot me alive* named among them, no *Devil sucke me through a Tobacco-pipe*" (p. 6). *A Full Answer to a Scandalous Pamphlet* more adeptly picks up and transforms Cleveland's own terms into praise of Cromwell as the hero of Marston Moor: "It is true that [either] his complexion, or his Valour, so dazled their young Eagle, that he durst not looke him in the face at *Long-Marston*, but it was his bloody Sword, not his bloody Beake, which made them run almost toward every point of the Compasse."[11] The author reconnects military prowess and piety: "Sacriledge is not entailed upon him, but Religion, Vertue, and the Spirit of Reformation runs in his blood: For as his noble Ancestor overthrew those Houses of Superstition, Sloth, and Sensualitie, so he labours to purge Cathedrals of those abuses which threaten ruine to true Religion" (p. 10). Verbal devices such as alliteration ("Superstition, Sloth, and Sensualitie") are now turned against not Cromwell but the forces that he opposes. Revising and correcting Cleveland, the text transforms Cromwell from iconoclast to pious reformer.

Yet royalist texts kept alive the figure of Cromwell as iconoclast. Some of these texts eschew the humor and irony of satire to denounce directly alleged abuses. Cromwell makes an appearance, along with a number of other parliamentarians, in Bruno Ryves's *Mercurius Rusticus* (1647). Ryves offers an extended account of Cromwellian iconoclasm: "The Cathedrall Church of *Peterborough* robb'd, defac'd, and spoyl'd by Cromwel, and his Schismaticall Adherents."[12] Ryves compares Oliver with his ancestor, Thomas Cromwell, noting, however, that "this *Cromwel* hath so farre outvied in acts of Pietie his Precedent, that *Cromwel* in Henry the eighth's time, this place hath now suffered in so great a manner for its Loyaltie, as that we know not where to enter upon the narration of the same" (p. 245). Inverting the classical *imitatio*, Ryves's Cromwell goes beyond his predecessor in being not better, but remarkably worse.

Ryves's tale of Cromwell's troops begins with their destruction of the "great West-window" in Peterborough. Here, "his Souldiers made their first breach and entrance . . . as will evidence them to be deformers of that thorough Reformation in our blessed Queenes time of happy memory, whom notwithstanding they so highly cryed up" (pp. 245–46). From the window, the soldiers turn to demolishing the choir-loft, the books of divine service, the seats of the auditors, and even the pulpit. At last, some bystanders attempt to intercede, being moved to "request Cromwell, that he would please to stay his Souldiers from further defacing and ruining the place" (p. 246). Yet Cromwell's attitude is "but a provocation to further mischief, replying, That his gods were a pulling down, and when the other answered, *That the God he served was beyond the reach of Souldiers, Cromwel* told them, *That they did God good service in that action*" (p. 246). Although he is only one of a number of parliamentary iconoclasts represented, Cromwell stands out in Ryves's account not for his actual participation in physical violence, but for his canting hypocrisy.

Indeed, the incident demonstrates a kind of providential rebuke to such pious humbug, as Ryves explains: "but observe the wages that Divine Justice repayed one of them for their worke, which may testifie how he accepted of the same"; one soldier, "espying in the roof right over the *Communion Table*, our *Saviour* pourtrayed, comming in glory with his holy Angels . . . he charged his Musket to shatter them down, but by the rebound of his own shot was struck blind" (pp. 246–47). Ryves concludes sardonically that "if he did his God good thereby, he did himselfe an ill turne, his wickednesse falling on his own pate" (p. 247). The unexpected outcome utterly deflates Cromwell's pious sentiments.

Historians have been concerned primarily with determining whether the Peterborough account is factually correct. Geoffrey Nuttall and, more recently, Margaret Aston have quite plausibly argued that Cromwell could not possibly have been guilty of all the iconoclasm attributed to him.[13] Yet to focus on precisely what aspects of the account are true is to miss its symbolic and political impact. Even in their mockery and derision, royalist texts create Cromwell as a public figure, evoking the kind of populism that transforms their own cause.

The Machiavellian Cromwell: parliament and politics, 1646–48

In the cessation of actual fighting after the first civil war, royalist satire continued to take the lead in constructing a popular image of Oliver Cromwell.[14] Indeed, rather than simply including him as only one target among many, such texts began increasingly to single Cromwell out, as he actively mediated between the army and the Presbyterian-dominated parliament in an attempt to reach a settlement with the king. Charges of Machiavellianism originated with the Levellers, but soon became a central mode of royalist attack in various forms of popular print.[15] Such texts constructed Cromwell as a stage Machiavel who envied rather than genuinely opposed kingship. Literary discourse became increasingly politicized as the figure of Machiavel moved from the theater into closet drama as a means of exposing an allegedly hypocritical and ambitious Oliver Cromwell.[16] But, as in a long history of stage Vices and Machiavels, there was an increasing danger that, once given the stage, the comic and devious Cromwell would run away with the show.

Ironically, it was again royalist satire, rather than parliamentary print, that publicized the figure of Cromwell. The tragicomedy *Craftie Cromwell* (1648) opens with a mock-encomium: "Shall *Cromwell* not be famous made / Unto the after-times, / Who durst a THRONE for to invade, / And Act the worst of Crimes?" But the lilting verse itself makes Cromwell "famous": "Shall not his Nose DOMINICALL, / In Verse be celebrated?"[17] In moving from the irony of the opening address to the personifications of drama, the text constructs an enterprising and ebullient, if also scheming and ambitious, figure in Cromwell the Machiavel.

While it does not focus exclusively on Cromwell, *Craftie Cromwell* gives him a central, dynamic role. Although "doom'd for evermore to frie in flames," John Pym, early leader of the Commons' opposition to Charles I, returns to survey the sleeping Cromwell and pronounce him *"borne to be / His Countries Bane, the Fate of Monarchie"* (p. 6). Awakened by Pym, a newly energized Cromwell immediately reveals his impiety and singular ambition to "ascend a throne" (p. 7), beginning with the iconoclastic destruction of law and monarchy:

> So please yee, yee all-powerfull *Destinies*, that my Heart faile not, nor my Sinewes shrink till I have brought to passe what I intend, til I have made my selfe Lord *Paramount*, and quite eradicated all those Lawes which many Ages past have beene ador'd, till I have quite dissolved all *Monarchy*, and topsi-turvey turn'd all *Regall Power.* (pp. 6–7)

Cromwell's very language, an accumulative list of dire deeds, embodies the forcefulness of his actions and plots. No longer Cleveland's warrior against church windows, this Cromwell more dangerously aims at the monarchy itself. Yet the very text that attacks Cromwell also allows him to dominate, to address and to draw in a broad audience.

The final act of *Craftie Cromwell* similarly puts forth a potent and effective Cromwell. The play evokes the recent parliamentary debate over the Vote of No Addresses, but here it is Cromwell alone who breaks off negotiations with the king: "Ile have no more *Proposalls* sent to the *King* and so let them at *Westminster* be told" (p. 13). And he does so solely to further his own ambition: "What Law is there that can obstruct our hopes now, we have *conquered* our *Conqueror*? And if none have a true and legall right to the outward benefits of this life (save *Saints*) then none ought to enjoy their Sweets, BUT WEE" (p. 13). Cromwell aims directly at the crown: "*And then, though Heaven and Earth say no such thing, / Yet spight of* FATES *and* MEN, *I will be* KING" (p. 14). The wily, ambitious Cromwell implicitly contrasts with the true king, Charles, saint-like and imprisoned on the Isle of Wight. But Charles remains in the shadows and through this very means of attack Cromwell replaces him as a central figure in the public sphere.

A sequel to *Craftie Cromwell*, *The Second Part of Crafty Crumwell* (1648) again places an ambitious Cromwell center-stage. Although a guilt-ridden Fairfax appears, pursued by Furies, and the Leveller Rainsborough stages a mock-triumph, the play presents Cromwell, "Metamorphiz'd, to a King," as the main antagonist to Charles.[18] But once again the energetic figure of Cromwell complicates the play's royalism, and its popular form exists in tension with its anti-republican message.

Paradoxically, this satire employs a popular form to advance the most extreme form of divine-right ideology. Focusing on Charles's enemies, *The Second Part of Crafty Crumwell* both conveys and mystifies divine-right kingship. The drama opens with a dialogue between Ismeno, an Independent, and Solon, a Royalist, the latter of whom argues that Charles "is the head, and we the members be, he is our Father, and wee are his Children, Kings of their Kingdomes as the Centers are" (p. 4). Center and origin, Charles grounds all meaning.

And yet the text represents not the king at the center, but the people at the margins. The very form of the text itself reveals the fragility of this alleged origin. To represent Charles directly would be to open him up to interpretation, to bring the sacred icon into the world of history and change, print and the public. Finding direct representation too dangerous, the text defines Charles through difference from his opposite, Oliver Cromwell. But in so doing the text also moves Charles to the background and sets Cromwell loose in the unpredictable medium of popular print.

Pointing to true royalty through the image of the mock-king, much of *The Second Part of Crafty Crumwell* focuses on Oliver's parodic kingship. In the final scene, Cromwell's accomplices crown him in a burlesque ceremony, accompanied by this song:

> Now OLIVR Ascend the throne
> Feare not to tumble downe
> Come all you Furies every one
> And bring the burning Crowne.
> But look how ore thy head doth hang
> A sharp and threatning sword
> Denouncing terror to thy gang
> And thee their perjurd Lord.   (p. 15)

The satire incorporates inverted ceremony, evoking the contrast with the sacred true rites of Stuart kingship. The mock-king over whose head the sword of Damocles hangs defines by contrast the true king Charles, of whose presence the song reminds us: "What follie prompts you, yee pro-phane / To usurp CHARLES his Right / But thus you tamper with your bane, / And play with aconite" (p. 15). Yet Cromwell, not Charles, is onstage.

In the dialogue with which *The Second Part of Crafty Crumwell* concludes, Cromwell shows the high spirits and inventiveness of a Richard III. Again, the dramatic form presents an energetic if self-incriminating figure. Thanking his accomplices for "this glorious wreath, that circles now my temples," Cromwell readily acknowledges the hypocrisy of his appeal to the people:

> And if wee can the peoples pleasures gaine,
> Wee may perchance, in peace and quiet Reigne,
> Else wee are lost, and O I greatly dread,
> At once to loose my Kingdome, and my head.   (pp. 15–16)

The Chorus again explicitly contrasts Cromwell and Charles: "Kings do admit no fellowes if thou Reigne, / CHARLES must surrender, but I surely hope / To see him Rule, thou Ruled in a Rope" (p. 16). Satirizing Cromwell, then, by contrast elevates Charles. Charles's legitimacy and piety are not simply contrasted to, but dependent upon, the represented impiety of his dissembling foes. Yet by placing Cromwell on the public page / stage, such royalist texts keep Charles in the shadows and make Cromwell into the very populist figure they distrust and fear.

While oppositional print in the late 1640s has received most of the atten-tion of historians and literary critics, royalist satires such as the *Crafty Cromwell* plays complicate assumptions about the democratizing role of print and the public. Such texts turned drama and the figure of the Machiavel to new political uses for the king rather than for the parliament. Anonymous and cheap, they could be dispersed to a wide audience. Royalist satire mediated the contradictions between divine-right ideology and the form of popular appeal to the people by circulating the image not of the king, but of his enemies. Yet this very construction of Cromwell fixed him in the public imagination as a key military and political player long before he had such power in actuality. Royalist propagandists may well have contributed to the demise of their own cause.

"Is Cromwell dead?": images in the second civil war

In the spring of 1648, as the parliamentary army moved against new uprisings in England, Scotland, and Wales, royalists continued to employ the weapon of popular satire, with complex effects. As Cromwell left London and parliamentary politics to put down opposition in Wales, newsbooks ridiculed him as a mock-king. *Mercurius Elencticus* (15–22 March), for example, wishes: "Now you *K. Noll*, with your *Bacon-flicht-face* need not make more hast then good speed Northward: The *Fire* will burne there without the helpe of your Nose."[19] The following issue of *Mercurius Elencticus* (22–29 March) derides Cromwell as about to lose his usurped crown: "How now King NOL? is't so indeed, / that you *Depos'd* must be, / And none of all your *Barmy-seed*, / enjoy the *Soveraignty?*"[20] Royalists tried to show in print the differences between Cromwell and the true king, imprisoned on the Isle of Wight. The inverted forms of satire sought to redress the topsy-turvy world of Westminster, a world turned upside-down by civil war.

A Case for Nol Cromwells Nose, and the Cure of Tom Fairfax's Gout (June 1648) more extensively deploys mock-elegy, burlesque epitaph, and caricature to hold up Charles's enemies for widespread ridicule. By eschewing dramatic form, the tract avoids the danger of having the lively Vice / villain figures run away with the show. Rather, the tract diminishes its subjects through coarse material satire.[21] Nonetheless its very focus and mode of attack enhanced and publicized the figure of Cromwell.

Although Cromwell remained second-in-command to Sir Thomas Fairfax, *A Case for Nol Cromwells Nose* takes him to be the real power, with Fairfax as "Prince and head of all the rout, / Who honour'd *Cromwell* and his Snout."[22] Entertaining, albeit with a bite, the text dwells on everything that is not regal about Fairfax and Cromwell. Unlike the timeless body of the sacred monarch, their bodies are pointedly mortal. *A Case for Nol Cromwells Nose* opens with a Cryer searching for the bodies of Fairfax and Cromwell, the latter of whom is to be found "by his refulgent copper nose, which he ever kept well burnisht, that so he might not be constrained to trouble the devill to light him, or grope out his way to hell" (p. 2). The tract goes on to contrast Cromwell, Fairfax, and the mock-saints with "Christs beloved, and his fathers Anointed our most deare and dread Soveraigne" (p. 2).

But Charles himself does not appear. Rather, *A Case for Nol Cromwells Nose* defines true kingship by contrast with the moral, spiritual, and physical excesses of Cromwell on which it elaborates. Since Cromwell, "that great nos'd Champion," has died upon the rumor of a counter-rebellion, the writer prepares an elegy in suitably colloquial language and doggerel verse: "Am I awake or dreame? can it be sed, / Englands Arch Traytor thus to hell is fled?" (p. 3). The writer professes amazement that Cromwell's nose did not frighten off Death itself:

> Is *Cromwell* Dead, durst Death his eyes to close,
> Did he not tremble, to behold his nose,
> Whose radiant splendour, (if Fame) doth not lie,
> Shone brighter, than a Comet in the Skie.   (p. 3)

The satire again reaches the fantastic dimensions of the grotesque as Cromwell's nose, reflecting his copper brewing-pots and his lower-class origins, shines more brightly than a comet. Yet the excesses of his body merely emblematize his moral excess. The writer wonders ironically: "Who now shall rob the Church, pull windows down, / Who now shall dare to trample on a Crowne?" (p. 4). Cleveland's warrior against church windows now dangerously turns his attack on an even more sacred icon: the crown itself.

The final image of Cromwell in this tract places him in a history of iconoclasm, reminding readers of the history of reformation that Cromwell claims to follow but actually perverts:

> Farewell *Olliver Cromwell* a name that hath been ever ominous to the Church; for in *Henry* the eights daies (you may remember) that a *Cromwell* was the hammer that beat downe the monasteries, and religious Houses, and in the raigne of our most pious Soveraigne Lord, unfortunate King CHARLES, this *Cromwell* hath been chiefly active in defacing, demolishing, and levelling Churches, in persecuting, robbing and imprisoning all learned and knowing men: but enough of him whose infamie will ever last. (pp. 4–5)

The long periodic sentence with its triple verbs (defacing, demolishing, levelling; persecuting, robbing, imprisoning) imitates the cumulative force of the destruction dealt by the two Cromwells. Yet while *A Case for Nol Cromwells Nose* clearly endorses a royalist perspective, the figure of Cromwell takes over the text much as he dominates the dramas that we have been exploring. The author reminds us that Cromwell's iconoclasm occurs during the reign of the pious and unfortunate Charles. But the king seems a distant and pallid figure in contrast to the active (albeit destructively active) Cromwell, as he defaces, demolishes, and levels. Satire preserves the mystique of divine-right kingship, keeping Charles from the public stage / page. But it does so at the cost of giving vitality and recognition to his enemies.

The Machiavel and the martyr-king: regicide

On 30 January 1649, Charles Stuart, having been convicted of high treason and other high crimes, was put to death "by the severing of his head from his body."[23] His body was staged in a graphic display of punishment and justice. Recent scholars have linked such a display with theatrical monarchy and the politics of tragedy. Franco Moretti argues that the regicide completed theatrical tragedy: monarchy, desacralized by tragedy, came to its logical conclusion.[24] Nancy Klein Maguire shows how the regicide was understood and assimilated as tragedy, making comprehensible the traumatic event.[25] The king's courage enhanced the theater of regicide, and his speech on the scaffold affirmed his faith in the Anglican church for which he died.

Yet in emphasizing spectacle and the tragic theater of monarchy, scholars have neglected the supplementary role of print. Although the display was witnessed by a large crowd, printed texts including elegies, sermons, and engravings brought the event to a much larger audience. Charles's scaffold speech, heard by few, was more widely dispersed in print. Other private events, such as the king's poignant parting from his children, took public form only in print.[26] Both parliamentarians and royalists appealed to the people at the point of regicide, culminating in the printing sensation of the century, *Eikon Basilike*.[27] Transformed into the martyr of *Eikon Basilike* and dozens of accompanying elegies and sermons, Charles I became more powerful in death than in life.

Charles I, at least before 1640, was by no means a man of the people. Recent scholars have sharply debated the issue of Charles I and public relations. In response to early arguments, Kevin Sharpe and others have shown that Caroline masques, panegyric, and paintings were not as insular, inward-looking, and escapist as once had been thought; that they were intended to hold up a model of virtue to the nation.[28] Nonetheless the

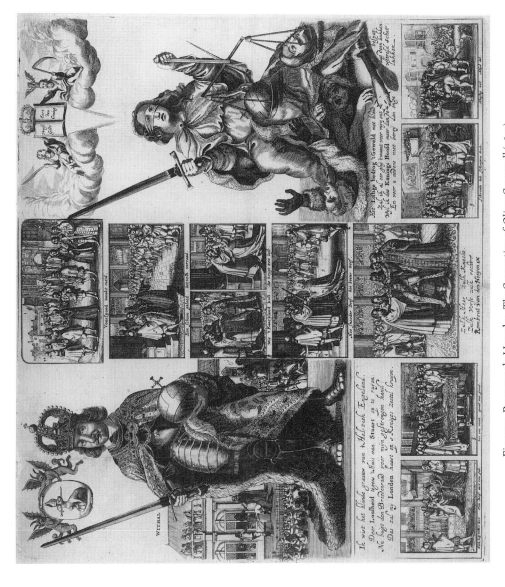

Figure 1 Romeyn de Hooghe, *The Coronation of Oliver Cromwell* (1649).

image of the king before 1640 was largely court-centered, hierarchical, and mystical, in keeping with divine-right kingship and Charles's own sense of order and decorum.[29] The events of the 1640s and the regicide itself decentered the image of the king in elegy and newsbook, engraving, woodcut, ballad, and pamphlet.[30] *Eikon Basilike* transferred the virtues of the masque into the world of popular print.

At the same time, royalists continued to construct satiric images of Charles's enemies. Both visual and verbal satiric texts juxtaposed Cromwell to the martyr-king. Visual satire on the regicide, for the most part printed on the continent (especially in Holland) rather than in England, quite literally foregrounded the duplicitous Cromwell and shielded Charles from the full glare of public scrutiny. A Dutch satire by Romeyn de Hooghe, *The Coronation of Oliver Cromwell* (1649), reveals Cromwell's guileful and self-serving actions since the death of Charles I, and his overall designs for securing the crown of England for himself (fig. 1). Cromwell, crowned and wearing regal ermine, stands in the foreground of the execution of Charles I. Signifying his usurpation, he holds the sword of justice in his right hand and the orb of sovereignty in his left.

Cromwell stands in the foreground of a complex and active iconographical scene. Behind him is a miniature rendition of the execution of Charles before Whitehall: two executioners stand on the scaffold: one wields the axe, while the other holds up the the bleeding head of the king. Based on a painting by Weesop (that I shall discuss later), this background scene shows the people crowded around the scaffold, on the ground, in windows, and on the roof of the Banqueting House. In the upper corner, showing the unsanctioned appropriation of forms, two winged devils hold an escutcheon, on which is a mitred dog with a sword in his mouth.

Cromwell not only quite literally overshadows the regicide, but he also seizes upon another monarchical ceremony: the coronation. Inset engravings depict the various stages of an illicit Cromwellian coronation: the processional to Westminster Abbey, presentation to the people, the oath, the anointing, receiving the sword, and the actual crowning. A subsequent image represents the ensuing coronation feast. The various vignettes show the (deluded) people acclaiming and rejoicing in their new, false ruler.

Yet the satiric print also offers a moral judgment absent in the dramas. On the right of the print, blind Justice holds the sword and balance in which Charles's head outweighs the orb of sovereignty. The pair of figures seated on the cloud above Justice's head in the upper right have an important iconographic function. The figure on the left personifies Virtue, whom we rec-

ognize from her simple mantle and the palm frond in her right hand. The
figure on the right personifies Time, with a scythe in his left hand and a
winged hourglass upon his head. These two figures, the image they frame –
a crowned book bearing the words "Vreest Godt / Eert den Coning" ("Fear
God / Honor the King") – and the light that connects that book to the head
of Justice relate the central moral of the entire engraving: in time, God will
reward the virtuous (those who fear Him and honor the memory of their
king) by restoring the balance of Justice.[31] Yet for the moment the wicked
have center-stage.

Cromwell also thrives in a ballad juxtaposing the Machiavel and the
martyr-king.[32] *A Coffin for King Charles, A Crowne for Cromwell: A Pit for the
People* (April 1649) sets a boastful and unrepentant Cromwell against the
pious martyr Charles. Juxtaposed in the text, Cromwell gets the best lines.
As the ballad opens, he is in high spirits:

> So, so, the deed is done,
> the Royall head is severd
> As I meant, when I first begunne
> and strongly have indeavord.
> Now Charles the I. is tumbled down,
> the second, I [do] not feare:
> I graspe the Scepter, weare the Crown,
> nor for Jehovah care.[33]

The language is that of a plain-spoken villain, evoking both public drama
and irreverent figures (Momus, for instance) from the Caroline masques.
The forceful villain for the moment takes over in print, as he also (allegedly)
controls the political scene. Hence, Cromwell's boast to the people: "In
vaine (*fond people*) doe you *grutch*, / and *tacitely repine*. / For why, my *skill*
and *strength* is such, / both *Poles* of heaven are mine." Yet at the time the
ballad was written Cromwell did not have the senior military, much less
civil, position. The ballad wholly ignores the new republican government,
using a royalist lens to focus on single-person plotting. But such satire gives
visibility and new life to the very person it derides.

That the ballad includes a speaking part for Charles is somewhat of an
innovation – and a risk. The danger comes in putting the king on the same
level as Cromwell and the people. Charles initially does seem pallid in comparison to the energetic Cromwell: "Thinkst thou, base slave, though in my
grave, / Like other men I lie: / my sparkling fame and Royall Name / can
(as thou wishest) die." Nonetheless, Charles expresses resentment for his
wrongs:

> Thrice perjurd Villaine, didst not thou
>   and thy degenerate traine,
> By mankinds saviours body, vow
>   to me thy Soveraigne,
> To make me the most glorious King
>   that ere ore England raignd.

Yet even such complaints attribute great power and influence to Cromwell (more, undoubtedly, than he had in reality). Cromwell lords it over the people, warning them: "You *must be props* unto our *pride*, / and *Slaves* to our command." Demonizing Cromwell made him central in a popular medium that was, at best, unpredictable and difficult to control.

Exposing the hypocrisy of Cromwell's pandering to the people, *A Coffin for King Charles, A Crowne for Cromwell* is itself a "low" form designed for oral circulation and consumption. Further, such a text popularizes Charles, radically departing from the mystique and distance of the elegant Van Dyck portraits, the masques of Davenant, Shirley, and Townshend, and the civic and ecclesiastical ceremonies. As such, *A Coffin for King Charles, A Crowne for Cromwell* and other satires transform royalism through the very means by which it is communicated and preserved.

Texts that focused on Cromwell without representing the king avoided making Charles into a construction of popular print. The playlet *The Famous Tragedie of King Charles I* (1649) stages only the king's enemies.[34] This drama alludes to Charles only as an absence, the true icon standing behind the parodic images of Cromwell and his associates who plot and carry out his murder. Much of the text exposes Cromwell, who evinces irreligion to the point of being an arch-Machiavel: "A King and Kingdome is my valours prize, / By both their ruines, I intend to rise."[35] Nonetheless, the place of center-stage mattered, and again a lively and comic Cromwell complicates the play's royalism.

Surprisingly, given its title, *The Famous Tragedie of King Charles I* contains farce and sexual high-jinks, scheming and various shenanigans presented in a comic manner. The play opens with a tried and true formula of the comic pair: Cromwell and his accomplice, the Independent preacher Hugh Peters. Their conspiracy undercuts the justification for regicide, reduced here to a Machiavellian plot. Like a Vice figure, Cromwell exudes high spirits and energy: "My fine *facetious Devill*, who wear'st *the Liverie* of *the Stygian God*, as the white *Embleme* of thy *innocence*; Hast thou *prepar'd* a pithie *formall Speech* against the *essence* and *the Power* of KINGS?" (p. 1). Peters in turn praises his "Most valiant, and invincible Commander" in terms that make evident (to the reader) Cromwell's vices and moral flaws. Peters's long panegyric, includes, for instance, a comic tribute to Cromwell's large red nose: "thy Nose, like a bright Beacon, sparkling still (the *Aetna*, that doth fame our English world) hangs like a Comet o're thy dreadfull face, denouncing death and vengeance" (p. 2). Alliteration underscores the increasingly hyperbolic praise: Cromwell's nose, red from drinking and reflecting the copper pots of his former profession of brewing, becomes a source of light, then a volcano famous through the land, as Etna is in Italy; finally, the nose expands beyond national to cosmic significance, metamorphosing into the celestial form of a comet, and portending danger to the king.

At once outrageous and entertaining, Cromwell and Peters simultaneously plot the seduction of Mrs. Lambert and the murder of the king. As Peters dubs Cromwell "*Englands* best Patriot, and my noble Patron" (p. 2), Cromwell in turn lauds his accomplice in evil: "Thou art that Load-stone, which shall draw my sense to any part of policy i'the Machiavilian world" (p. 4). Cromwell believes none of the republican arguments against kingship, but schemes solely so that "thee and I, and those whom we create / Will Reigne like Princes, and the Lords of Fate" (p. 4).

The comic character of Cromwell takes a more central role in *The Famous Tragedie* than in the pre-regicide satire sometimes bearing his name in the title. Having revealed his Machiavellianism in an earlier soliloquy, Cromwell boasts to his new love, Mrs. Lambert, of his plot to kill the king:

> As for the Man (they call the KING) He hath not foure and twenty howers to live, I've hyr'd a dapper Lad, a neat-tongu'd (but inexorable Fellow) for fifteene hundred pounds, to ease Him of the burthen of His cares, good King, he's fitter farre for to converse with Saints and Seraphims, than with erronious and ambitious Mortalls, and 'twere a sinne (a grand one) for to deferre the hopes Celestialls have for to enjoy his presence. (p. 33)

Cromwell admits that he hopes simply to replace the king with himself: "once perform'd, then I am Lord alone, though not a King by Title, yet by Power" (p. 34). As Cromwell schemes against the king, the play itself indeed removes Charles to the celestial realm, allowing the energetic and diabolically clever Cromwell to supplant him.

By focusing only on Cromwell, *The Famous Tragedie of King Charles I* sustains the mystique of kingship in a text designed for a popular audience. Charles himself remains at a distance, adumbrated in the other royalist martyrs and shown only in death, in an interpretive framework provided by the Chorus. Yet bawdy, comic, and lively, the play concentrates its energy not on the absent king but on his diverting if diabolical substitute. In the aftermath of regicide, such royalist satire paradoxically contributed to the republicanism it abhorred by relegating the king to the heavenly shadows and offering up a populist figure of Oliver Cromwell.

In a similar vein, John Crouch's *A Tragi-Comedy called New-Market Fayre* (June 1649) meditated on the regicide by lampooning Charles's enemies, who nonetheless to some extent run away with the show. Taking the popular form of the marketplace or fairground, with its hawkers of goods and buyers of wares, *New-Market Fayre* satirizes the dispersal and sale of the king's goods. Such a sale had indeed taken place. As early as February 1649, *Mercurius Elencticus* reported that "the Commons (as they call themselves) assembled in Parliament [ordered] That it be referred to the Committee of the Navy, to raise money by the sale of the late King's Crown, Jewells, Hangings (they might have reserv'd the Hangings for themselves), and all his other goods." The newsbook then trains its sights specifically on the brewer Cromwell:

> Nor is the malice of that bloody Brewer *Cromwell* yet half satisfyed with the last *Gyle* of Blood Royall, drawn off from the Father, but is now a *Brewing* more mischief towards his Royall Sonne King CHARLES the *Second*, who (in spight of all the Brewers and Bakers, Coblers, Pedlers, and Tinkers in the Parliament and Army) is rightfull King of *Great Brittayn, France,* and *Ireland.*[36]

Brewing imagery and the language of grotesque materiality mirror social upheaval: when the "proudest Rebell in the pack, (even Crumwell himself)," reads the titles of the new king, "his black perjur'd soul should make way through the very Bung-hole of his Hoggs-head, to its double Damnation, for Fear and Shame."[37] The text degrades Cromwell in material, sometimes scatological, terms. Like the passing of the malt through the opening at the bottom of a barrel, or the passing of excrement through the "bung-hole" of the body, Cromwell's soul makes its way downward to damnation. Cromwell's very material body contrasts with the ethereality of the martyr-king and his son.

A Tragi-Comedy called New-Market Fayre extends to Cromwell and Fairfax the money-grubbing proclivities of the soldiers said to have made money by displaying the dead body of the king. But once again the form of the drama complicates the play's royalism. As an adept and flourishing schemer, Cromwell engages the audience, even while they (presumably) disapprove of his character and actions.

While the First Cryer's wares recall the martyred king, the spotlight soon moves to the Grandees who fight over the symbols of kingship. The First Cryer enters "with a Crowne and Scepter, a Cabinet of Jewells, Suites and Roabes belonging to the late King."[38] The sale goes beyond these emblems of royalty to include relics that poignantly recall the royal martyr, Charles's "bloody handkerchers," his "*Meditations* and *Prayer-Booke*," and his "*Haire, and royall blood*" (p. 85). The Cryer is confident in his sale of kingship: "Here you may all things *buy* / That belong to *Monarchy*" (p. 85). Entering with the other Army Grandees, Cromwell and Fairfax fight over the trappings of royalty, above all the crown. The Cryer assures Cromwell that the crown, which he has seized and tried on, has transformed him: "So, now 'tis sure, / And makes you look more like a *King*, then *Brewer*" (p. 86).

Yet the ensuing squabble over the crown highlights not the absent king (who disappears from view) but his comic and entertaining replacements. Cromwell takes full control of the crown – and the dramatic action – as he avers: "A Crowne admits no Rivall; Ile *all* or none, / He sits unsafe that doth divide his Throne" (p. 86). His quarrel with Fairfax escalates as Lady Fairfax and Mistress Crumwell join in, engaging in a lively verbal skirmish. Lady Fairfax, for instance, scorns the former brewer's wife:

> What wood ye Mistris *yest* and *graynes*;
> Marry foh, come up *small-beer*:
> You'd make your nose as red hot as your husbands,
> And thrust it into his *fizzling-place*,
> Woo'd ye not, mistris *Brazen-face*?   (p. 87)

Mistress Crumwell's defence – "Call me Mistris brazen-face; thou *Rotterdam* slut, thou; call me brazen-face? Thou look'st more liker a *Mistris foolsface*, or like thy *Husbands-face*" (p. 87) – reveals her lack of class in contrast to the true absent monarch. Nonetheless the brawling ladies upstage the monarch, who moves even further into the shadows.

Building upon the success of *New Market Fayre*, Crouch's sequel, *The Second Part of New Market Fayre* (July 1649), makes Cromwell more Machiavellian and further idealizes – and distances – the absent Charles. The play opens with a reminder of the martyred king by the character Constantius, who professes astonishment at "what they have done by Butchering Sacred Majesty."[39] A necromantic scene in which a Faustus-like Hugh Peters calls up the ghost of Isaac Dorislaus, the murdered English envoy to the Netherlands, underscores the contrast between England's old and new rulers. When Peters naively inquires whether "the late King be in these lower Regions," Dorislaus eulogizes the king and blackens by contrast his opponents:

> No, thou Viper, he reigns in Heaven; in Hell there are new torments pro-
> viding answerable for that damn'd Crime without all presidents but
> *Bradshaw*, *Cook*, and *Steel*, and such as those have forg'd:
>> Knaves hired by *Cromwel* to corrupt the Laws:
>> Now all made food for *Hells* devouring jawes. (p. 220)

Indeed, a special place has been reserved in hell for *"Fairfax, Cromwel, Ireton, Pride,"* and Dorislaus looks forward to the day when they too, like him, will "rue their damn'd *Regicide*" (p. 220). With straightforward invective, the play embodies and conveys royalist ideology.

Yet if damnation awaits Cromwell, in the play itself he is very much alive and well, diverting the audience and duping the naive and gullible Fairfax. Cromwell's profession of loyalty – "Wee're now at Amity, and made both one; I hope there will remain no Jealousies or Fears each of other?" – utterly deceives Fairfax, who embraces Cromwell as "my second Self" and admires his wit and policy: "Oh that I could by this embrace beget a wit like thine; the State wants *Policy* as well as *Money*; and mine's but little, thine a full *Magazine*" (p. 217). Although the play turns dark and tragic for Fairfax, betrayed to the people and taken off to be hanged, Cromwell himself remains the conniving Vice figure, whose double-entendre lets the audience enjoy and appreciate his dissembling. As with the earlier playlets we have explored, the satire of the two parts of *New-Market Fayre* does not so much contain Cromwell as unleash him as a popular comic figure in print.

The public execution of the king was a traumatic event that brought to culmination all the upheaval of the civil war years. Along with the (now) more familiar elegies, the higher literary forms that grappled with the execution of Charles I through the paradigms of the theater, tragedy, and sacred martyrdom, royalists deployed "lower" and more popular printed forms of satire. Such forms transformed Cromwell the pious military victor into an iconoclast who attacked church windows and tombs, defacing God's image with his own unsightly appearance. By making Cromwell a Machiavel, royalist satire defused principled opposition to monarchy: in these texts, Cromwell did not oppose, but simply envied, kingship.

What would be the purpose of such satire once the king was dead? Royalist satire attempted to stem what Barry Coward has called the "functional radicalism" of civil war, to keep *de facto* regicide from becoming doctrinaire republicanism.[40] Popular royalist print constructed an ambitious and duplicitous Cromwell to explain why the regicide had occurred without giving any legitimacy to the arguments of *either* regicides or republicans. Rather than literature reflecting life, here life borrowed from literature the stock type of the Machiavel to explain and manage the unpredictability of contemporary events.

How effective were such paper bullets? Readers undoubtedly appropriated texts for their own purposes, and it is difficult precisely to align popular print with political thought or action. But by tracing the ambiguities and complexities of a range of cultural texts, we have seen that royalist representations of Cromwell may paradoxically have helped to undermine their own position. As the success of *Eikon Basilike* suggests, the impulse to insulate the figure of the king from the demystifying effects of popular print may have backfired. At the same time, the image of a powerful Cromwell with royal pretensions served to create a common conception of Cromwell as a key military and political figure long before that was actually the case in reality. Royalists created their own worst enemy.

Two

Portraiture, print, and the republican heroic

In chapter 1 we saw how the contested realm of popular print both preserved and transformed royalist ideology during the latter years of civil war and at the opening of the English republic. In this chapter I want to look, conversely, at how the republic appropriated and revised monarchical forms of portraiture, panegyric, and ceremony. How did Cromwellian portraiture both appropriate and change Caroline forms? How did Charles's own visual image change with military defeat and regicide? How did printed texts incorporate, challenge, and interpret the heroic portraiture? Did the visual images drawn from the Caroline court help to make the new state acceptable to the people, or did they inevitably remind viewers of regicide and usurpation?

Early representations of Cromwell in portrait, ceremony, medal, and print borrowed from the court of Charles I. But Caroline images were not simply duplicated. Rather, they were appropriated and revised for a republican state. Both portrait and ceremony moved into popular print culture which not only promulgated but fiercely contested the heroic image of Cromwell.

Representations of Cromwell fit into the broader aesthetics of the new English republic which critics have recently debated. Sean Kelsey has argued that the new republic successfully invented itself with icon, palaces, spectacle, and material objects such as the symbolic mace; Kelsey sets Cromwell largely in opposition to this new culture, as a figure who abruptly dissolved the Rump in a grab for power, just as the civilian government was about to take deep root.[1] But Kevin Sharpe sees the same period as dominated symbolically by ongoing monarchical images and forms, including the image of the martyr-king and imitations of monarchical portraiture.[2]

31

How can one adjudicate between these seemingly contrary views? Representations of Cromwell were, I would argue, an integral part of, rather than opposed to, the republican aesthetic that Kelsey traces; but such representations dislocated and challenged rather than (as Sharpe suggests) imitated monarchy, in the service of a republican cause.

Nonetheless, the use of monarchical forms evoked the absent monarch, and printed and visual satire attacked the new republican hero, Cromwell, reiterating his role in the regicide and his inadequacy in comparison to the martyr-king. In the face of fierce attacks, Andrew Marvell defended both the republic and its iconoclastic hero, not by avoiding the regicide but by boldly juxtaposing martyr-king and military conqueror to show the former acceding to the latter. After Cromwell's victories in Scotland, Payne Fisher employed a syncretic classicism to portray Cromwell as instrument of the republic, while John Milton depicted Cromwell as a victor over "crowned Fortune." With Cromwell's abrupt dissolution of the Rump in April 1653, the question of monarchy re-emerged. The display of Cromwell's portrait on the Exchange in May 1653 evoked sharply divergent responses that made clear the political and representational stakes: was this an icon or an icono-clast?

Walker's Cromwell and Caroline forms

Early in March 1649, the Council of State requested that Cromwell lead an expeditionary force to quell the uprising in Ireland. Cromwell did not immediately agree. He explained his position in a long and self-deprecatory speech to the General Council of the Army at Whitehall, in which he insisted that "it matters not who is our Commander-in-Chief if God be so; and if God be amongst us, and His presence be with us, it matters not who is our Commander-in-Chief."[3] Characterizing himself as "a poor man that desires to see the work of God to prosper in our hands," Cromwell insisted on his role as mere instrument of a higher cause and power.

Cromwell's public humility and self-denial contrasted with the courtly portrait that appeared in 1649. The earliest and by far the most widely circu-lated image of Cromwell was a painting by Robert Walker.[4] In this three-quarters-length portrait (fig. 2), the viewer looks up from below at a gracefully elongated martial figure, whose body is turned at an angle and counterpoised (in some versions) by a young page tying on his sash, both symbols of rank. Cromwell holds a baton of military command and wears a full suit of black plate armor of a style normally associated with the early sixteenth century. The armor itself was an artistic prop; during the civil

Figure 2 Robert Walker, *Oliver Cromwell* (1649).

wars, only the cuirass (with detachable breast and back plates) was normally worn, with a buff-coat and helmet.

The graceful and naturalistic pose of the Walker portrait evoked the aristocratic portraiture of Anthony Van Dyck, who died in 1641 just before the outbreak of the first civil war. Brought to England by Charles I, himself a passionate connoisseur and collector, Sir Anthony Van Dyck represented in a series of paintings the majesty, splendor, and elegance of the Caroline court.[5] Van Dyck's paintings of Charles I and various courtiers in armor follow Peter Paul Rubens's *Thomas Howard, Earl of Arundel* (1629 or 1630), which closely resembles Titian's *Alfonso d'Avalos, Marchese del Vesto, with Page* (1533), and the *Allocution of Alfonso d'Avalos, Marchese del Vesto* (1539–41), but whose ultimate source is Titian's own lost *Salvius Otho*.[6]

Walker's various poses of Cromwell not only evoked but in fact borrowed bodies from Van Dyck portraiture. The portrait of Cromwell in armor with a page most strikingly paraphrases Van Dyck's 1636 portrait of a key figure in the years of personal rule, Thomas Wentworth, Earl of Strafford, in a military setting as Lord Deputy of Ireland.[7] As with the Strafford, the portrait shows Cromwell embarking from the west coast of England or Wales to cross to Ireland as commander-in-chief (the shore and sea can be seen on Cromwell's right). Strafford (with Laud) was a central figure in the formation and implementation of royal policy during the years of personal rule and, by the time Walker borrowed his body, had been tried and executed for treason.[8] Variations on this Walker pose of Cromwell in cuirassier armor were also taken directly from Caroline court portraiture, including *Sir Kenelm Digby*, *Sir Edmund Verney*, and the *Duke of Hamilton* (all c. 1640).[9]

There is irony, of course, in republican appropriations of Caroline court images. Taken to task for his blatant imitation of Van Dyck, Walker responded with blunt honesty worthy of his subject: asked "why he did [not] make some of his own Postures, says he if I could get better I would not do Vandikes."[10] Yet Walker's frank answer should not be taken as proof that he simply duplicated monarchical forms. There are significant differences as well as links between the Walker portrait and Van Dyck portraits, particularly those of Charles. Although Charles himself was sober and retiring and did not provoke the criticisms of extravagance that his father James I had, Van Dyck portraiture displays luxurious and elegant apparel, a concomitant of Stuart majesty.[11] No such splendor appears in Walker's portrait of Cromwell. Although Walker has attached Cromwell's head to an elegantly apparelled body, the head itself is plain, the hair uneven, the chin spotted with tufts of hair. Cromwell's head contrasts to the bland, idealized visage of the page tying his sash. And the very fact of the borrowing challenges the exclusionary claims of the Caroline court to images of power and authority.

At the same time, Cromwellian portraiture employed a mode no longer available to Charles I himself, since after military defeat the image of Charles had become civil and regal. In the early years of civil war, engravings of Charles followed Van Dyck's martial portraiture. Hence, *Military Orders, and Articles Established by his Majestie*, a 1643 tract on the regulations of the royalist army, had as a frontispiece an equestrian print of Charles in full armor (fig. 3). "The High and Mighty Monarch Charles" closely resembles in dress and pose (if not in exact placement of the subject) Van Dyck's great equestrian portrait of *Charles I with M. de St. Antoine* (1633). The king, mounted on a lavishly chased and caparisoned horse, faces the viewer's right and looks into the distance. He wears plate armor, a sash, an elaborate lace collar, the lesser George on a ribbon, and soft cavalry boots with spurs. In his right hand the king holds a long stick or crop, and his sword in its scabbard hangs behind his right leg. Behind the king is London, clearly taken from Hollar's famous engraving of the cityscape. The engraving thus captures the full elegance of early Stuart kingship in a martial and imperial mode.

Military defeat dramatically transformed the iconography of Charles I. By 1647, regal engravings had replaced the martial mode. *The Divine Right of Government Naturall and Politique* (1647) reproduced perhaps the most commonly engraved image of Charles after the first civil war (fig. 4). The text corroborates and explicates the image: "Charles par la grace de Dieu Roy de la grande Bretaigne, &c." The king, looking very handsome, is turned to the viewer's right as he looks into the distance. He wears his ermine-trimmed robes of state and an exquisite lace collar. His hair is gathered on his left shoulder, in his characteristic lovelock style. No longer martial, the image of Charles moves toward the regal image that would define the martyr.

The William Marshall frontispiece to *Eikon Basilike* culminated the iconography of Charles as martyr (fig. 5). *Eikon Basilike* was on sale in London shortly after Charles's execution, and this picture became one of the most famous engravings of the seventeenth century for the way it simply and powerfully re-enacts its iconographic model: Christ in the Garden of Gethsemane. The king kneels in profile on his left knee, facing to the viewer's right, his eyes fixed upon a glowing crown above which has been inscribed "Beatam et Æternum" and upon it the word "GLORIA." Charles wears his robes of state that all but conceal his doublet, plain collar and cuff, stockings, and shoes. In his right hand he holds a crown of thorns ("Gratia"), the world ("Mundi Calco") rests beneath his right foot, while his earthly crown ("Vanitas") lies toppled at his right toe. Behind the king are

The high and Mighty Monarch CHARLES by the
Grace of GOD King of Great Brittaine
France and Ireland. Defender of the Faith etc.
1643.

Are to be sould by Rich. Peake.

Figure 3 "The High and Mighty Monarch Charles," from *Military Orders, and Articles Established by his Majestie* (1643).

Figure 4 "Charles par la grace de Dieu," from *The Divine Right of Government Naturall and Politique* (1647).

Figure 5 Charles I, from *Eikon Basilike* (1649).

symbols of his constancy: the rock amid raging waters ("IMMOTA TRIUM-PHANS") above, and the palm tree upon which weights were traditionally placed to steady its growth ("CRESCIT SUB PONDERE VIRTUS") below. A ray of light ("Clarior è tenebris") breaks from the stormclouds in the upper left and shines upon the back of Charles's head. Widely circulated and copied, the frontispiece powerfully shaped the popular conception of Charles the martyr.

An engraving of Weesop's well-known painting of the execution of Charles I similarly shows the traumatic force of regicide and the emotive power of the image of the martyr-king (fig. 6). Hundreds gather to watch the execution, pressing up to the scaffold and gathering even on the roof of the Banqueting House at Whitehall, with a deep press of soldiers carrying pikes closest to the scaffold; but the primary emotional shock of the execution is registered in a fainting woman (in the bottom right corner) who is being supported by three bystanders. David Howarth has suggested that this image was intended to evoke the fainting Mary Magdalene at the crucifixion of Christ.[12] The caption below identifies the participants on the scaffold. Portraits of Fairfax, Charles, and Cromwell in the style of the miniature decorate the top of the engraving. Such a powerful visual image, then, like the frontispiece to the *Eikon Basilike*, transformed defeat and loss into moral and spiritual triumph.

Cromwellian portraiture countered and attempted to replace the emotive power of the Caroline visual image. Yet by borrowing visual forms from the Caroline court to legitimate a new republican hero, Cromwellian portraiture also reminded viewers of that court and of the fate of its king. Although the images were infused with new meaning to celebrate the English republic, the Caroline origins of Cromwellian portraiture were not undone and cancelled. Contaminated by the discourse of its monarchical precedent, Cromwellian portraiture was especially vulnerable to irony and parody. Various texts countered the Cromwellian heroic by exaggerating Cromwell's martial and masculine mode into grotesque sexual promiscuity. Such attacks, as we shall see, took both visual and printed form.

"Quod utile honestum": contesting Walker's Cromwell

In the world of print, Robert Walker's Cromwell was challenged and reinterpreted as well as copied and circulated. Clement Walker included a quite remarkable satiric engraving in *Anarchia Anglicana* (1649), the second part of his *History of Independency*. Walker was a parliamentarian who had

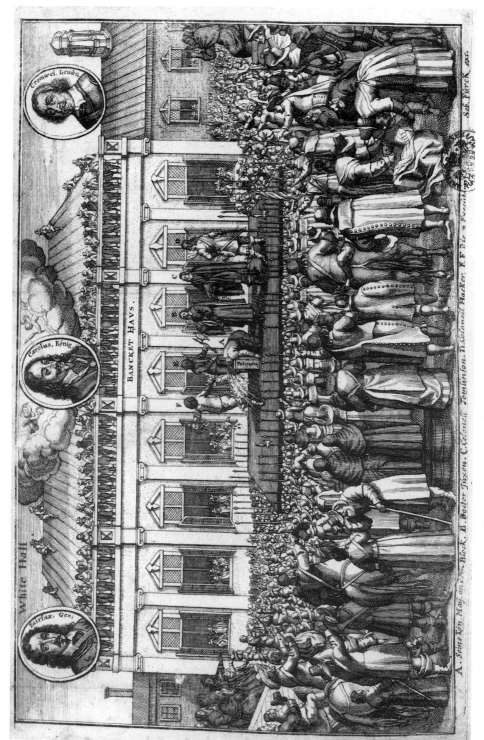

Figure 6 Engraving after Weesop, *Execution of Charles I* (1649).

been accused of fomenting apprentice riots during the army revolts of 1647 and who was ousted at Pride's Purge in December 1648. This complex and elaborate engraving, entitled *The Royall Oake of Brittayne* (fig. 7), transposed Cromwell from a martial setting or a neutral frame to an incongruous civil scene in which he attacks, not a military opponent, but a tree: the sacred Royal Oak of Britain. Cromwell, dressed in the Van Dyck / Walker armor and sash of the Walker portrait, is shown full-length, revealing that his feet stand on a ball, *"locus lubricus"* (slippery place), which emerges from the bottomless pit of hell. Inspired by hell, he creates anarchy in order to take possession of the crown for himself.

This engraving overturns Cromwell's apparent piety by linking him with notorious biblical figures: here, the wicked king Ahab and the husbandmen of Christ's parable of the householder and his vineyard. Cromwell's "Kill and take possession" echoes the word of the Lord to the prophet Elijah in 1 Kings 21:18–19: "Arise, go down to meet Ahab king of Israel, which is in Samaria: behold he is in the vineyard of Naboth, whither he is gone down to possess it. And thou shalt speak unto him, saying, Thus saith the Lord, Hast thou killed, and also taken possession? And thou shalt speak unto him, saying, Thus saith the Lord, In the place where the dogs licked the blood of Naboth shall dogs lick thy blood, even thine." After he had refused to sell his vineyard, the inheritance of his fathers, to King Ahab, Naboth was murdered at the instigation of Ahab's notorious wife, Queen Jezebel. Cromwell, going beyond Ahab's sin, has no Jezebel, but himself orders the destruction of the sacred oak, giving the order to three men armed with axes.

The second biblical quote (by the tree), "Let us kill him and seyse his Inheritance" (Matthew 21:38), links Cromwell with the evil husbandmen left in charge of the vineyard in Christ's parable of the winepress. The husbandmen kill first the householder's servants and then his son, saying, "This is the heir; come, let us kill him, and let us seize on his inheritance" (Matthew 21:38). Christ's parable, foreshadowing the crucifixion, here links Charles I with Christ, and Cromwell with Christ's crucifiers. As with Ahab, dire punishment is predicted, for the master of the vineyard "will miserably destroy those wicked men" (Matthew 21:41).

Cromwell's martial figure is deceptively appealing in the engraving, neither distorted nor grotesque. His position to the left of the centrally placed royal oak, however, indicates the illegitimacy of his actions. The engraving reveals Cromwell to be a hypocrite, motivated by ambition and greed: written alongside his head and shoulders are the words "Quod utile honestum" (how profitable honesty is!).

Figure 7 "The Royall Oake of Brittayne," from Clement Walker, *Anarchia Anglicana* (1649).

Clement Walker's inclusion of visual satire in his printed attack on Cromwell was the exception in England during the Commonwealth, although many satiric engravings of Cromwell were produced on the continent, especially in Holland. And indeed, Walker's fate served as an exemplary warning: he was arrested for *Anarchia Anglicana* and charged with high treason, although his case never came to trial and he died in the Tower in 1651.

At the same time, other heroic portraits of Cromwell continued to draw upon and revise earlier monarchical forms. In a second painting done around this time by or after Robert Walker, Cromwell's head was set upon a different body of a horseman, which is much less courtly in apparel and stance (fig. 8). Cromwell is dressed as a cavalryman, in padded trousers, oxhide jacket, spurs, pull-up boots, and fringed gauntlets. He wears a cuirass and sword, and holds a martial baton and hat. Once again, there is both continuity and change from Van Dyck and the Caroline court. While lacking full armor, the pose and execution of this portrait are nearly identical to Van Dyck's *Frederik Hendrik, Prince of Orange* (1631–32), a replica of which Van Dyck presented to Charles I in 1632.[13] Van Dyck's original is only half-length, which perhaps explains why the portrait of Cromwell is so oddly elongated below the waist. And the Cromwell pose is also noticeably plainer and more sober, as the portrait draws upon but also revises the culture of the Caroline court.

It was also around this time that Samuel Cooper painted his (now) famous unfinished miniature watercolor of Cromwell (fig. 9).[14] Cooper's Cromwell wears a buff coat over a shirt with a simple white collar; he is looking away, preoccupied, even other-worldly. Again, there was influence from the court of Charles I: Horace Walpole later wrote that Cooper "owed great part of his merit to the works of Van Dyck, and yet may be called an original genius, as he was the first who gave the strength and freedom of oil to miniature . . . if his portrait of Cromwell could be so enlarged, I don't know but Van Dyck would appear less great by the comparison."[15] Most immediately striking about the Cooper miniature, however, is its visual realism. Cromwell's hair is receding; his face is lined, and his cheeks are blotched and paunchy. In contrast even to Van Dyck's naturalistic if aristocratic portraiture, this is a startlingly honest and plain depiction. Such an image coheres closely with Cromwell's own plain-spoken biblicism and piety. But many of the images to follow contrasted with, rather than followed, this plain style.

Figure 8 *Oliver Cromwell*, attributed Robert Walker (n.d.).

Figure 9 Samuel Cooper, *Oliver Cromwell* (c. 1650).

"To worship mighty snout": satire on Cromwell and Ireland

Classicized ceremony as well as portraiture produced the heroic in the early years of the republic. Having put down Leveller-inspired unrest in the army and having finally completed his preparation of troops and supplies for Ireland, Cromwell was given a hero's send-off in June 1649, when the London authorities held a feast at Grocers' Hall for the new Council of State and all officers above the rank of lieutenant. *A Modest Narrative of Intelligence* reported the ceremony: the procession, the trained bands standing along the passage, the symbolic exchange of the City sword, the "stately dinner," and the gifts: "to the Lord Gen. [Fairfax] a Bason and Ewer of beaten gold and to the Lieut. Gen. [Cromwell] a sute of plate to the value of 300l and a purse with 200l in gold." According to this account, all was "joy."[16] But not all observers agreed.

Rather, royalist newsbooks and pamphlets ridiculed the ceremonies, deflating the solemnity with scatological or otherwise insulting descriptions of the participants themselves. *The Man in the Moon* scoffs: "This Thursday comming, the great Solemnity or City Thanksgiving is Celebrated at Grocers Hall *London*, where Alderman *Shit-breech*, and the right doubty *Mayre* are to be dubb'd Knights of the *burning-Pestle* in *Cromwells* face, his Black *Majesty*, King Gowey-leggs is to be Master of the Ceremony."[17] *Mercurius Elencticus* suggests that following his entry "drawne by Flanders-Mares," Cromwell should be drawn by a "*Hang-man*."[18] Despite the pomp of a "sumptuous Coach drawne by six lustie gray Mares," with life guard "well habited and well mounted," the participants seem to be only "*Coblers* or *Tinkers*"; equally preposterous is Cromwell's wife, "*Pusse Rampant* of *Ely*, cloathed all over in *Innocent white* (her *Beloved's* owne colours) with the *Clerke* of the *Kitchen* both in a *Coach*)."[19] For some, the lavish display only underscored the inadequacies of those it was meant to honor.

Other texts took the form of mock-encomium in doggerel verse. *The Loyall Subjects Jubilee*, a broadsheet published just after Cromwell's departure for Ireland, countered the classicized heroic with satire on Cromwell as an "insatiate Monster, that doth swallow downe / At once a Kingdome and a glorious Crowne."[20] The writer wished that Cromwell's nose might light the way not to Ireland but to hell:

> May the day look black, and soon convert to night,
> Onely thy ruby Nose to give thee light;
> And that thou mayst to shipping safely get,

> Hell for thy life-guard shall the Furies set,
> Charon thy ferry-man shall be, and once being ore,
> Mayst thou nere come to vex the English shore.   (broadsheet)

Printed satire opposed the heroic image and ceremonial display, deploying the language of the material grotesque to link Cromwell's bodily protuberances (his ruby nose) with the lower parts of the world: the hell that was his proper abode.

A Sad Sigh, with some Heart-Cracking Groanes sent after the Lord Governour (July 1649) similarly deployed the language of the grotesque to ridicule the heroic Cromwell. Evoking a *"Parliament of Fiends"* that belches out votes and has substituted *"Our Calves-head Gods of England"* for the true sacred king, the writer alleges that had Cromwell not left for Ireland, "this reforming rout" would have "compeld all to worship mighty snout."[21] Quite at odds with the actual complexities of the situation, *A Sad Sigh* presents Cromwell as Charles's single antagonist:

> This was thy work, how had we done to bring
> To th' fatall block, so wise, so just a King,
> If *Peters* had not stablisht strong thy heart
> In that rare doctrin, that King-killing art?   (p. 4)

The charges resonate in simple, monosyllabic language, underscored by two opening spondees. The poem focuses clearly if briefly on the means and moment of the king's death: on that "fatall block."

Significantly, the text brings up the subject of regicide to blacken and demonize Cromwell as solely responsible: "And may we not well mourn to part with thee, / Whose blood-shot eyes have out-star'd Majesty" (p. 4). In contrast to the emphatic monosyllables that condemn Cromwell, Charles remains mysterious and sacred: he is simply "Majesty," the unique trisyllabic word underscoring his regal difference. Yet Cromwell dominates both trial and execution:

> And though thou Basilisk like, with poysonous spight
> Couldst not confound him with thy hideous sight.
> Yet thou couldst force thy Imps the traiterous *Commons*
> To warn him rudely by an unjust summons,
> T' appeare before a perjur'd Convocation
> Of *Brewers, Tapsters, Tinkers*, of good fashion.   (p. 4)

By labelling Cromwell a basilisk, a legendary serpent with fatal glance and breath, the satire draws upon a powerful myth to interpret a contemporary figure. The writer may also be punning on the etymology of basilisk as "little king" or kinglike; while this serpent, according to Pliny, was so called because of a golden spot on its head that resembled a crown, Cromwell is a basilisk for his ambitious and inappropriate striving after the crown. But the writer does not allow Cromwell to remain in the realm of the legendary; unlike a basilisk, his hideous sight alone is insufficient, and he is reduced to strong-arming and manipulation. The diction diminishes the rebels, making them ignominious and finally ludicrous: the Commons are "imps" (small demons), not only traitors but lower-class upstarts, brewers, tapsters, and tinkers, in contrast to regal majesty.

Through 1650, as he forcefully put down Irish opposition to the new English republic, Cromwell was both praised and satirized in print.[22] Significantly, such satires neither defended the Irish nor attacked Cromwell for the massacres at Drogheda and Wexford that now mar his reputation; rather, they were openly skeptical about Cromwell's alleged victories or ridiculed him as a false king.[23] *The Right Picture of King Oliver* (January 1650) opens with mock-encomium, an elevated style to sing about a nose:

> Of *Nolls Nose* my Muse now sings,
>   his *power, force,* and *might*:
> Subduing Kingdomes, murthering Kings,
>   and winning all by fight.[24]

The reprehensible deeds for which Noll uses his *"power, force,* and *might"* signal the mock-heroic. Most reprehensible of all is, of course, "murthering Kings," the regicide.

Countering the heroic with a grotesque image, *The Right Picture* dismembers Cromwell one body part at a time:

> *Nolls Nose* is toasted, his *Jowle* is roasted,
>   his *Hornes* doe feare no knocks,
> His *Eares* hang downe, from his bald *Crowne*
>   made bare with the *French* P— (p. 1)

The author dwells on Cromwell's protruding body parts, jowl, ears, and especially his phallic nose, constructing him as a cuckold ("*Hornes*"), a libertine ("*French* P—"), and a social climber to boot. Such inter-line feminine rhymes as "toasted" / "roasted" heighten the exaggeration of the mock-praise, and a final spondaic foot ("French P—") calls attention to the venereal disease that has caused all this physical disfigurement.

Citing his Muse in mock-heroic style, the author goes on to laud Cromwell as brewer in terms that humorously mix elevated praise with low style and subject-matter.

> Of all the *Brewers*, my *Muse* assures,
>   *Noll* beares the comly grace
> His *Lips* doe blopper, he beares his Copper
>   In his Brazzen *Face*.   (p. 1)

Rhymes become increasingly contrived and comic ("*Brewers*" / "assures"; "blopper" / "Copper"). Noll bears the comeliness, deflatingly, of brewers. The nonsense word "blopper" calls further attention to its rhyming match: the copper of the brewer's nose.

In particular, *The Right Picture of King Oliver* challenges the republican heroic by depicting a licentious and sexually profligate Cromwell. The tract recounts Noll's various offenses in sexual terms:

> Nols Shoulders full, like a Town-Bull,
>   can beare the *State* a pick-pack
> His *Lips* can meet, and the *Sisters* greet
>   when he is at Tub-tick-tack.   (p. 2)

Double rhymes and onomatopoetic nonsense words underscore the sexual innuendo. At the same time the text goes on to emasculate Cromwell by showing him as so afflicted with venereal disease that he has lost the use of his "Pizzle" and can neither whore nor "doe / the *Sisters* any pleasure" (p. 2). The colloquial language and sing-song verse make Cromwell's moral and bodily excesses comically vivid to the reader.

The grotesque body counters the heroic image of Cromwell, produced in civic ceremony and epitomized in the Robert Walker portraits. But such satire also explicitly recalls a sacred image of Charles I. Thus *The Right Picture of King Oliver* concludes by contrasting the cruelties of "Knave *Cromwel*, Foole *Fairfax*, and Beggerly *Bradshaw*" to the paradise under the late king. Significantly, the form itself changes into alliterative, balanced, and patterned prose that embodies the monarchical order that is being praised:

> Now let me draw you the *Picture* of *England* what it was: The Paradice of *Europe*, the Patterne of Piety, *Beati Populi*, a Blessed People; Where our King like the *Sun* in the Firmament, by his bright raines of Honour gave light to our prosperity, where the Queen like the *Moon* kept a just motion in her *Orb* and received her light from that Fountaine of Justice her Loyall-hearted *Spouse*; Where their Progeny as numerous as the Planets kept their royall Station in this Earthly Heaven. (p. 6)

Parallel phrases and clauses highlight the cosmic harmonies and order reflected in the monarchical universe. The king and queen epitomize the natural order, in sharp contrast to the aberrant and disgusting images used to represent Cromwell. The royal virtues and blessings praised here recall the encomiums of Caroline masques on royal piety, honor, justice, and prosperity. But now such praise serves to challenge and counter a new republic that has destroyed and replaced the Caroline court.

"Still keep thy Sword erect": Andrew Marvell and panegyric on Cromwell after Ireland

The appropriation of monarchical ceremony for the republican state continued with the lavish welcome for Cromwell upon his return from Ireland in May 1650. *A Speech or Declaration of the Declared King of Scots* (June 1650) described the ceremonies at Windsor, where Cromwell was "entertained with many vollies of shot" and greeted by a distinguished delegation: "many persons of eminency, Members of Parliament, and of the Councel of State, and chief Officers of the Army."[25] While these dignitaries congratulated him on "the prosperous success wherewith it hath pleased God to crown his undertakings," Cromwell showed characteristic self-deprecation: "but his Lordship expresseth much humility, and when any Victory obtained is spoken of, he acknowledgeth God to be all in all, and saith, that which is of God shall stand, but if it be not of God, 'twill come to naught" (p. 5). This was not, then, simply a repetition of monarchical forms, but ceremony with a difference. The self-denying figure at the center transformed the meaning of the visual display. Although he expressed reservations about the "Pomp and Glory," Cromwell participated in the ceremony, commenting that "it may be decent and seemly, for such as are well-wishers to the common good, to testifie their affections this way, which may be done without ostentation in the one, and ascribing more than is due by the other" (p. 6). But, as we shall see, while some observers lauded Cromwell in print, others found the spectacle neither decent nor seemly.

Printed text and image complemented and further disseminated the public ceremonial. One engraving, from *A Perfect Table of One Hundred Forty and Five Victories Obtained by the Lord Lieutenant of Ireland* (August 1650), shows Cromwell astride a rearing stallion, wearing full armor, a sash tied over his right shoulder, and carrying his baton in his right hand (fig. 10). The horse is simply caparisoned, and Cromwell is unarmed. The printed text gives a factual account of Cromwellian activities in Ireland: skirmishes, battles, and victories. But the equestrian engraving idealizes Cromwell, and an inscription in the upper left corner guides the viewer to admire "The Right Honorable and undaunted Warrior."

Figure 10 Oliver Cromwell, *A Perfect Table of One Hundred Forty and Five Victories* (1650).

Criticism of Cromwell also continued, although it retreated from print to manuscript, as unsympathetic contemporaries exaggerated Cromwell's martial and masculine virtue into grotesque excess. A private letter in June 1650 from W. Dillingham to Mr. Sancroft fixated with increasing intensity on Cromwell's nose:

> Yesterday I saw the great excrement of the Kingdome, that unnatural nose which is grown beyond the head, the epitome of the East Indies, one contrary to that in Erasmus; instead of casting a shadow, it illuminates the aire so far about, & is the original of al new lights: a truth clearer then the Sun, the shame of the Moon, & the router of al the stars; Yet that which somewhat abates the edge of its Splendour, is the vicinity of gold and spangles wherewith he has bedaubd himself, unless happily the riches of his nose have propagated themselves thither.[26]

The text uses cumulative detail, an extravagant catalogue of hyperbolic epithets, to ridicule and diminish Cromwell, reduced to a single protruding feature. The body image that we have seen in the earlier satire is transposed onto the kingdom: Cromwell has become the excrement, literally that which is sifted out (*excernere*) but with all the unappealing connotations of waste matter. His brewer's nose shines brighter than the sun, moon, and stars, albeit "bedaubd" (both ornamented with vulgar excess and besmeared) by ill-gotten gold and silver. Such an unnatural image contrasts sharply with the natural image we saw earlier of the king and queen as sun and moon.

A month later, Dillingham uses similar nose imagery in a second letter, describing Cromwell as "Samsons foxes firebrands & al beaten together into an intolerable nose," as "the Elephant of reformation that can easily catch all plots against the state in his ~~nose~~ snout," and as "the devils breeches turn'd wrong side upwards & clapd by a mischance to the Generals face."[27] Through biting repetition, Dillingham finds various animal and diabolic figures with which to objectify and ridicule Cromwell. The oil on Cromwell's nose replaces the sacred rites of the coronation: "and shall that oily nose at last goe for the Lords annointed?"[28] Such satire both counters the martial images of Cromwell and keeps faith with the sanctity of true kingship: by so egregiously parodying true kingship, Cromwell underscores its validity and necessity.

The context of fiercely contested representations sheds new light on perhaps the best-known literary text on Cromwell, Andrew Marvell's *An Horatian Ode upon Cromwel's Return from Ireland*. Educated at Cambridge, Marvell (1621 to 1678) was abroad during much of the civil war period, from

1643 to 1647; upon his return to England, he participated in London literary circles and was friends with royalists. From 1650 to 1652, he served as tutor to Mary Fairfax, daughter of Sir Thomas Fairfax, who was, at the time of the *Ode*, still head of the armed forces (he would soon resign and be replaced by Cromwell). Marvell would later be tutor to Cromwell's ward, William Dutton, before accepting an official position in the Cromwellian government as Latin secretary to the Council of State (assisting the blind Milton).

In the *Ode*, which remained unpublished, Marvell engages and directly rebuts what Milton would call the "detractions rude" of satire on Cromwell, and in particular the attacks on Cromwell as Machiavellian hypocrite, destructive iconoclast, and sexually rampant, big-nosed brewer. In so doing, the poem also addresses the juxtaposed visual images: Charles the martyr-king versus Cromwell the martial hero. But Marvell did not put his own work into print; rather than presenting a new image of Cromwell, *An Horatian Ode* calls for an active reader to see and judge rightly, to partici-pate in the process of constructing a new republican hero – and aesthetic.

An Horatian Ode has attracted more commentary and, perhaps, more dis-agreement than any other poem on Cromwell. In the 1940s, Cleanth Brooks used the poem to epitomize the new critical ideal of a literary icon, bal-anced, detached, and self-referential, and a number of critics have followed this general approach.[29] But more recent studies by Blair Worden, Michael Wilding, and David Norbrook argue that the poem is not detached, but politically engaged.[30] While the theatricality of the poem has been recog-nized, it has not been situated among the very material forms of representa-tion of Cromwell and of Charles. My recontextualization shows how Marvell boldly transforms negative stereotypes into praise of a republican hero, reinstating Cromwell in a martial and masculine mode.

In the *Ode*, Marvell challenges the unchanging virtues of royalist iconog-raphy with the movement of time and history embodied in the martial figure of Cromwell.[31] Hence, unlike images of Charles in peace, or the passive martyr-king, Marvell's Cromwell is "restless," constantly in motion:

> So restless *Cromwel* could not cease
> In the inglorious Arts of Peace,
>   But through adventrous War
>   Urged his active Star.[32]

Although the verse is lucid and highly controlled, the run-on lines under-score the forward movement of the restless Cromwell, who (notably unlike Charles during the years of personal rule) is not content with peace. While royalists, as we have seen, constructed and publicized a negative image of Cromwell as iconoclast, Marvell links Cromwell with "three-fork'd Lightning, first / Breaking the Clouds where it was nurst" (lines 13–14), a natural and unstoppable and hence unblameable force:

> Then burning through the Air he went,
> And Pallaces and Temples rent:
>   And *Cæsars* head at last
>   Did through his Laurels blast.   (lines 21–24)

Marvell's richly allusive language transforms Cleveland's disturber of dust and monuments into an instrument of the irresistible heavens: "Tis Madness to resist or blame / The force of angry Heavens flame" (lines 25–26). Marvell replaces the royalists' Machiavellian Cromwell, who boasts that "a King and Kingdome is my valours prize," with a heroic image of the Machiavellian prince who:

> Could by industrious Valour climbe
> To ruine the great Work of Time,
>   And cast the Kingdome old
>   Into another Mold.   (lines 33–36)

The activist founder of new states contrasts sharply with the perfidious stage Machiavel, who hypocritically schemes to send the king to a better realm in order to take possession of the crown for himself.[33] *An Horatian Ode* corrects misreadings of Cromwell as Machiavel, showing the viewer how to see and judge his actions.

Yet Marvell does not avoid the regicide or the martyr-king: rather, he shows how Charles himself, the *"Royal Actor* born," acquiesces in his fate:

> *He* nothing common did or mean
> Upon that memorable Scene:
>   But with his keener Eye
>   The Axes edge did try:
> Nor call'd the *Gods* with vulgar spight
> To vindicate his helpless Right
>   But bow'd his comely Head,
>   Down as upon a Bed.   (lines 57–64)

The initial placement and stress ("*He*") heightens the focus on the royal actor, and the unhesitating actions of the king are impelled forward by enjambment, assonance, alliteration, and the syntax of the single long sentence. But the king's actions are, significantly, non-actions: *not* doing anything common or mean, *not* calling on the gods, acting only in his patience, bowing down. In contrast to Old Noll who "Of all the Brewers . . . beares the comly grace," Charles here has the real thing: beauty, dignity, and grace. But Marvell transforms the image of the martyr-king, the most powerful icon from the royalist lexicon, by causing Charles to accept his fate before the activist Cromwell, who in turn serves the needs of the republic.

An Horatian Ode recuperates even Charles's bleeding head from satire against Cromwell, putting it into the framework of the new republic. The head becomes part of the story of the founding of a new Rome:

> This was that memorable Hour
> Which first assur'd the forced Pow'r.
>> So when they did design
>> The *Capitols* first Line,
> A bleeding Head where they begun,
> Did fright the Architects to run;
>> And yet in that the *State*
>> Foresaw it's happy Fate.   (lines 65–72)

Again, the syntax itself heightens the forward movement of the founding of a new state: as Charles accedes to his fate, so Cromwell subordinates his own interest to the republic: "Nor yet grown stiffer with Command, / But still in the *Republick's* hand" (lines 81–82). Marvell praises Cromwell for subordinating his own will to the state, as he lays his conquests at the feet of the republic: "What may not others fear / If thus he crown each Year!" (lines 99–100). Marvell both evokes and rewrites royalist satire, as his Cromwell, rather than seeking a throne for himself, "crowns" each year with victories in service of the republic. If Cromwell is a martial figure, he is so in the service of others, not to gain a crown for himself.

Finally, *An Horatian Ode* ends with a positive heroic and martial image, staging Cromwell in a new republican triumph:

> But thou the Wars and Fortunes Son
> March indefatigably on;
>> And for the last effect
>> Still keep thy Sword erect:
> Besides the force it has to fright
> The Spirits of the shady Night,
>> The same *Arts* that did *gain*
>> A *Pow'r* must it *maintain*.   (lines 113–20)

Marvell's poem powerfully opposes satire on the Machiavellian mock-king by representing Cromwell as active, masculine, and iconoclastic. Here, the erect sword evinces a positive image of masculinity and martial skill, countering the parodic excesses of the grotesque body. Marvell builds a positive image of martial endeavor, a fit commentary on the heroic portraiture and a rebuke to the satire of the preceding years.

In the context of contemporary political culture, Marvell employs a sympathetic image of the martyr-king Charles only to invert its usual meaning: rather than supporting royalism, he shows Charles acquiescing to his fate as sacrifice to the new republic. Recuperating both Cromwell and Charles within the larger context of the republic, Marvell *depersonalizes* what the satirists had been turning into a character conflict. Cromwell and Charles together become instruments of a higher destiny.

Scotland and the heroic image of Cromwell

As Cromwell proceeded to Scotland to put down continuing opposition to the new English republic, ongoing representations continued to draw upon and revise monarchical forms.[34] To some extent, Cromwell's own iconoclasm and resistance tempered such representations. After his stunning defeat of the Scots at the battle of Dunbar on 3 September 1650, Cromwell wrote to William Lenthall, Speaker of Parliament, in his usual pious terms: "It hath now pleased God to bestow a mercy upon you, worthy your knowledge, and of the utmost praise and thanks of all that fear and love His name."[35] Similarly, he wrote to Richard Mayor, "This is the Lord's doing, and it is marvellous in our eyes. Good Sir, give God all the glory."[36] But the members of parliament turned to the human instrument as much as to a merciful divinity. Declaring 8 October a day of thanksgiving, they also appointed a committee to commission a medal for all who took part in the battle.

Cromwell resisted having his image on the medal. In response to parliament's having commissioned Thomas Simon to copy his likeness, he wrote that "it was not a little wonder to me to see that you should send Mr. Symonds so great a journey, about a business importing so little, as far as it relates to me."[37] Urging that the medal be made with the image of parliament on one side and the army on the other, with the inscription "The Lord of Hosts," Cromwell asked that his own figure not appear: "I do think I may truly say, it will be very thankfully acknowledged by me, if you will spare the having my effigies in it."[38]

Despite Cromwell's suggestion, the medal was made with his own image and a small token skirmish on the front, underneath the caption, "The Lord of Hosts" (fig. 11).[39] The face of the medal shows Cromwell in left profile,

Figure 11 Oliver Cromwell, Dunbar medal (1650).

with the phrase "THE LORD OF HOSTS" inscribed over his head. The reverse of the medal shows parliament in session. The medal captured the paradoxes of Cromwellian iconography: the more that Cromwell demurred, the more he was praised and commemorated. "The Lord of Hosts" remained, but the portrait was of his instrument.

The republican heroic image of Cromwell culminated in the public celebrations, panegyrics, and poems that followed his second and decisive victory over the Scots army at Worcester on 3 September 1651. The victory brought the civil wars to a close, fully consolidating the power of the new English Commonwealth and establishing Cromwell as a figure of considerable political stature. Two weeks after his victory at Worcester, Cromwell entered London to great public acclaim. *Another Victory in Lancashire* recounts how Cromwell, met by all the dignitaries of the city, received "a congratulatory speech in behalf of the whole City."[40] The spectacle was widely attended, and "many thousands of Citizens both horse and foot . . . filled the ways and places best scituate for beholders four or five miles together" (p. 2). As Cromwell progressed from Knightsbridge to Piccadilly, great volleys were fired by the soldiers and "a mighty shout of the people ecchoed again to the earth," four times over (p. 2). Further, "the people all along as he went, put off their hats, and had reciprocal respects return'd from him again" (p. 3). The ceremonial entry and public acclaim marked

Cromwell's political ascendancy in a mode that flirted with the more elaborate monarchical entries.

Yet *Another Victory in Lancashire* insisted on difference, on a kind of self-denying revision of the triumphal mode: "his Excellency chose rather to come in as privately as he could in a coach then openly on horseback, to avoid the popularity and applauses of the people, desiring rather that the good he doth to this Common-wealth may be heard and felt then seen, [lest] that the people should attribute or ascribe too much unto him, who desires to carry on the work of the Lord in all meeknesse and humility" (p. 3). Cromwell's own reservations modified the spectacle, denying the iconic figure at the center. If monarchical forms were evoked, they were also modified, even transformed.

Not only ceremonial display, but engravings and printed texts constructed the heroic image of Cromwell in 1651. A version of Walker's plate-armor portrait (with the addition of Cromwell's personal arms in the upper left) appeared in *A Perfect List of all the Victories Obtained by the Lord General Cromwell* in October following the Worcester victory (fig. 12). The printed text reflects Cromwell's own providential interpretation, as it recounts, for instance, that in June 1650, Charles Stuart, son of the late king, "had agreed with the Scots to be their King and was come to them in Person, but by the providence of God kept out of England," or that in September 1650, "The Lord was pleased to give His Excellency that memorable Victory near Dunbar."[41] But the addition of "His Excellency" dramatically changes Cromwell's own self-representation.

Payne Fisher's *Irenodia Gratulatoria*, probably published in late January 1652, moved to a classical mode of praise that sidestepped the issue of the crown and offered an image of Cromwell as servant of the republic. Although a former royalist, Fisher began composing for the parliamentary side after Marston Moor, and he became Cromwell's unofficial poet laureate, producing a series of Latin panegyrics on state occasions and anniversaries.[42] Rather than a visual or prose icon, Fisher's *Irenodia Gratulatoria* is deliberately syncretic, shifting, and paradoxical, challenging and revising the smooth harmonies of monarchical portraiture and verse.

Reworking the monarchical icon into the printed image, Fisher opens with two engravings. The first engraving (fig. 13) is an equestrian image of Cromwell on a rearing stallion. Cromwell's head is unnaturally large and his sugarloaf hat crudely sketched on, revealing that the body has once again been borrowed from an earlier source. He cuts a military figure, wearing full armor and soft boots, and carrying a baton in his right hand. As in *The*

The Portrayture of His Excell.^{cie} Oliver Crumwell Capt Gen.^{all} & Commander in chief of all y.^e Forces of y.^e Comon-wealth of Engl. Scotl. & Irel. Chancell.^r of y.^e Universiti^e of Oxford &c.

Figure 12 Oliver Cromwell, from *A Perfect List of all the Victories Obtained* (1651).

Figure 13 Equestrian engraving of Cromwell, from Payne Fisher, *Irenodia Gratulatoria* (1652).

Royall Oake of Brittayne, a written gloss interprets and defines the visual image: a disembodied hand beneath the horse's raised right forehoof refers the viewer to Psalms 91:13: "Thou shalt tread upon the lion and adder: the young lion and the dragon shalt thou trample under feet." To direct the reader from the instrument to his divine source, Cromwell speaks the words *Duce, et Auspice Christo* ("With Christ as leader and under his religious authority").[43]

A second engraving in the Fisher text (fig. 14) replicates Walker's painting save for the addition of the Cromwell family arms at the bottom center and a combined land–sea operation in the background. Beside Cromwell are the lines: *Similem Quæ protulit Aetas Consilio vel Marte Virum* [What age has produced a man of similar counsel and military genius].

Yet following Cromwell's own self-deprecation, Fisher focuses on actions not icons. Hence, although the text opens with a frontispiece, it does so to direct the reader away from the visual image to Cromwellian deeds and virtues:

> *Accedite Lectores; & Docemini*
> Quid Icones mutas, vel umbratiles has Effigies
> Sic hiantibus inhæretis oribus?
> Invictissimum si nosse desiderabitis CROMWELLUM
> Non *Vultus*, sed virtutes contemplemini
> Potiores Auro, perenniores Ære.   (Sig. A1r)

[Come close readers and be instructed. Why do you gaze openmouthed upon silent paintings or these shadowy (elusive) statues? If you want to know the invincible Cromwell you will not contemplate his appearance but rather his courageous deeds (*virtutes*), which are more precious than gold, more lasting than bronze.]

Fisher invites the reader to a more active participation than that of simply gazing on the visual icon. Deeds, and not works of art, have lasting value.

Further, Fisher goes on immediately to subordinate Cromwell to the public good: "Qui Communi *Bono* natus, Communi vixit" [Who, having been born for the common good, lives for the public] (Sig. A1r). Having dedicated his poem to the Council of State, Fisher continually reminds Cromwell that he fights for his country's liberty and rights, and for religion. In the verse itself, Fisher concentrates on how Cromwellian victories have fully consolidated the new English republic.

In keeping with its representation of a hero who serves the republic rather than fighting to gain glory for himself, *Irenodia Gratulatoria* refuses to focus on a single, stable image or precedent for Cromwell. Rather, the poem

Figure 14 Engraving of Cromwell, after Walker, from Payne Fisher,
Irenodia Gratulatoria (1652).

sets out multiple heroic precedents while denying their adequacy. Fisher evokes a range of heroes – mythological and historical – only to assert their insufficiency in comparison with Cromwell. This eclectic syncretism merges conventional *imitatio* with Cromwell's own radical distrust of a single fixed image.

In this context of multiple references, repeatedly qualified, Fisher does not make a sustained or straightforward comparison between Cromwell and Julius Caesar. Rather, he both links and dissociates the two:

> Sed Tu magne Pater, Romano Cæsare Major
> Virtutum Imperium late protendis, & Iras
> Sub Ditione premens, positis compescis habenis.
> Te nec Avarities damnosis circinat hamis,
> Non lucrum, Tibi vel infoelix imperat Aurum.   (Sig. HIr)

[But you, great father, greater than the Roman Caesar, you extend far and wide the authority / empire (*imperium*) of your noble deeds and, holding back your anger in a controlled fashion, you check it with a touch of the reins. Avarice does not circle you with her destructive hooks, nor does love of gain or even ruinous gold rule over you.]

Fisher draws upon, but does not idealize, Caesar, pointing directly to his violation of the temple for monetary gain. This simultaneous comparison and contrast, assertion and denial, marks *Irenodia Gratulatoria* throughout, as Fisher refuses to fix Cromwell with a single, stable image.

Likewise, Fisher recounts battles – sometimes at great length – while at the same time denying the need to recount them. He praises Cromwell for not needing praise:

> Fortunate *Heros*! cui temperat omnia candor
> Qui virtute *animi* pompa meliore triumphans,
> Mobile suffragium, populi & plaudentis honores
> Despicis, aeriæ damnans crepitacula famæ.   (Sig. CIv)

[O blessed hero, whose majesty governs all things. You who scorn the fickle approbation and honors of the applauding masses, rejoicing in the courage (*virtute*) of your soul more than in a triumphal procession, condemning the empty rattle of a fame that is here today, gone tomorrow.]

Fisher argues that no argument needs to be made regarding Cromwell's virtues. He praises Cromwell for not seeking praise. He adduces all the precedents that do not apply to Cromwell. And he publishes two detailed engravings that he insists are a barrier to rather than a mirror of Cromwell's virtue.

As such, *Irenodia Gratulatoria* does not simply move the triumph into print, eliciting the reader's unthinking assent. Rather, the complexities and paradoxes of the text demand active participation and judgment. Fisher calls upon his reader to discern and assess how Cromwell both embodies and transforms heroic precedent. With its syncretic, shifting images, *Irenodia Gratulatoria* revises rather than duplicates earlier monarchical iconography. By refusing to align Cromwell with a single, stable image, Fisher depicts him as active in the service of the republic, not an icon in himself. Yet such open-endedness (like Cromwell's own) could have unforeseen effects: Thomas Manley's English translation of Fisher, *Veni, Vidi, Vici*, heightened the imperialism and the links with Caesar, moving toward a more iconic and courtly mode.[44]

The developing and contested images of Cromwell in the early English republic illumine John Milton's highly crafted sonnet, *To the Lord General Oliver Cromwell* (May 1652).[45] By the time he wrote his sonnet to Cromwell, Milton (1608–74) was widely and notoriously associated with the causes of both regicide and republicanism.[46] He was friends with Marchamont Nedham, whose *The Case of the Commonwealth of England, Stated* had set out the rationale for the new republic, significantly, without mentioning Cromwell. Milton's unsolicited *The Tenure of Kings and Magistrates* (1649), published shortly after the regicide and defending the right of the people to punish a tyrant who had broken his contract with them, had won the attention and favor of the newly formed Council of State. Milton was appointed Latin secretary and officially responded to *Eikon Basilike* in *Eikonoklastes* and to Salmasius in *Pro Populo Anglicano Defensio* (only the latter mentions Cromwell and then only briefly). Especially in *Eikonoklastes*, Milton fiercely attacked the idol of kingship. He would not remake that idol, even in a republican mode.

Milton appeals to Cromwell as the defender of liberty and conscience, offering Cromwell both specific advice and conditional praise. *To the Lord General*, which like Marvell's *Ode* was not published, praises Cromwell while eschewing all the traditional elements of a public and ceremonial triumph. Rather, the poem shows a figure who serves as instrument of the divine:

> Cromwell, our chief of men, who through a cloud
> Not of war only, but detractions rude,
> Guided by faith and matchless Fortitude,
> To peace and truth thy glorious way hast plough'd,
> And on the neck of crowned Fortune proud

> Hast rear'd God's Trophies and his work pursu'd,
> While Darwen stream with blood of Scots imbru'd,
> And *Dunbar* field resounds thy praises loud,
> And *Worcester's* laureate wreath.   (lines 1–9)[47]

Like both Marvell and Fisher, Milton shows a Cromwell in constant motion: he ploughs through clouds, rears trophies, and pursues God's work. The single long and complex sentence, with its multiple subordinate phrases and delayed, emphatically placed verbs, evokes the Cromwellian forcefulness and movement that it describes. The cumulative force of the run-on lines takes the sentence beyond the usual sonnet break at the end of the eighth line. Milton praises Cromwell as an unstoppable force: whether bursting through detractions or winning so spectacularly that even the bloody streams and fields praise him. The image of Cromwell standing triumphant on the neck of crowned Fortune takes direct aim at the "detractions rude" with which Cromwell has been afflicted. Rather than the Machiavel, hypocritical and ambitious, this Cromwell has utterly conquered Fortune as instrument of a higher, divine power.[48]

But Milton paints an image of an heroic Cromwell for specific ends. Milton wants Cromwell to prevent the Rump from passing what he viewed as anti-toleration legislation. In February 1652 Cromwell's chaplain John Owen proposed a plan for the "propagation of the gospel" that would eventually become the system of Triers and Ejectors, a central commission set up to examine candidates for the ministry and local commissioners charged with examining existent clergy. Although Milton and Cromwell agreed on the general goal of liberty of conscience, they had very different views on the role of church and state in preserving that liberty.[49] Milton opposed the imposition of doctrinal unity upon the church, and found himself in difficulties with the Rump over his approval, as licenser, of the anti-trinitarian *Racovian Catechism*, cited by Owen's committee.[50]

The praise of the poem is, then, if not conditional at least radically qualified by the turn to the wars of peace. Hence, Milton turns from praise of the past to an appeal to Cromwell to continue to fight on the side of liberty:

> yet much remains
> To conquer still; peace hath her victories
> No less renown'd than war, new foes arise
> Threat'ning to bind our souls with secular chains:
> Help us to save free Conscience from the paw
> Of hireling wolves whose Gospel is their maw.   (lines 9–14)

Three vivid metaphors and run-on lines, as indeed the same sentence continues, now convey a sense of urgency, incompleteness, and danger. The impetus is now behind not the emerging Cromwell but the new foes, whose "Threatening" is emphasized by metrical substitution and placement of the word at the beginning of a line. Milton simultaneously evokes and challenges the image of Cromwell as martial conqueror, making it conditional on his continuing to pursue "God's work" in peace, implementing reform and protecting liberty of conscience. Milton's Cromwell is an activist and iconoclastic figure, part of a new aesthetic that contrasts with, rather than imitates, the monarchical icon.

Was Cromwell's dissolution of the Rump Parliament a little less than a year later an answer to such pleas for the preservation of liberty and conscience? Did Cromwell dismiss the Rump because he chafed under the slow pace of reform in church, state, and society?[51] Or did he, as Sean Kelsey has recently argued, dissolve the civilian government because it was about to strike deep ideological and cultural roots, threatening the power of the military?[52]

Representations of Cromwell from 1649 to 1653, I would argue, complicate and alter parts of Kelsey's picture. The range of texts that we have explored, from Walker's paintings and subsequent engravings to Marvell's *Horatian Ode*, Fisher's panegyric, and Milton's sonnet, show that republican ceremonial, visual image, and panegyric incorporated the figure of Cromwell. Cromwellian representation was not opposed to, but a part (however fraught) of the new aesthetic. Indeed, we have also seen that Cromwell's own self-representation tended to be more radical than that of others, that he evaded the icon and stressed his role as instrument. Such evidence does not detract from Kelsey's ground-breaking work on other republican cultural symbols and images. But it does give Cromwell a more positive role in relation to republican culture, thus also making his relationship to the Rump less antagonistic than Kelsey envisions. The classic accounts of the military man chafing under delay and restraint and concerned to protect liberty still seem best able, in my view, to account for the complex and troubled situation of April 1653.

Portraiture and the appropriation of the monarchical once again came into play immediately following Cromwell's abrupt dismissal of the Rump. Like the images of kings before and after him, Cromwell's portrait was placed on the Exchange in May 1653 by a mysterious gentleman in black, with an appended verse exhorting him to assume the throne:

> Ascend three Thrones great Captaine and Divine
> By th[e] will of God (o Lyon) for they are thine
> Come Preist of God, bring Oyle, bring Robes, bring Gold
> Bring Crownes and Scepters, 'tis high time t'unfold
> Your cloysterd baggs (you states cheate) least the rodd
> Of Steele and Iron of this your King and God
> Pay you in's wrath with Interest: Kneele and pray
> To Oliver the Torch of Syon, a Starr of day.
> Shout then you Marchants: Citty and Gentry sing
> And all bareheaded cry
> God save the King.[53]

Such was an attempt to make the picture into a monarchical icon. Although the inscription was manuscript not print, it nonetheless entered the public realm, reinterpreting the visual image not as a republican hero but as monarch. As "great Captain and Divine," Cromwell needs only the external accoutrements of kingship: oil, robes, crown, and scepter. The gentry and city kneel and pray as to a divine-right king. Full of sacred symbols and powers, the poem explicates the portrait and directs the response: "God save the King."

Yet as a written gloss, a supplement to what was almost certainly a non-monarchical portrait of Cromwell, the verse both guided and dangerously opened up interpretation of the visual text. Hence, a second manuscript verse reinterpreted the material object. In this second account, Cromwell does not have a crown and scepter because he is not a king at all. Or, rather, he is a mock-king, a grotesque parody of true sacred kingship. A second writer copies not only the preceding verse but "The Answer" that begins: "Ascend three Gibbetts, other Right thou hast none, / Two in effigie, and in Person one." As "Rebell to God, to King, and Parliament," Cromwell deserves this triple hanging. The verse goes on to urge Cromwell to take, not the three thrones of England, Scotland, and Ireland, but

> Antichrists three Crownes, for they are thyne
> To which we wish three Headds like Cerberus grim
> For thou art fiend enough to be like him.
> And to each Head a face too, wish we thee,
> For thou hast Nose enough for them all three.[54]

This second verse attempts to undo the sacred image of Oliver as monarch, piece by piece. The writer replaces the throne with three gibbets, marking Cromwell's rebellion against God, king, and parliament. Sacrilege replaces the divine icon. The satire is graphic and visual: three crowns of the

Antichrist, three heads of Cerberus, and three faces to boot, since Cromwell's nose is (like his out-of-proportion actions) "enough for them all three."

At the same time, the satirist envisions a parodic ceremony in which Independent preacher Hugh Peters "shall ayde thy Coronacon / And in the Pulpit thy damnd Acts rehearse / Whilst all the People cry / Goe kisse myne Arse." With this final written comment, we are back in the realm of the grotesque body, albeit arse rather than nose. The sacrilegious and the scatological mingle: Hugh Peters serves as a parodic priest, and the people bare not their heads but their posteriors in an obscene gesture: "Goe kisse myne Arse."

The written glosses on Cromwell's portrait on the Exchange in May 1653 set out two options: king or mock-king. But Cromwell, allegedly, declined both. Another manuscript reports that "after it had been gazed at for a long time," the picture was taken down and brought to the mayor, who in turn brought it to Cromwell. Pressed by the mayor to disclose his role in the display of the picture, Cromwell remained resolutely noncommittal: "his Excellency smiled, and made merry with the Mayor, saying, It was some odd fellow to make sport, &c, but such trifles as these were not to be considered these serious times, and so dimissed the Mayor unsatisfyed and the world unresolved."[55] As earlier, Cromwell refused to fix – or unfix – his own image.

In the early years of the English republic, Caroline portraiture and ceremony were appropriated and revised to praise a heroic Oliver Cromwell. But the effect of such appropriation was double-edged, as such forms also reminded viewers of the absent monarch. Violent satire opposed the heroic image, and only after the consolidation of the republic with Cromwell's victories in Ireland and Scotland did a new, transformed poetic image emerge in the syncretic activism of Andrew Marvell, Payne Fisher, and John Milton. Refusing to define the new hero with a single, stable image, such texts cohere with Cromwell's own anti-formalism and his view of himself as instrument, whether in the service of a divine master or the Commonwealth state. After the dismissal of the Rump, and the calling and resignation of the nominated parliament, the challenge of the Protectorate would be to construct an aesthetic that mediated between republicanism and royalism, that reformed rather than duplicated the image of the king.

Three

"Riding in Triumph": ceremony and print
in the early Protectorate

On 16 December 1653, Oliver Cromwell was installed as Lord Protector under the Instrument of Government, a new written constitution that provided for mixed government by a parliament, council, and Lord Protector. For this office, to which he had assented after accepting power back from the short-lived nominated parliament, Cromwell could claim neither hereditary nor divine right. If, as he insisted, he wished to rule by consent and not by military force, Cromwell needed the legitimation of authoritative languages and symbolic forms even more than the monarchs whom he followed and preceded. Although royal entries have received sustained scholarly attention, the inception of protectoral ceremonial forms has been largely overlooked.[1] How did Charles I serve as antecedent for Cromwellian forms? How successful was the Cromwellian triumph staged in the opening months of the Protectorate? What visual image of Cromwell was produced in the early Protectorate? To what extent did Cromwell control his own image?

Drawing upon Caroline antecedent, the London authorities and Cromwellian officials participated in a public triumph to consolidate and celebrate the Protectorate. But the monarchical forms both helped to legitimate and called into question the new regime. Charles had participated in few public ceremonies: he entered London only twice, and even these ceremonies, as we shall see, were shaped by the king's near-obsession with hierarchy, order, decorum, and divine-right authority. Appealing directly to the public, the Cromwellian regime boldly reworked Caroline conservatism in a civil ceremony focused on the people, performance, and print.

In this chapter I trace the interaction of print and ceremony, beginning with Cromwell's installation as Lord Protector. The Caroline entry into London in November 1641 was an antecedent for Cromwell's contested entry into London and reception at Grocers' Hall in February 1654. Intervening in the disputed images of the early Protectorate, Payne Fisher claimed that the Protector Cromwell had actually saved the republic, while John Milton stressed Cromwell's piety and refusal of the crown in his *Defensio Secunda*. Andrew Marvell's *The First Anniversary of the Government under O.C.* masterfully reworked the anti-triumph of Cromwell's riding accident. But in the months that followed, Cromwell's image became increasingly iconic and imperial.

Cromwell himself was remarkably passive in shaping a protectoral image. Far from directing his own image as had his predecessors Elizabeth, James, and Charles, Cromwell resisted representation. The wide range of conflicting texts that represented Cromwell in the early years of the Protectorate attested to the degree to which his image was constructed from without, in popular print and engraving.

The inception of protectoral ceremony

Despite his reputation as an iconoclast, Cromwell did not neglect the rites of state. But neither did the Protectorate simply ape and hearken back to monarchy. The inception of the Protectorate drew upon the power of display, oral proclamation, and the printed word. Appropriated to celebrate a new mixed form of government, the ceremonies were nonetheless initially colored by their monarchical antecedents, producing resentment and skepticism rather than assent and acclaim.

The ceremony of installation included a public procession in which Cromwell passed from Whitehall to Westminster in his coach. Soldiers lined the street, and he was preceded by numerous dignitaries. *Mercurius Politicus* reported that Cromwell arrived at Westminster attended by state, civic, and military officials. At the ceremony, Cromwell listened bareheaded as "a large writing in Parchment, in the nature of an Oath, was read; there being the power with which his Excellency was invested, and how his Excellency is to govern the three Nations."[2] After Cromwell had accepted and subscribed to this oath, the Lord Commissioners gave him the purse and seals, while the Lord Mayor of London gave him his sword. Accompanied by the Lord Mayor, the aldermen, sheriffs, and troops, Cromwell proceeded to the Banqueting House at Whitehall.

Newsbook accounts describe a joyous response. *Great Brittain's Post* concludes: "Thus, after a stately solemnization, the fame thereof soon eccho'd forth with great acclamations of joy both from the souldiery, and others;

the Bells ringing, the Muskets ratling, and the Canons roaring."[3] *Severall Proceedings of State Affaires* reports that as Cromwell rode back to Whitehall in his coach "there were great acclamations and shoutings all along the streets as they passed" and that "there is more then ordinary joy, in and about *London* (both by the Inhabitants and the Souldiery) for this happy day."[4] The ringing of church bells and lighting of bonfires further commemorated the investiture.[5]

Yet despite the optimism of the newsbooks, other evidence points to a mixed response to these displays of new protectoral power. The papers of John Thurloe, Cromwell's Secretary of State, contain an intercepted letter of 22 December designed for Paris. The letter claims that Cromwell "hath lost much of the affections of the people, since he tooke the government upon himselfe"; the writer asserts that no one except the soldiers, and not even all of them, responded to the proclamation of the new Lord Protector and indeed that the people "publiquely laughed and derided him without being taken notice of."[6] The writer goes on to give an example of the popular distaste for Cromwell's new civil position in the witticism of "an ordinary fellow at Temple-bar" who, having been informed by a trooper that "they were proclaimeing his highnesse the lord protector Cromwell," retorted that Cromwell "protects none but such rogues as thou art."[7] The ceremonial forms, in this account, elicited only disbelief and mockery from the people to whom they were designed to appeal.

The Venetian envoy, Paulucci, similarly wrote in cipher that the people were dissatisfied despite the formal acclamation from the Lord Mayor, sheriffs, and army officers: "But I noticed that the people seemed rather amazed and dashed than glad, and no shout of public or private satisfaction was heard."[8] Indeed, Paulucci alleges that "some have been heard to mutter, We deserve this for our foolish action, putting to death our legitimate king in order to submit to a base born fellow of no standing."[9] The envoy did not expect the new regime to last: the new government had "been received with so little enthusiasm at the outset that one may expect, in its career, to see it either treated with contumely or fall with a great crash."[10] Without the reciprocal participation of the people, the display that was intended to legitimate and strengthen the new protectorate also exposed its vulnerability.

The solemn display evoked even more bitter protest from radical millenarians or fifth monarchists, Cromwell's former allies, who attacked him for not permitting a Rule of the Saints (in the nominated assembly) and, in this sense, replacing King Jesus with himself.[11] At a meeting in Christ Church, Vavasor Powell and Christopher Feake called Cromwell "the dissembleingst perjured villaine in the world" and threatened that "his raigne was but short, and that he should be served worse than that great tirant the last lord protector was, he being altogether as bad, if not worse than he."[12] At a second meeting, the two preachers brought a full panoply of scriptural allusion to bear on the historical moment, bitterly denouncing Cromwell as "that man of sin, the old dragon, and many other scripture ill names." Feake discoursed on "the little horn" of Daniel 7 who made war against the saints, and, although he insisted "I will name nobody," he gave many "desperate hints" that transparently pointed to Cromwell.[13] Following Feake, Powell made further invidious comparisons, concluding, "Let us go home and pray, and say Lord wilt Thou have Oliver Cromwell or Jesus Christ to reign over us?"[14] In their view, Cromwell was a false king and usurper, for he "tooke the Crowne off from the heade of Christ, and put it upon his owne."[15] For these radical sectarians, Cromwell had replaced not King Charles but King Jesus.

But Cromwell himself was remarkably passive in the performance of the protectoral inauguration. Later, speaking to his refractory first protectoral parliament, he thus defended himself: "When I had consented to accept of the government there was some solemnity to be performed, and that was accompanied by some persons of considerableness in all respects . . . who accompanied me, at the time of my entering upon this government, to Westminster Hall to take my oath."[16] Passive constructions underscore Cromwell's representation of his own compliance and passivity; he insists that the initiative comes from elsewhere, that the ceremonies recognize an office, not a person. There was, he maintains, "an explicit consent of interested persons, and an implicit consent of many, showing their good liking and approbation thereof."[17] Although the ceremonies drew upon monarchical precedent, they reworked the symbols to cohere with constitutional changes in the state.

The relatively restrained ceremony of the protectoral inauguration was enhanced in a symbolic entry into the City of London early the following February, when the Lord Mayor, aldermen, and liveried companies invited Cromwell to a reception and banquet at Grocers' Hall. Such a public ceremony served to negotiate and legitimate civic and state power, to stage and publicize harmonious and mutually supportive Protectoral–City relations.[18] As such, the entry paralleled the coronation entry of previous monarchs, although the Cromwellian mode both drew upon and revised monarchical forms.

Charles I as precedent

For much of his reign, Charles avoided the theatrical public display. He did not participate in an entry into London after his coronation in February 1626; nor did he go on progress through the kingdom. After his return from negotiating with the Scots in November 1641, however, Charles entered London in an elaborate public triumph, to be received by the populace and by the civic dignitaries.

Charles's relation with the City of London had been strained by the personal rule of the 1630s. Particular to Crown–City relations, there were conflicts over the alleged mismanagement of the Londonderry plantations in Ulster, over the sale of royal lands to pay off creditors of the crown, over Charles's support for splinter craft groups, and over the royal creation of a Corporation of the Suburbs. But by the fall of November 1641, Charles had recalled parliament, acquiesced in the execution of the Earl of Strafford, and agreed to abolish such hated fiscal measures as Ship Money and such institutions as Star Chamber. Seemingly full of good will and concessions, he had gone to make peace in Scotland, and public opinion swung back in the king's favor. Now struggles within the City Corporation and parliamentary assaults on Charles made the ceremony beneficial to both the king and the Lord Mayor.[19]

Charles impressed his own stamp upon the royal entry, as he did with portraiture and (as we shall see) with other royal ceremonies. Caroline forms embodied the harmony and order of hierarchy in church and state. Hence, while the entertainment for Charles I showed a dynamic interaction between the king, the civic elite (as represented by the Lord Mayor, the Court of Aldermen, and the livery companies), and the populace, the reciprocity was within carefully controlled limits. The Caroline entry served as a kind of ceremonial version of the masques and Van Dyck portraiture: the king at the center dissipated all disorder and disharmony.

The public display of mutual affection and loyalty in the Caroline entry both expressed and constituted the newly harmonious relations of power. In keeping with the traditional forms of the royal entry, the Lord Mayor, the aldermen, and about five hundred members of the livery companies met Charles at the City Wall. In symbolic acknowledgment of Charles's authority, the Lord Mayor presented him with the sword and keys of the city, which Charles, reinvesting that authority, then returned. The lavish procession moved on to Grocers' Hall for feasting and music.

Such public displays undoubtedly did cultural work in and of themselves. But printed texts also circulated and interpreted the royal spectacle. Such texts focused, first of all, on the magnificence and splendor of the spectacle, which was in keeping with the elegance and majesty of early Stuart kingship. Lawrence Price's *Great Britaines Time of Triumph* conveyed, on its title-leaf alone, the splendor of the display, "Shewing in what a magnificent manner, the Citizens of London entertained the Kings most excellent majestie, and how the honourable Lord Mayor of London, with the warlike Artillery men in their glittering armour, gave his Majestie a Martiall-like welcome."[20] Although the entry eschewed elaborate pageantry, the glittering and magnificent display reinforced hierarchical power relations and the mystique of Charles's divine-right kingship.

Other texts emphasized the king's quasi-divine place as the symbolic center of power, acclaiming Charles in conventional sun imagery. John Bond's *King Charles his welcome home* develops the traditionally monarchical sun analogy in verse that embodies the decorum, control, and restraint that marked Caroline style:

> Welcome thou Sun of glory, whose bright beames
> Doe so illuminate those obscure dreames
> Of adverse Fortune, unto which we were
> Late incident, by our quotidian feare.
> But the bright raies of your returne absolv'd
> Us from that passion, and sweetly dissolv'd
> That cloud of feare into the glorious day
> Of triumph.[21]

Even in the opening lines, judicious metrical substitution in the iambic pentameter couplets emphasizes key terms: the trochaic "Welcome," the spondaic and alliterative "bright beames" and the opening stressed feet that underscore both the adversity ("Late incident") and its resolution ("But the bright raies"). The verse idealizes, glossing over the tensions and stresses of the personal rule. The appearance of the sun-king dissolving the clouds of disorder and fear functions much like the dispelling of an antimasque in that characteristically Caroline dramatic form, the court masque.[22] The author uses the symbolic images of traditional royalist panegyric to reconstruct hierarchy, insisting that the failure had been in their own vision, not in the true light of their king as sun. In form, imagery, and message, the text puts forth the ideals of Caroline kingship.

The Recorder's speech, as recounted in *Ovatio Carolina*, stresses the joy of the City and their love and affection to their king above all: "We present unto you our *hearts* and affections, *hearts* of true *Subjects*, full of *loyaltie* to you our King and Sovereigne."[23] The speech acknowledges recent strains. Having urged Charles to "uphold and countenance that ancient forme and frame of *Government*, which hath been long establisht in the *Citie*," the Recorder promises that "wee shall be thereby the better enabled to serve Your Majesty, and constantly to render to you the fruits of a true *obedience*" (p. 10). Despite or perhaps because of the strain of this conditional praise and the precepts for the king, the Recorder ends with great emphasis upon the people's loyalty and joy:

> These Expressions of *joy*, of *love*, of *loyaltie*, and these hearty wishes & desires, which I have mentioned, I meet with everywhere from your *Citizens* of London. They are the soft and stil *Musique* prepared for your *Majesties* welcome and Entertainment this day: the joyfull *acclamations* of your people, upon the sight of your *Royall* Person, will make it lowder, and all cheerfully bearing their agreeing parts together, shall I hope this day make up to your *Majestie* a full and pleasing *harmonie*. (p. 10)

The printed text of *Ovatio Carolina* coheres strikingly with Charles's own concern with decorum, order, and unquestioned authority. The author converts the crowd itself into musical harmony; in keeping with the Caroline view of sacred kingship, the people offer assent and acclaim. Form embodies content here, as the doubling of synonymous nouns or adjectives ("wishes & desires"; "soft and stil"; "welcome and Entertainment"; "full and pleasing") express the harmony that the speaker finds in the people's acclamation.

The symbolic center of the display, Charles, not only accepted the acclaim and advice, but actively cooperated and participated in the pageant, albeit within limits. He responded graciously to the Recorder's speech, desiring the Recorder "to give most hearty *thanks* to all the good Citizens of London, for their hearty expressions of their *love* this day to me" (p. 11). Yet the reciprocity was neither spontaneous nor wide-ranging. Unlike earlier entries for James I or Elizabeth, there were no dialogues or pageants. There is no suggestion that, like Elizabeth, Charles stopped to receive petitions from or converse with his subjects. Nor did the pageant come alive in response to the entry of the king, as it had with James. Rather, the entry was ceremonial, elegant, and restricted. Charles interacted with the Lord Mayor and with the City Recorder; only in print did his words reach a wider public.

Ovatio Carolina goes on to record that despite his graciousness in receiving the homage, Charles's response to the City Recorder also evinced discomfort with the people. Given the display of affection, he remarked that he now realized that "all these former *Tumults* and disorders, have only risen from the meaner sort of people: and that the affections of the better and mayne part of the *Citie*, have ever beene *loyall* and affectionate to my *person*, and *government*," before reiterating "as *heartie* and kind affection to my *people* in generall, and to this *Citie* in particular, as can be desired by loving *Subjects*" (p. 11). Charles did not appeal to the people *per se*, but rather enacted in public form a masque-like ceremony, symbolically dispelling disorder by the display of royal virtue.

Yet if in the court masque the antimasquers disappeared for good, here trouble remained on the horizon. The easy assumptions about virtue and harmony, the almost liturgical celebration of majesty evinced in the Caroline entry, could not calm the political and religious discord. Late October had marked the outbreak of the Catholic rebellion and massacre of Protestants in Ireland; on 8 November, parliamentary leader John Pym brought before the Commons the Grand Remonstrance, a massive indictment of Caroline misgovernment since 1625; passed on 23 November, the Remonstrance was subsequently printed, stirring up apprentice riots in London. On 21 December the City held new elections, ousted its conservative leaders, and elected a new Common Council more sympathetic toward the cause of parliamentary reform. By January 1642 Charles was rebuffed in his attempt to extract the leaders of parliamentary opposition from their hiding-places in the City. Charles fled London for Oxford and the beginning of civil war. Caroline ceremony had failed to effect lasting change in the public sphere.[24]

The Cromwellian entry

The Caroline ceremony, a decade before the Cromwellian entry, was to all appearances calm, but in reality circumscribed and limited, taking little hold; in the appeal directed to the people lay both the strength and vulnerability of the Cromwellian forms. With the figure at the center refusing to give interpretive direction, a range of contested views can be found. For some observers, both supporters and opponents, the entry evoked the monarchy. But others saw the beginnings of a new kind of power and began to fashion a protectoral iconography that resisted the static, iconic forms of monarchy.

In form, the Cromwellian entry was closer to the entertainment for Charles upon his return from Scotland than to the coronation entries of earlier monarchs. No elaborate pageantry marked the Cromwellian triumph. There were no magnificent arches or tableaux, no devices with speeches. Such tableaux helped to fix the allegorical meaning of the specta-cle: Elizabeth as Deborah, James I as Augustus. Noticeably reduced in splen-dor, the Cromwellian entry celebrated not divine-right monarchy but a new civil state based, at least ostensibly, on the will of the people.

Cromwell's ceremonial entry was intended to display harmonious rela-tions among the new Protector, the city elite, and the people. *Mercurius Politicus* reported how Cromwell travelled by coach to Temple Bar, attended by his council and officers of the army. At Temple Bar, the boun-dary between Westminster and the City of London, the Lord Mayor and other civic dignitaries, dressed in ceremonial robes, waited to greet Cromwell before a large group of spectators. There, the Lord Mayor pre-sented Cromwell with a sword in recognition of his authority, which he returned again. Following the traditional ritual of the royal entry, the Recorder expressed the citizens' loyalty and presented the allegiance and duty of the City in a formal speech.[25]

With Cromwell now on horseback, the procession traveled on to Grocers' Hall. Here, the Recorder made another speech "to let his Highness understand how happy the City were in the enjoyment of his Person." After being "entertained (besides Cheare) with Musick, Voices, Drums, and trum-pets," Cromwell was conducted to "a noble Banquet" after which he knighted the Lord Mayor. *Mercurius Politicus* concludes: "This being done, his Highness departed, being plaid out by Hoboys and other loud Musick. In all which this famous City have by these solemn expressions of affection to his highness, given a good example to the rest of the Nation, being sensible of the great benefits they are like to enjoy under his Protection and Government."[26] In print, at least, the ceremony was a highly successful display of reciprocal affection.

Several elements made the Cromwellian ceremony more resonant of the royal entry than the installation itself had been. Cromwell's clothing was much more ornate than before, as were the lavishly caparisoned horses. The delivering of the sword of the city was a ritual, as we have seen, with monarchical precedent. Knighting the Lord Mayor was another apparent assumption of monarchical prerogative.[27] Yet the protectoral display bor-rowed only to transform. The differences between Cromwell's entry into London and coronation entries are as striking and as significant as the simi-larities. The ceremony itself made self-conscious reforms or distinctions. Hence the Recorder's speech to the Lord Protector pointed to the good of the people, *salus populi*. And while stressing that the ceremonies attested to the "Affections of the People," he nonetheless insisted that the day's pageantry was distinct in kind:

> They leave it to other Nations to salute their Rulers and Victorious Commanders with the names of *Cæsares* and *Imperatores*; and after Triumphs, to erect for them their *Arcus Triumphales*. But if I mistake not, their end this day is not any such outward Pomp or Glory, but that those who have been delivered together might rejoyce together; and to express their Desires that the Civil Sword might be as prosperous for Publick Ends, in the Hand where it is placed, as the Military Sword hath been in the same Hand.[28]

In this account, then, Cromwell was not a Caesar but a new kind of ruler, whose power drew upon the consent of the people.

Other accounts similarly offered a non-monarchical Cromwell. *Mercurius Politicus* (9–16 February) included a Latin panegyric by Marchamont Nedham that lauded Cromwell for his refusal of the crown:

> Barbara Cæsareæ sileant Magnalia *Romæ*,
> *Cæsar* adest melior, Sidus ut orbe novum.
> *Cæsare* major adest, quia noluit esse: Coronam
> Arripiant alii; Se potuisse sat est.
>
> [Let the barbarian greatness of Caesar's Rome be silent
> One greater than Caesar is present, as a new star in the sky
> Greater because he did not wish to be (Caesar): a crown
> Others may seize. Sufficient that he could have.][29]

Nedham attempts to have it both ways: to deny Caesar as an ideal (barbarian greatness) and yet to praise Cromwell by saying that he is even greater than (the presumably great) Caesar. The triumphing Caesar / Cromwell brings laurels and scepters stripped from the tyrant not to advance himself, but as great trophies of liberty ("*Libertatis* magna trophæa"). Nedham shifts the focus from the triumphator to the people, who, having been slaves to kings, now must learn how to be free citizens ("primum Cives").

Nedham's shift to the people coheres with Cromwell's continued self-abnegation. Stressing the approbation of the City and public, Cromwell later referred to the ceremony as an important witness to protectoral power, "for it was very great [and] high, and [very] public; and as numerous a body of those that are known by names and titles (the several corporations and societies of citizens in this City) as hath been at any time seen in England, and not without some appearance of satisfaction also."[30]

Cromwell did not so much as mention his own figure, riding in triumph into the City. Rather, he focused on the initiative and participation of the City elite, who thus showed their approval of the Protectorate. And, in his own modest terms, such wide participation on the part of the corporations and city officials showed "some appearance of satisfaction."

Yet the Cromwellian entry did not evoke an unequivocal expression of loyalty and harmony. Far from satisfied, John Evelyn disapproved sharply of "the Usurper Cromwell" being "feasted at the L[ord] Mayors on Ash-Wednesday, riding in Triumph through the City."[31] A written newsletter likewise represented the people as sullen and resentful:

> The only newes we have here is that of our Ashwednesdays Pageantry which was a Tryumph made up of Durt and Multitude; But ye silentest I beleeve that London ever saw of that kinde; not an acclamation, nor one God save from Whitehall to the Grocers, nay nor so much as a Mordecai to put off his hatt. And therefore no mervaile if Haman could not sleepe that night.[32]

According to this account, nobody applauded. Rather, the crowd offered "Curses" and threw dirty pieces of cloth and leather: "nor were there wanting Tiles and Filthy Cloutes to accompany the pompe."[33]

Similarly, the Venetian envoy, Paulucci, asserted a lack of enthusiasm at the entry: "although the entire population of London came forth to view the pageant, not the faintest sound of applause was heard, nor were any blessings invoked on the head of his Highness," and he noted that the scene was "very different from what happened when the kings similarly appeared in public."[34] Paulucci claimed that a large stone was thrown at Cromwell's coach as he returned to Whitehall, materially evincing the disaffection and discontent of the onlookers: "the incident serves to give Cromwell an idea of the spirit of the malcontents and to induce him to be more cautious for the future in placing himself at the mercy of the populace, which, if intimidated into submission certainly bears him no love."[35] The ceremonial entry was intended to celebrate and consolidate harmonious relations between the Protector, the civic elite, and the people. Yet in the view of this (admittedly jaundiced) observer, the ceremony evoked a response opposite to what had been intended.

Designed to manifest the joy of the subjects in the rule they acclaim, the Cromwellian entry depended as much upon the people as upon the visual spectacle. But the joy was apparent only in print. And even in the printed word and image, as we shall now see, Cromwell was contested.

Contested visual images

Complementing the ceremonial triumph of the early Protectorate, a visual image of Cromwell circulated more widely in paintings, engravings, and medals. But unlike the unity of monarchical portraiture, the classicized James I, the youthful mask of Elizabeth, or the elegance and hauteur of the Van Dyck Charles I, images of Cromwell were varied, shifting, and contested.[36] Cromwell apparently made no attempt to create a new mode of protectoral representation after he took office in December 1653. In all of Cromwell's letters and speeches, he makes no comment on the commissioning, circulation, or reception of his portraits. Rather, the Commonwealth mode of appropriating and reforming Caroline forms continued. Sir Peter Lely (1618–80) painted his head-and-shoulders oval portrait of Cromwell (fig. 15) just after the inauguration of the Protectorate.[37] The portrait is in the round, but without a coat of arms or any decoration. The body is again closely modelled on Van Dyck. Lely gives Cromwell a martial image, retaining a plain style of collar and black armor. Unusually, Cromwell's eyes do not meet ours or even look up. Instead, they look down and to his left, giving the portrait a somewhat distant, contemplative tone.

It was to Sir Peter Lely that the (now) well-known advice of Cromwell regarding his portraiture was allegedly given: "Mr. Lilly I desire you would use all your skill to paint my picture truly like me & not Flatter me at all. But (pointing to his own face) remark all these ruffness, pimples warts & everything as you see me. Otherwise I never will pay a farthing for it."[38] The anecdote was first recorded by George Vertue early in the eighteenth century and is thought by some to refer not to Lely, but to Cooper, whose watercolor miniature evinces Cromwell's warts even more prominently. Although its authenticity cannot be proved, the account of Cromwell urging that his portrait be "truly like me," without flattery and even with "ruffness, pimples [and] warts," coheres with Cromwell's own professed piety and humility. In the event, the portraiture was never wholly "warts and all": while eschewing the gaudy trappings of power, Lely elongates Cromwell's face, smooths over some of the roughnesses, and adds the cultural prestige of the cuirassier armor.

A medal also commemorated the installation of the Lord Protector (fig. 16). On the front was an elegant head-and-shoulders profile of Cromwell, while the reverse showed the new protectoral arms. A shield, guarded by a lion, shows in its quarters the cross of St. George for England, the saltire of St. Andrew for Scotland, and the Irish harp for Ireland. In the center of this

Figure 15 Peter Lely, *Oliver Cromwell* (1654).

shield, a much smaller shield showing Cromwell's own arms, a lion rampant, is placed over the heraldic arms of his dominions.

Copies also continued to be made of Robert Walker's portrait in black-plate armor and of the unfinished Samuel Cooper miniature. Such engravings, with altered inscriptions, differed in kind from the more controlled

Figure 16 Lord Protector medal (1654).

and stable iconography of monarchy. The protectoral image became subject to the contingencies of time and history, assimilated into popular culture, made familiar. Engraved images of Cromwell were produced in a political or commercial context, not controlled by the court. No longer mythologized icons, images of Cromwell were part of an unpredictable and public world of print.

One further case, or rather object study, should clarify the ongoing development of the Cromwellian visual image. With the inception of the Protectorate, continental images of Cromwell also evolved and changed. Sometime in the early Protectorate, an anonymous equestrian painting showed Cromwell astride a barb stallion, a pistol in a saddle-holster near his left knee (fig. 17). The painting was clearly not done from life, as Cromwell's head was placed on a short and rather portly body. Cromwell carries a long crop or stick in his right hand, and wears high cavalry boots with spurs. Behind him is a copy of Hollar's engraving of the cityscape of London. The image itself is significantly non-monarchical, more like that of a Dutch burgher.

But satires raised the spectre of usurped kingship. Hence, an undated engraving of this image portrays a youthful, rather portly Cromwell in half length (fig. 18). Cromwell's body is turned to the viewer's left, and his head turned to face the viewer. He wears the clothes of a well-to-do merchant: matching velvet jacket and breeches, the jacket with a long row of many buttons. The only military item in his costume is the gorget around his

Figure 17 Anonymous equestrian painting of Cromwell (*c.* 1654).

Figure 18 Engraving of Oliver Cromwell, half-length (n.d.).

neck, over which peeks his characteristic plain falling collar. He wears an understated gold chain and medal about his neck, carries a cane in his right hand, and sports a lavishly plumed sugarloaf hat atop his head. Although this engraving, with its honorific caption, was apparently intended to present a positive image, not all observers were convinced. Beneath the caption, a contemporary has written the words "traidor à dios y à in Rey."

Another version of the continental image depicts "Oliverius Cromwel Vice Generalis" in half length, his body turned slightly to our right, the left hand holding a small book, the right resting flat on his chest (fig. 19). Facing the viewer, he wears his characteristic plain falling collar and a simple doublet with a sash or shoulder-belt over his right shoulder. Around the picture is inscribed "Sat Doctus Versare Dolos. Oliverius Cromwell Vice Generalis Exercitus Parlam.ᵗⁱ in Anglia." Below the picture is written

> En CROM-WEL, curvum potuit qui dicere rectum,
> Ille erebo et furiis peior cacodemone pestis
> Ductorum his animat dictis, tota Anglia nostra est,
> Tollamus CAROLUM REGEM, paribusque petamu[ii]s
> Insidiis PROCERES, populus nostræ omnia dextræ
> Permittet, fortes sortem tentasse iuvabit.

[Behold Cromwell, who could say the crooked was straight. That creature from Hell and demonic plague worse than the furies inspired his followers with these statements: "all England is ours; let us depose Charles the king; let us seek out the nobility with plots similar [to theirs]; the people will grant everything to our right hand; it will aid the brave to have tried [their] fortune."]

The vicious Latin inscription attacks Cromwell and reminds the reader of the betrayal of King Charles. Adroit word choice and punning heightens the polemic: *Erebo* recalls Erebus, Latinized from a Greek synonym for Hades; *Pestis* connotes plague and disease, but also has the common rhetorical sense of "anarchist, subversive." The final phrase, *fortes sortem tentasse iuvabit*, cleverly but bitterly evokes the famous Virgilian (*Aeneid* 1.203) line: *forsan et haec olim meminisse iuvabit*. Future commentators will look back sardonically upon the Cromwellians' supposed bravery in gambling everything to seize power for themselves. Visual additions to the engraving also recall the martyred king. On each side of the stylized scroll that contains these lines is a jumbled pile of heads. The foremost head in the left-hand pile is that of Charles I, the crown still on it.

Another engraving similarly reflected the vicissitudes of history to undercut Cromwell's authority (fig. 20). Although originally a non-satiric engraving, a number of visual additions jeer at the Lord Protector.

Figure 19 Engraving of Oliver Cromwell, with heads (n.d.).

Figure 20 "Oliver Cromwel, Proteckteur Geeweest" (1654).

Cromwell wears plain civilian dress, with a fur-lined coat, simple collar and cuffs, and a beaver hat. But now a raven perches atop Cromwell's broad-brimmed hat, to which stag's horns and a feather have also been added. Spectacles are perched on his oversized nose, and a smoking pipe is in his mouth. To further ridicule the figure of the Protector, an owl, who likewise sports a horned cap and spectacles, perches on Cromwell's right shoulder.

Cromwell's visual image was shifting and contested, subject to interpretation and change, in contrast to the largely unchanging divine-right icon. In the weeks and months following the triumph at Grocers' Hall, the heroic image of Cromwell as conqueror was also refracted into a spectrum of printed texts. Not only did some see Machiavel, Antichrist, or Jeroboam rather than Caesar, but the figure of Caesar was itself contested.

Ceremony in print, Payne Fisher, and Milton's *Defensio Secunda*

Roman history continued to be a prominent and debated mode of representation of Cromwell in the early Protectorate.[39] In May 1654, Ralph Josselin heard a rumor that Cromwell would be made emperor.[40] That same month, a skeptical Edward Hyde wrote that "Cromwell no doubte is very busy in the tyringe-house, but very silent upon the stage. They are without question upon a deepe consultation for some new title, and in their whispers there is one mentioned: *Oliverus Maximus Insularum Britannicarum Imperator Augustus.*"[41] Similarly, John Thurloe received a report from Cologne that Cromwell had been dubbed "Oliver, the first emperor of greate Britaine, and the isles thereunto belonging, allways Caesar."[42]

Royalists and republicans alike saw Cromwell as a mock-Caesar. "The Character of a Protector" (May 1654) queries: "What's a Protector? tis a stately thing / That Apes it in the non-age of a King / A Tragick Actor, Caesar in the Clowne / Hee is a brasse farthing, stamped with a Crowne."[43] Also in May 1654, John Streater published a cleverly ironical anti-protectoral tract that used the figure of Caesar.[44] *A Politick Commentary On the Life of Caius July Caesar* gives excerpts from Suetonius that represent Caesar as a Machiavel in terms transparently applied to Oliver Cromwell:

> *Cæsar* made use of the discontents of the people as a footstep to ascend, together with pretending to ease them from servitude: he alwaies, untill he attained the Empire, pretended all that he did to be in favour of the people, which begot in them the more Willingnesse to assist him. A people are alwaies deceived by these two Vizards, *viz.* pretence of Liberty, and Religion.[45]

Streater offers a disclaimer that (by his very denial) makes the contemporary application even more clear, pointedly commenting: "Reader, thou mayest wonder that in this discourse, I should undertake to prove *Cæsar* a Tyrant and a Usurper, my Author saith little better of him," but "I shal not comit treason against him in my undertaking, I am told he is dead long since" (p. 8). Nonetheless, Streater implicitly suggests that a discerning reader could find the treason for himself: "by this smal work thou shalt see the picture of all Governments and Governers: if they be just and good thou mayest see how far they differ, thou mayest judge colours by their contrary, and if not contrary, how near they are one unto another by comparing" (p. 8). Streater thus calls upon an active reader to see between the lines and judge rightly.

Unlike Streater, Payne Fisher employs Roman history in praise of Cromwell, although that praise is both more daring and more fraught than has been recognized. Fisher's *Inauguratio Olivariana*, like his earlier *Irenodia Gratulatoria*, employs both republican and Julio-Claudian imagery to formulate a Cromwellian iconography. Upon the occasion of the Protectorate, Fisher does not straightforwardly make Cromwell an Augustus; rather, he continues to deploy a synthesis of figures to argue that Cromwell has saved and continues to nurture the republic. To maintain this perhaps surprising argument, Fisher modulates the classical images through a focus on piety that seems more indebted to puritan godliness than to classical *pietas*. Fisher's portrayal of a humble and self-negating Cromwell responds to attacks from royalists, republicans, and radical sectarians alike.

Fisher needs, first of all, to explain Cromwell's present position and his earlier dissolution of parliament, especially since he had praised the Council of State so highly in his previous work. To do so, Fisher represents the divisions and fighting within the parliament as parallel to the divisions of civil war, both of which Cromwell must calm. Hence, as in *Irenodia Gratulatoria*, Fisher portrays Cromwell as bringing peace after war, order after chaos and destruction, harmony reflected as well in the Latin verse:

> O fortunatam, tali de Principe, Gentem!
> Qui male fraterno gavisos sanguine Fratres
> Nexuit, & nexos concordi lege ligavit.   (p. 2)

[O blessed people [living] under such a ruler! A ruler who reconciled brothers who sinfully took pleasure in fraternal blood and a ruler who, once brother was reconciled to brother, bound them together under harmonious rule.]

Fisher then employs the language of civil strife to describe the parliament, hence legitimating Cromwell's dissolution of it as once again bringing control and order after disorder:

> (Ille *Senatorum* rixas & jurgia deflens)
> Perdite divisis in mutua viscera *membris*
> Arbiter emicuit.   (p. 2)

> [When the limbs [of the senatorial body] were divided against their own flesh, that man (bemoaning the quarrels and spats of the senators) stood out as a mediator.]

Fisher thus transforms Cromwell's dissolution into its opposite: the parliament is divided and riven *before* Cromwell acts to restore unity.

Quite audaciously, given the circumstances, Fisher portrays the parliament itself as dissolving (*liquare*) the storm-tossed ship of state, which Cromwell then rescues:

> Propria cum sponte *Senatus*
> Obstreperus surgens, *Navim* Rectoris egentem
> Liquerat, ambiguis & caligantibus undis,
> *Ille* insperato *Cynosura* eluxit olympo,
> *Ille* idem *Palinurus* erat. *Navarchaq*; gnarus
> Admisit vidui; clemens moderamina, clavi.   (p. 2)

> [When the senate, noisily revolting by its own free will, had dissolved the ship of state when it was in need of a leader, while unpredictable waves were enveloping it (the ship of state) in darkness, that man, like the constellation Ursa Minor, shone forth unexpectedly from Olympus, that man was a second Palinurus. Like a skilled ship captain, he gently took up the controls of the abandoned rudder.]

Boldly employing the traditional "ship of state" metaphor, Fisher makes Cromwell's act of dissolution an act of recovery.[46] Cromwell becomes a second Palinurus. Or, rather, a Palinurus who survives, since Aeneas' helmsman, in the course of saving Aeneas' ship from sinking in a storm, gets swept over the side, a necessary sacrifice for the founding of the Roman state. Significantly, Fisher had commended Bradshaw and the Council of State as steering the ship of state in *Irenodia Gratulatoria*; he now transfers the praise to Cromwell himself.

Fisher also elaborates the ship of state metaphor to show that, far from destroying the republic, Cromwell has brought it at last into a safe port:

> Talem *Anglus* poscebat inops; Qui vindice dextra
> Assereret salvum, tuta in statione reponens:

> Talem *Templa* Ducem; Talem petiitque Popelli
> Sanguine parta salus; nequiit sine Remige tanto
> Turbidi, tranquillos *Respublica* tangere, *Portus*.   (p. 3)

[Hapless England was begging for such a man: the sort of man who would restore England to health by means of his avenging right hand, setting her down in a safe harbor. The sanctuaries [churches] sought such a leader; prosperity, obtained by the blood of the common people, sought such a leader. The troubled republic was unable to arrive at calm ports without such a great oarsman.]

Fisher does not avoid but boldly appropriates republican language and themes. Indeed, he later argues that the heroes and defenders of the Roman republic could have learned from Cromwell.[47] No one need be a republican martyr under Cromwell, who himself guarantees the state of liberty.

Yet Fisher does more than simply praise Cromwell as one who has saved the republic. Rather, *Inauguratio Olivariana* synthesizes and melds various historical and mythological figures in praise of Cromwell. Most notably, Fisher rewrites the history of the Roman republic, praising Cromwell as a ruler under whom Brutus would have been happy to live:

> Vivere sub tali gauderet Principe, *Brutus*;
> *Brutus* grande decus, Libertatisq; repertor
> *Ausoniæ*, qui Jura suis *fascesque* reduxit.   (pp. 43–44)

[Brutus would rejoice to live under such a ruler (*Princeps*), Brutus who is a great source of glory and the founder of Italy's freedom, who reinstituted the legal system and political offices for his fellow countrymen.]

The key republican hero was Lucius Junius Brutus, who drove out Tarquinius Superbus from Rome after the rape of Lucretia by Sextus, son of Superbus. But rather than praising Cromwell as a Brutus, Fisher daringly praises him as a ruler who himself preserves the law and political offices, obviating the need for a Brutus. The description of Cromwell as *Princeps* (a term adopted by Augustus to represent his status as the leading citizen rather than *imperator*) seems key here, and seems to be implying a contrast between a Caesarian model of absolute rule and an Augustan model of cooperative rule. It is not a coincidence that Augustus himself claimed to have restored the republic in 23 BC.

As Fisher elaborates his portrait of Cromwell, the implied contrast with the Tarquins continues. First, Fisher praises Cromwell for his self-control and moderation. In protectoral England under Cromwell, there is no threatened rape of Lucretia:

> Non ibi deformis *Lucretia* damna rapinæ
> Lugebit, castræ nec solvet vincula zonæ
> Virgo Pudicitiæ compos.   (p. 44)

[In that place Lucretia will not bewail the harm of foul rape, nor will the maiden in full control of her modesty, loosen the bonds of her chaste girdle.]

Rather, Cromwell as protector himself preserves the laws so that there is no need for a Brutus: "Te *vindice* servat / Jura *Torus* Thalamusq; *fidem*" (p. 44) [with you playing the role of avenger (*Vindex*), the marriage bed and bedroom preserve the laws and guard their fidelity]. Fisher also draws here upon distinctively Augustan language. *Vindex*, related to *vindico, vindicare*, is the same word used to describe the action of the head of the household giving freedom to a slave. Augustus himself uses the term in *Res Gestae*, although this text was not known in the seventeenth century. Augustus – and also Cromwell's supporters – collapse the distinction between father of household and father of country.

Finally, Fisher reinforces the continuity between Cromwell as republican military hero and his role as protector by depicting him as embraced by a personified liberty in his new role as Protector:

> Hinc nova *Libertas* rapidis peritura favillis
> Tutior illuxit, tantosq; experta tumultus
> Apparans tandem positis pacatior armis,
> Te PROTECTOREM passis complectitur ulnis.   (p. 45)

[For this reason a new freedom, on the brink of destruction among the swift-burning embers, shone forth without fear and, after undergoing such great upheavals and finally, once the weapons were set aside, peacefully making herself visible, she embraces you as her protector with open arms.]

Fisher's bold syncretism constructs Cromwell as an activist figure in the service of republican ideals.

Largely restricting their treatment of Fisher to Thomas Manley's translation of his *Irenodia Gratulatoria*, scholars have assimilated him to a bland Augustanism, in turn assimilated to monarchy. But, as our examination of *Inauguratio Olivariana* has shown, Fisher does not drop the republican ideals of liberty with the inception of the Protectorate. Rather, in the tradition of panegyric that guides, advises, and even cautions, Fisher draws upon a range of figures and times to exhort Cromwell to continue to protect *Libertas*. Fisher remained more republican in spirit than has been recognized, and his use of Augustus can be seen as not so much monarchical as *avoiding* the issue of the crown. Perhaps disingenuously, he takes Augustus'

professed ideals, his anti-monarchism and claim to have restored the republic, at face value. Cromwell too must live up to his professed claims.

Placed alongside Fisher, Milton can be seen as participating in a shared
project of constructing a new protectoral aesthetic marked by anti-formalism, syncretism, and the refusal of a single, fixed image or icon. Recent
accounts of a republican Milton have extended and deepened Austin
Woolrych's classic account of Milton's eventual disillusionment with
Cromwell.[48] Milton's panegyric to Cromwell in his *Defensio Secunda*, published in Latin in May 1654, has been increasingly seen as containing conditional praise and veiled critique, laying the groundwork for repudiation.[49]
But too strict a focus on republicanism underestimates the shared
Protestant ideals. Recontextualized in the complex and shifting political
culture of 1654, Milton's *Defensio Secunda* can be seen as responding to
attacks on Cromwell by stressing above all his piety. Yet in the process of
praising Cromwell's piety, Milton also holds him accountable for the future,
pointing to a series of specific actions that will protect liberty of conscience
and promote ongoing reform.

Milton thus crucially praises as a central Cromwellian trait a piety that
goes well beyond the classical *pietas* to draw upon godliness and self-
denial.[50] At the same time, he characterizes his opponent as impious in the
very sentence preceding the discussion of Cromwell: "major enim cumulus
ad impietatem tuam accedere non potuit" [for your impiety could not by
any measure be increased].[51] Milton denies royalist charges of Cromwellian
ambition and duplicity, allegedly shown in such actions as his persuading
the king to flee to the Isle of Wight. Rather, he argues, the royalists continually blame the results of their own errors on Cromwell's trickery and deceit
(*doli & fraudes*).

Milton represents Cromwell as following in the tradition of reformation,
linked with his ancestor Thomas Cromwell (a linkage that we have seen
used negatively in royalist satire). Milton's Cromwell is "nulla re magis
quam religionis cultu purioris, & integritate vitae cognitus" [known for
nothing so much as his devotion to the Puritan religion and his upright
life].[52] Even martial prowess transmutes to piety:

> Ut omnes ad sua castra tanquam ad optimum non militaris duntaxat sci-
> entiæ, sed religionis ac pietatis gymnasium, vel jam bonos & fortes
> undique attraheret, vel tales, ipsius maxime exemplo, efficeret.

> [(So) that to his camp, as to the foremost school, not just of military
> science, but of religion and piety, he attracted from every side all men
> who were already good and brave, or else he made them such, chiefly by
> his own example.][53]

While the royalist troops are characterized by *vis, vinolentia, impietas atque libidines* [violence, drunkenness, impiety and lust], Cromwell's troops are welcomed as *virtutis etiam omnis & pietatis hortatores* [men who actively encourage every virtue and piety].[54] Rather than a Machiavel who has conquered Fortune, Milton's Cromwell is guided by God himself: "Te enim salvo, Cromuelle, ne Deo quidem satis confidit, qui rebus Anglorum, satis ut salvæ sint, metuat; cum videat tam faventem tibi, tam evidenter opitulantem ubique Deum" [for while you, Cromwell, are safe, he does not have sufficient faith even in God himself who would fear for the safety of England, when he sees God everywhere so favorable to you, so unmistakably at your side].[55] Cromwell serves not for his own ends, but as an instrument of the divine.

Lauding Cromwell above all for his rejection of the idol of kingship, Milton simultaneously praises and advises, commends and cautions. As Cromwell takes on the position of single head of state, he will be crucially tested to see "vivatne in te vere illa pietas, fides, justitia, animique moderatio, ob quas evectum te præ cæteris Dei numine ad hanc summam dignitatem credimus" [whether there truly live in you that piety, faith, justice, and moderation of soul which convince us that you have been raised by the power of God beyond all other men to this most exalted rank].[56] In the end, Cromwell's actions alone can refute the charges of deceit and ambition.

In the eloquent plea that follows for the restoration and preservation of liberty, including the separation of civil and ecclesiastical powers, law reform, and moral reform through education, Milton broadens his exhortation and warning to include the people. They too must be pious to be free:

> Scitote, quemadmodum esse liberum idem plane est atque esse pium, esse sapientem, esse justum ac temperantem, sui providum, alieni abstinentem, atque exinde demum magnanimum ac fortem, ita his contrarium esse, idem esse atque esse servum.

> [Rest assured, I say, that just as to be free is precisely the same as to be pious, wise, just, and temperate, careful of one's property, aloof from another's, and thus finally to be magnanimous and brave, so to be the opposite to these qualities is the same as to be a slave.][57]

Carefully paralleled infinitive phrases enumerate and underscore the multiple responsibilities upon which true freedom depends. Milton's balanced syntax reflects the self-discipline and order that he praises.

Milton exhorts both Cromwell and the English people to develop inner virtues in order to be free. Milton's Cromwell is thus a part, and always a subordinate part, of his epic of the godly English nation. That Milton would become bitterly disillusioned with Cromwell, lashing out cryptically in the final prose works, goes against his consistent concern with holding the people themselves to account. Milton both allies himself with Cromwell and challenges him to live up to his professed ideals. But Cromwell faced even more severe challenges in the months that followed.

Satire on Cromwell's riding accident and Marvell's counter-image

The first protectoral parliament that opened on 3 September 1654 did not quell criticism of the new regime; indeed, the members set about challenging the very basis of protectoral rule in the Instrument of Government. In this fraught political climate, Cromwell's riding accident in Hyde Park in November 1654 provoked a representational as well as a political crisis, underscoring the malleability and vulnerability of the protectoral image. In contrast to the early protectoral ceremony that had displayed Cromwell (to some) as a triumphing Caesar, the riding accident appeared to be an anti-triumph. The public participated actively in offering (mostly negative) interpretations of the event. Andrew Marvell strikingly foregrounds this process of interpretation to dissociate Cromwell from kingship in his *The First Anniversary of the Government under O.C.* But subsequent interpretations of the Protectorate were more imperial and more contested.

The riding accident was by its very nature an event observed by few, but it was circulated widely in manuscript and print. Cromwell wanted to take the reins of a team of horses in Hyde Park, but he lost control and was dragged for some distance. Even more dangerously, the pistol in his pocket went off. Newsbooks reported the accident, but glossed over the danger.[58] *The Faithful Scout*, for instance, stated that "This day his Highness the Lord Protector went in his Coach from White hall, to take the ayr in Hide-park; and the horses being exceedingly affrighted, set a running; insomuch that the Postilian fell, whereby his Highness was in some danger; but (blessed be GOD) there was little hurt."[59] The newsbook omitted both the seriousness of the injury and any details that might discredit Cromwell.

Nonetheless, rumors circulated. Although he terms the incident a "miraculous escape," the Venetian envoy, Paulucci, goes on to write that "many do not scruple to assert that this adventure should warn his Highness that bad driving leads to a bad end and that those who meddle with what does not belong to them experience what they do not expect or even imagine."[60] Paulucci reports that "malcontents" ridiculed the accident and asked their preachers "to pray and implore the prayers of their congregations for an ill advised coachman who had undertaken to manage three kingdoms, with other satirical expressions."[61] Manuscript text and oral word thus functioned as a form of opposition, ridiculing and questioning Cromwellian rule.

Manuscript verse deriding Cromwell as unfit to rule directly countered the triumphal ceremony and the heroic portraiture. These verses depict Cromwell as a mock-king who cannot guide six horses, much less a kingdom. Such texts replace the larger-than-life heroic conqueror with a tyrant and brewer.[62] Satire undercuts the spectacle of the triumph, showing its falsity. It is striking that a number of these satires focus not on Cromwell himself, but on sardonic reactions (which presumably the reader can share) to the accident. Hence, "The Coachman of St. James" dramatically depicts not just spectacle, but spectator:

> I'm pleased to fancy how ye glad compact
> Of Hackney coachmen sneare at ye last act
> Hark how ye scoffing concourse hence derives
> The Proverb needs must goe when th' Divel drives.[63]

Adopting colloquial language and a direct first-person point of view, the author confides in the reader, who shares the joke. The text imagines the overheard reactions to be taking place in the present tense: "hark." Simultaneously, the reader overhears another common voice, the "Whipster" who recognizes the irony in Cromwell, who has turned out the parliament, being "turned out" himself by a team of horses:

> Yonder a Whipster cryes, Tis a plain Case
> He turn'd us out to put himselfe in's Place
> But God a mercy Horses once for ye
> Stood foot and turn'd him out as well as wee.[64]

The colloquial and monosyllabic "plain" speech underscores the "plain" truth that the whipster speaks. A third observer is equally derisive: "Another not behind them with his Mock's / Cries out, Sir faith you were in ye wrong box." The speaker confides to the reader that Cromwell belongs not in a coach box but in a brewer's cart:

> He did presume to rule because forsooth
> Has bin a Hors Commander from his youth
> But he must know there's difference in the rains
> Of Horses fed with Oates and fed with granes.
> I wonder at his frolick for be sure
> Four pamper'd Coach Horses can fling a brewer.[65]

Vernacular language, a highly dramatic present tense, and contrived disyllabic rhymes (be sure / brewer) comically expose Cromwell for what he is: a brewer accustomed to working not with coach but with dray horses. The minced oath ("forsooth") and pretended surprise ("I wonder at") align the speaker with a common point of view. The text deflates the accident from dangerous or potentially tragic to comic: a "frolick."

Literary texts responded to both the riding accident itself and the apparently widely circulated manuscript satire. George Wither (1588–1667) had long seen himself as a prophet–poet, although he had been repeatedly frustrated in his bid for Stuart royal patronage, no doubt in part because of his blunt satire and outspoken critique of such favorites as the Duke of Buckingham. During the civil wars, Wither was an early and active supporter of opposition to the king, continuing to write prolifically and serving as a major in the parliamentary army. His *Vaticinium Causuale*, countering various negative readings of the riding accident, was the first of several texts he composed about and to Cromwell.[66] Asserting that "when GOD *Acts*, or *speaks*, each *Word* and *Deed* / Should be observed, with some *useful heed*" (p. 1), Wither depicts not an accident but a "Miraculous Deliverance" with providential meaning.

Vaticinium Causuale begins as a defense of Cromwell against the detractors who mocked the riding accident:

> For many *Lookers on*,
> And (some, who love to trumpet forth *Mischances*,
> With Descantings, on all their *Circumstances*)
> Have publish'd what befell. Thence, *Rumour* spreads;
> Puts various *Fancies*, into Peoples heads;
> And every one draws *Uses*, or, *applies*
> As *Malice* fools him, or, *Love* makes him wise. (pp. 1–2)

As he counters negative views, Wither's disjointed rhythms, abrupt caesurae, unpoetic language, and egregiously forced rhymes ("undone" / "*Lookers on*"; "*Mischances*" / "*Circumstances*") underscore his anticourtly message. The balanced symmetry of the final line contrasts with the striking asymmetry of what precedes it.

Wither reads the accident as providential, a reminder to the people of the divine source of Cromwell's power. But he offers no easy praise to Cromwell. Rather, the accident serves to evince Cromwell's own mortality. Wither warns against "the *stumbling stones*, / Environing th' Ascent, to *Earthly Thrones*" (p. 9) and urges Cromwell not to abandon his divinely appointed mission "*for a Buble*, / *Which in vain hope begins & ends with trouble*"

(p. 13). Again, homely language and disyllabic feminine rhyme ("*Buble*" / "*trouble*") match style to content. Wither exhorts and admonishes Cromwell, focusing on divine agency and an apocalyptic future.

The context of this debate over the accident in Hyde Park and, more broadly, early protectoral heroic imagery, clarifies and illumines long-puzzling features of Andrew Marvell's *The First Anniversary of the Government under O.C.* Many previous scholars have noted and attempted to rectify in various ways the poem's disunified and shifting images.[67] But Marvell's poem, in my view, deliberately evokes and maintains syncretism and shifting imagery as alternatives to the stable, monarchical icon.[68] Going even further, Marvell foregrounds and problematizes the process itself of constructing a Cromwellian image. Much of the poem addresses the act of viewing, depicting the spectators or viewers as much as Cromwell himself. What has been seen as disunity and diffusion in the poem is a lesson in hermeneutics, showing the reader how to read, interpret, and judge rightly. And the right interpretation is that Cromwell is not a king.

Unlike the *Horatian Ode*, *The First Anniversary* was published, albeit anonymously, in 1655, and was advertised in the official newsbook *Mercurius Politicus*.[69] In *The First Anniversary* Marvell moves from the classicism of the *Ode* to a work infused with biblical imagery and energy. We shall see that both poems, however, are chiefly constructed as responses to attacks on Cromwell. In the same way that the *Ode*, as we have seen, counters the Machiavellian stereotype, *The First Anniversary* engages current debate on the Protector, answering recent attacks and royalizing panegyric alike.

At the thematic and structural center of the poem is an account of the much-disputed accident in Hyde Park. Marvell's account of the accident concentrates not on the spectacle alone but on the reactions of those who view it. In sharp contrast to the satires, Marvell envisions not mockery but grief and sorrow. Even nature itself mourns for the apparent loss of Cromwell:

> Thou *Cromwell* falling, not a stupid Tree,
> Or Rock so savage, but it mourn'd for thee:
> And all about was heard a Panique groan,
> As if that Natures self were overthrown.   (lines 201–04)[70]

Spondaic substitution ("Thou *Cromwell*") stresses the direct appeal to Cromwell; Marvell keeps the pathetic fallacy of mourning trees and rocks in control by compression and largely end-stopped lines. The control and balance of the verse even as it describes the panicked and passionate natural reaction to Cromwell's fall suggest that the loss may not be what it seems.

Thus Marvell goes on to employ biblical imagery to transform the scene of apparent humiliation into triumph:

> But thee triumphant hence the firy Carr,
> And firy Steeds had born out of the Warr,
> From the low World, and thankless Men above,
> Unto the Kingdom blest of Peace and Love:
> We only mourn'd ourselves, in thine Ascent,
> Whom thou hadst left beneath with Mantle rent.   (lines 215–20)

Here, the run-on lines imitate the urgency with which Cromwell is borne, like Elijah, into a new heavenly kingdom, while repetitions and balanced pairs ("firy Carr" / "firy Steeds," "low World" / "thankless Men") maintain stylistic and thematic control. The final lines shift the focus from Elijah / Cromwell to those who are left behind. In the figure of the mourners, left behind with mantle rent, Marvell indicates the failure not of leader but of nation: there is no Elisha to take up the mantle.

Indeed, most of those who observe Cromwell in the poem see and judge wrongly. In an implicit rebuke to those who ridiculed the riding accident, Marvell interweaves a series of misinterpretations of Cromwell and others. Hence, the "tumult blind" fail to recognize that Cromwell acts not on his own but as an instrument of a higher power:

> What since he did, an higher Force him push'd
> Still from behind, and it before him rush'd,
> Though undiscern'd among the tumult blind,
> Who think those high Decrees by Man design'd.   (lines 239–42)

Like the scoffers who mock the alleged brewer–Protector and his dray-horses, the "tumult blind" make noise without understanding; they fail to see the providence that guides Cromwell.

Marvell continues to comment on the process of interpretation by depicting various viewers and interpreters of Cromwell. Cromwell becomes a Gideon, misunderstood and ultimately let down by his own people:

> When *Gideon* so did from the War retreat,
> Yet by the Conquest of two Kings grown great,
> He on the Peace extends a Warlike power,
> And *Is'rel* silent saw him rase the Tow'r;
> And how he *Succoths* Elders durst suppress,
> With Thorns and Briars of the Wilderness.
> No King might ever such a Force have done;
> Yet would not he be Lord, nor yet his Son.   (lines 249–56)

Marvell holds up not only Gideon, but Israel watching Gideon, an Israel that reacts and misinterprets. After Gideon "beat down the tower of Penuel, and slew the men of the city [of Succoth]" for their refusal to give provisions to his army (Judges 8:16–17), the men of Israel desire to make Gideon king ("Rule thou over us, both thou, and thy son"). But Gideon refuses, insisting that "the Lord shall rule over you" (Judges 8:22–23). Marvell recounts the incident not only to align Cromwell with the victorious Gideon, but to evoke the nation's flawed reaction. The exclusively monosyllabic words, balance, and distinct caesura of the final line emphasize the point: Gideon would not, and Cromwell should not, be king.

Continuing the focus on seeing and interpretation, with its clear political overtones for viewing Cromwell, Marvell then tells another story of misreading, this time narrating a nautical tale. Taking the helm back from the "artless Steersman" who has mistaken the rocks for land, a "lusty Mate" with "more careful Eye" averts potential disaster: "And doubles back unto the safer Main. / What though a while they grumble discontent, / Saving himself he does their loss prevent" (lines 276–78). The story points to the importance of true vision and the danger of misinterpretation. The lesson is double: not only is the sharp-sighted mate a good model, but the reader should take warning from the bad example of shipmates who continue to see wrongly, grumbling and "discontent."[71]

Other misperceptions arise from more questionable motives. Marvell gives yet another exemplum of wrong viewing: those who desire to see the weakness and faults of others, like Ham, the youngest son of Noah: "such as to their Parents Tents do press, / May shew their own, not see his Nakedness" (lines 291–92). When a drunken Noah lay "uncovered within his tent," Ham looked upon the nakedness of his father and told his two brothers, bringing a curse down upon himself and his lineage (Genesis 9:20–26). If in the earlier examples of misreading, an obtuse nation or crew nonetheless finds security and safety, this later example of Ham more ominously portends retribution on those who willfully view wrongly.

The typological layering of *The First Anniversary* thus provides a lens through which to read Cromwell's own recent accident. And indeed, Marvell makes the contemporary meaning of the biblical type explicit, linking Ham with the fifth monarchists who had so fiercely objected to Cromwell's acquiescence in the end of Barebone's parliament and his assumption of single-person rule:

> Yet such a *Chammish* issue still does rage,
> The Shame and Plague both of the Land and Age,

> Who watch'd thy halting, and thy Fall deride,
> Rejoycing when thy Foot had slipt aside;
> That their new King might the fifth Scepter shake,
> And make the World, by his Example, Quake.   (lines 293–98)

Marvell swerves away from what was in fact widespread ridicule of the riding accident to focus on one particular *bête noire*, the fifth monarchists.[72] But their prognostications are wrong, and Cromwell as "great Captain" returns in a true reading of prophecy that corrects the false fifth-monarchist reading. Like Ham whose generation Noah curses, they too face retribution.

But Marvell does not close his discussion of the accident with a warning. Rather, he reimagines the accident yet again, employing a natural and innocent misreading to envision Cromwell in terms that both evoke and alter the traditional sun–monarch analogy. The text recounts another scene of misreading, as the first man misses the sun on the first night and "His weeping Eyes the doleful Vigils keep, / Not knowing yet the Night was made for sleep" (lines 335–36). Nonetheless Cromwell, like the sun, returns:

> So while our Star that gives us Light and Heat,
> Seem'd now a long and gloomy Night to threat,
> Up from the other World his Flame he darts,
> And Princes shining through their windows starts.   (lines 343–46)

Again the movement of the run-on lines embodies the action it describes. That the sun shines upon "Princes" is significant, for Marvell shows that foreign monarchs and their monarchical readings of Cromwell are the most mistaken of all.

From the opening lines of *The First Anniversary*, then, Marvell contrasts Cromwell with kings. An "indefatigable" Cromwell runs, springs, restores, shines, acts, tunes, and hies, in contrast to the "heavy Monarchs" whose orbits are "Longer, and more Malignant then *Saturn*" (line 16) and who "nor more contribute to the state of Things, / Then wooden Heads unto the Viols strings" (lines 43–44). Marvell records the observations of the foreign princes who "wisely court the Influence they fear" (line 104). One such foreign prince "reads" Cromwell as king, fixing and limiting his power:

> He seems a King by long Succession born,
> And yet the same to be a King does scorn.
> Abroad a King he seems, and something more,
> At Home a Subject on the equal Floor.   (lines 387–90)

The foreign prince wants to see Cromwell with the "title" of king, not because Cromwell already is a *de facto* king, but because he would then be limited and mortal: "he might Dye as wee" (line 392). The form of the verse holds in symmetrical balance but does not reconcile the antithetical views. The prince's words, furthermore, are corrected by Marvell's earlier observation regarding the riding accident, that "to be *Cromwell* was a greater thing, / Then ought below, or yet above a King" (lines 225–26). Like the poem's other poor interpreters, this prince judges wrongly.

Marvell does more in *The First Anniversary* than appeal to public opinion; he shows how representations of Cromwell are collective and participatory. Most of his viewers cannot see rightly. Yet the poem does not eschew the process of interpretation. Rather, Marvell calls upon his readers to become as active themselves as the Cromwell who moves unceasingly at the center of his poem. If the readers themselves participate, the meaning of the image is transformed, even when the image is that of a king.

Augustus Caesar and parodic responses

If, in January 1655, Marvell stressed the participatory, shifting, and often misguided constructions of Cromwell, later praise of Cromwell became more resolutely imperial. Edmund Waller's *A Panegyric to my Lord Protector* praises Cromwell as Caesar Augustus in courtly verse that eschews the syncretic images and anti-formalist techniques of Fisher, Milton, and Marvell. Although Augustanism may have been used as much to sidestep as to promote the issue of the crown, Waller's poem moved toward the icon that Cromwell himself conspicuously avoided.[73]

A kinsman of Cromwell's, Waller (1606–87) was a former parliamentarian and royalist arrested in 1643 for his part in a plot to seize London for the king. Whether, as some contemporaries alleged, Waller mortgaged his considerable fortune to bribe parliament or whether his craven behavior in informing on fellow conspirators saved his life, he escaped with a fine and banishment. In 1651 he petitioned parliament to be allowed to return and, perhaps with Cromwell's intervention, was pardoned. Upon his return to England, Waller re-employed on behalf of the Protector the poetic forms and skills with which he had earlier praised Charles I and would, in the future, praise Charles II. Warren Chernaik writes that Waller "changed his allegiances without changing his basic beliefs."[74] But the monarchical precedent was again double-edged.

If Marvell's poem offers variant readings, held in balance but not reconciled, Waller's highly crafted, skillful verses imitate the order and control brought by Cromwell. While Milton, Marvell, Wither, and, to some extent,

Payne Fisher incorporate Cromwell's own iconoclastic impulse, Waller's *A Panegyric* more straightforwardly constructs an icon:

> While with a strong and yet a gentle hand,
> You bridle faction, and our hearts command,
> Protect us from ourselves, and from the foe,
> Make us unite, and make us conquer too.[75]

Like the Cromwell he praises, Waller uses a strong yet gentle hand to craft a unified and carefully constructed image. The opening stanza evinces Waller's subtle but masterful control. To represent the contradictions embodied in Cromwellian rule, he uses oxymoron ("strong and yet a gentle"); Cromwell's various achievements are juxtaposed through chiasmus ("bridle faction" versus "hearts command"), the poetic turn ("make us unite, and make us conquer too") and zeugma (with "protect"). Such devices harmonize the paradoxes and ambivalences of Cromwellian rule.

Waller allows dissenting voices into *A Panegyric* only under firm control and thoroughly stigmatized for their partiality. The long sentence with which the poem opens thus continues:

> Let partial spirits still aloud complain,
> Think themselves injured that they cannot reign,
> And own no liberty but where they may
> Without control upon their fellows prey.   (lines 5–8)

Waller's balanced verse encloses the discontented spirits, whose lack of control nonetheless spills over in run-on lines with pejorative verbs ("complain," "prey") as stressed rhyme words.

A *Panegyric* shows peace and empire as a reconciliation and uniting of contraries, an achieved state, not a process in which the reader must participate or which he must interpret. The verse both exemplifies and praises control:

> Your never-failing sword made war to cease;
> And now you heal us with the arts of peace;
> Our minds with bounty and with awe engage,
> Invite affection, and restrain our rage.   (lines 109–12)

Characteristic of Waller, and crucially underscoring his message, are the craft and art that balance and unite disparities. Hence the use of paradox with the "never-failing sword" that ends war, and the symmetry in syntax and thought between the first and second lines. The use of zeugma with "engage" links what might seem conflicting qualities in Cromwell:

"bounty" and "awe." The balance of the final line imitates the balance Cromwell himself has achieved.

Waller extends and elaborates previous praise of Cromwell as an Augustus bringing peace after civil war:

> Your drooping country, torn with civil hate,
> Restored by you, is made a glorious state;
> The seat of empire, where the Irish come,
> And the unwilling Scotch, to fetch their doom.   (lines 13–16)

Here again Waller uses symmetry and inversion between the first two lines (moving from "drooping country" to "glorious state"). Such "smooth" verse aptly conveys Waller's message, as the compressed, balanced lines emulate the control and order of Cromwellian England / Augustan Rome.

Waller later makes the comparison with Rome explicit, when, after comparing Cromwell with such luminaries as Alexander the Great, he develops an extended analogy first with Julius and then with Augustus Caesar:

> As the vexed world, to find repose, at last
> Itself into Augustus' arms did cast;
> So England now does, with like toil oppressed,
> Her weary head upon your bosom rest.   (lines 169–72)

Line and thought parallel the vexed world and England, Augustus' arms and Cromwell's bosom. The rhyme of keywords underscores the transformation: "oppressed" to "rest." Waller refashions both Cromwell's own motto (*pax quaeritur bello*) and earlier heroic images into a new ideal of Cromwell as Augustus Caesar. No Cromwellian zeal intrudes upon the smooth verses. Waller's one use of the term "piety" was changed to "clemency" in published form.

Waller's smoothly crafted icon contrasts to the multiple views and voices of Marvell's *First Anniversary*, the admonitory prophecy of Wither's *Vaticinium Causuale*, Milton's precaution-laded praise, and Payne Fisher's syncretism. Perhaps not surprisingly, *A Panegyric* elicited a storm of protest from royalist and republican alike. Satiric verses used Waller's literary techniques against him, deconstructing the heroic image through witty but biting repetition and turn, balance, and antithesis. Richard Watson's collection, *The Panegyrike and The Storme*, turned the paradoxes of Waller's opening stanzas against him in form and in theme:

> Whilst with a *loftie*, yet a *flatering*, pen
> Thus highly you extoll *the worst of men*;
> Whilst *Nero* is by you, as *Trajan*, shown,
> And you, by praysing, make *his crimes your owne*.[76]

Rather than contrarieties reconciled in the forceful figure of Cromwell, the satirist depicts Waller's verse as itself paradoxical in its high praise of the lowest of men. The satirist's final paradox is that it is better to have no wit, than to use it as Waller has done:

> Let all impartial, that have eares or eyes,
> To heare or reade thy *abject flateries*,
> Be joyfull to be thought to have *no wit*,
> Rather then make such *sordide use* of it. (Sig. BIV)

The satire turns Waller's characteristic balance and symmetry against him, envisioning the readers who condemn his flattering verse.

The *Anti-Panegyrist* who follows also targets Cromwell himself, dismantling Waller's idealized image. He quotes Waller's praise of the Cromwellian empire that had brought the luxuries of paradise without the incommodities. Hence the *Panegyrist* (Waller) writes: "The tast of hot *Arabias* spice we know / Free from that scorching sun that makes it grow" (p. 8). But the *Anti-Panegyrist* turns such phrases into a witty if stock Cromwellian caricature: "The tast of hot *Arabias* spice was knowne / Before your *scorcht-nose-Master* climbd the *Throne*" (p. 8). Waller had compared Cromwell's private life to the early life of the biblical David – "Borne to command, your Princely vertues slept, / Like humble David, while ye flock he kept" (p. 17). But the *Anti-Panegyrist* denies the biblical precedent, inverting Waller's meaning: "Your *Oliver* had no *King Davids* call, / Nor was *King Charles* the first a *second Saul*" (p. 17). As for comparing Cromwell with Julius Caesar, "*Caesar* was no such *Monster*, tis not sed', / He did his Master *binde*, *lose*, then *behead*" (p. 19). In satiric form, compression works not for courtly polish but to heighten the attack.

The *Anti-Panegyrist* dismantles the imperial icon of Cromwell to reassert the Stuart line as the proper heirs of Augustus, looking forward to the time when "our *Augustus* by his birth and merit / Come the *usurped Chariot* to inherite" (p. 20). But Waller's kingly image evoked opposition from republicans as well as royalists. Lucy Hutchinson (*b.* 1620) rejects Waller in a manuscript satire that likewise parodies both the form and content of *A Panegyric*.[77] Hutchinson was a devout puritan, whose husband signed the death warrant of Charles I but withdrew from public life after Cromwell's dissolution of the Rump; Lucy herself viewed the Protectorate with distrust and left a vivid account of her reactions in her *Memoirs of Colonel Hutchinson*.[78]

Hutchinson rejects Waller's Cromwell in lines that dismantle through parodic imitation Waller's artfully balanced antitheses. Waller had praised

Cromwell with cool symmetry as "To pardon, willing; and to punish, loath; / You strike with one hand, but you heal with both."[79] Hutchinson inverts the verbs, changes from the intimacy of direct address to the distance of third-person, and substitutes a final verb with devastating effect: "To punish willing, but to pardon loath / He strikes with one hand, and he gripes with both" (p. 81). Here the compression is sharp and biting, as Hutchinson drops the antithesis and thus transforms Waller's meaning. Indeed, she rejects the Augustan ideal altogether:

> As by severe Augustus Rome at last
> Into Tiberius grinding lawes was cast;
> So England now opprest with the like curse
> Groanes under him, feares his Successors worse.

Hutchinson employs Waller's characteristic turn (repetition of a word with some variation in meaning) against him, as Rome is cast not into Augustus' arms, but into the tyranny of Tiberius. Waller's verse might indeed be seen as a move back to monarchical forms. But the very protests that it elicited demonstrated ideological and cultural change. The nature and form of the satire attested to a politically informed public and a new questioning of authority.

The political crises of 1655 made the image of Cromwell more contested than ever. Penruddock's Rebellion and an abortive royalist uprising in Wiltshire in mid-March, followed by the failure of the Western Design to take Hispaniola from the Spanish (the capture of Jamaica was not yet seen as significant), led Cromwell to impose the rule of the major-generals in England and Wales, both to keep order and to restore morality.[80] Printed texts continued to engage in unprecedented debate over the role and nature of Cromwellian rule.[81] The project of constructing Cromwell was a collaborative one in which protectoral images grew increasingly at odds with Cromwell's own pronouncements. Cromwell's failure to direct a mode of protectoral imagery meant that the initiative for representation moved from the court to the public sphere. As we shall see, Cromwell's own iconoclastic distrust of self and of set forms paradoxically kept alive the icon of kingship.

Four

Contesting Cromwell in the
late Protectorate

In April 1657, after months of speculation, Cromwell definitively rejected the proffered title of king. But, nonetheless, when on 26 June Cromwell was reinstalled as Lord Protector under a new constitution, the Humble Petition and Advice, the ceremony included many of the elements of a monarchical coronation. Was Cromwell made, in fact, a king in all but name? Did the spectacle instantiate or compensate for Cromwell's own point of view? How and why did the ceremony differ from the Caroline coronation of 1626? How did printed texts lead up to, participate in, and respond to the second installation?

Despite considerable interest in the forms of monarchical power, including the coronation, the Cromwellian appropriation has received little attention. Those few historians who have treated the ceremony of the second installation have assumed or argued that it was a clear and complete assimilation of kingship.[1] But differences mattered. The Caroline ceremony showed the imprint of the king's personality and beliefs, and the enhanced ritual and sacramentalism embodied Charles's high view of monarchy and church. On the contrary, the Cromwellian ceremony seemed to counter his own words and his public refusal of the crown.

In this chapter I trace the increasing tensions between Cromwell as subject and the objects (including print and display) by which others constructed him as a king. Rumors about Cromwellian kingship circulated in oral and manuscript form throughout the Protectorate. Printed texts variously urged Cromwell to accept or refuse the crown; hence, *The Unparalleld Monarch* depicted Cromwell as an uncrowned king, while James Harrington's republican utopia, *The Commonwealth of Oceana*, envisioned Cromwell as Lord Archon willingly giving up power. Although the Caroline coronation reflected Charles's own decorum and belief in sacrosanct kingship, the protectoral installation jarred with Cromwell's pronouncements and personality. Manuscript accounts and a late protectoral painting show that, despite lavish panegyric and renewed calls for Cromwell to take the crown, he retained much of his plain and humble character.

The coronation of Charles I: monarchical precedent

The closest antecedent to the Cromwellian forms was, of course, the 1626 coronation of Charles I.[2] In Charles's coronation, forms of power conveyed and embodied the monarch's own views; printed texts supplemented spectacle to produce a coherent and unified image. The ceremony reflected Charles's piety and his inclination toward the ceremonial and decorous, the hierarchical mystery rather than the popular public display.

The coronation pageant of Elizabeth I had been highly successful, even overshadowing the church ceremony, and James had established his imperial mode in a coronation entry.[3] But Charles eschewed the coronation entry altogether (although a lavish pageant was staged after his coronation in Scotland several years later and we have seen his 1641 entry into London). Indeed, Charles ordered the removal of arches and pageantry that had been constructed in anticipation of the coronation entry, much to the disappointment and even resentment of the citizens who had already paid for them.[4]

The coronation itself was in keeping with the king's own sense of decorum. John Chamberlain writes that "the coronation holdes on Candlemas day, but private without any shew or feast at Westminster Hall."[5] Although there were, of course, spectators in Westminster Abbey to observe portions of the ceremony and to acclaim the new king when prompted, a second account similarly describes the coronation as private: "the Coronation of the King was on Thursday (as passengers yesterday from London tell us) but private. The King went to Westminster Church by water. The Queen was not crowned, but stood at a window in the mean time, looking on; and her ladies frisking and dancing in the room. God grant his Majestie a happy reign."[6] Charles omitted the public street procession, choosing to arrive by water instead.

The ceremony reflected Charles's ecclesiastical conservatism and his views of sacramental kingship. Indeed, Charles replaced Bishop Williams, Dean of Westminster and Bishop of Lincoln, with Bishop Laud, whom he entrusted to draw up the coronation service. Charles and Laud concurred in their high ceremonial view of church and state: Charles supported Laud's ecclesiastical innovations, while Laud actively defended divine-right monarchy.[7] That the ceremony was primarily a religious rite, reflecting Charles's intense Anglican piety, was underscored by the refusal of his Catholic queen to participate.

Like the 1641 entry, the coronation of Charles I was both hierarchical and reciprocal. The ceremony called upon the people to recognize and acclaim their new king. At the Abbey, the Archbishop presented Charles to the people. Eyewitness Simonds D'Ewes noted that the people, unused to the ceremony, failed to respond at first: "whether some expected hee should have spoken more others hearing not well what he saied . . . not one worde followed, till my Lord of Arundel tolde them, They should crie out 'God save King Charles.' Upon which, as ashamed of ther first oversight, a little shouting followed."[8]

The coronation proper indicated the mystery and sanctity of kingship. The central rite of anointing, however, was private, not observed even by the people within Westminster. D'Ewes comments that "because the putting on of his crimson shirte, the anointing of his naked shoulders, armes, handes, and head were arcana, a traverse was drawen."[9] The heart of the service, then, was a sacramental and religious ceremony. Anointing was followed by a sermon and then communion following high Anglican rites. D'Ewes continues: "Then receaved his Majestie the Communion; and after, crowned, in his purple robes ascending the stage and Throne, tooke homage of all the Peeres; they putting ther handes into his and being kissed by him, did him both homage and fealtie."[10] Anointing, communion, homage, and fealty embodied the sacramental mystique of kingship.

The people were involved as audience to the display. The Lord Keeper's announcement of the traditional coronation pardon elicited "an exceeding acclamation." D'Ewes comments extensively on the props: rich clothing, regalia, stage, and throne. Charles, he writes, returned to an inner chapel and "ther put on black velvett roabes lined with ermine"; he wore a crown "narrower and higher then that my Lorde of Pembroke carried; yet both incomparablie rich."[11] The rich and elegant clothing in itself embodied the majesty and splendor of divine-right kingship.

Yet Charles imprinted his own ecclesiastical conservatism and authoritarian view of monarchy upon the traditional coronation ritual. Another eyewitness, Mr. Mead, points out a prayer that had been added to the ceremony, enhancing the sacramental nature of kingship: "One Prayer, therein, was used, which hath been omitted since Henry the VIIth's time . . .

It understands the King not to be merely laic, but a mixed person. The words, or some of the words, are these: *Obtineat gratiam huic populo sicut Aaron in tabernaculo, Elizæus in fluvio, Zacharias in templo. Sit Petrus in clave, Paulus in dogmate. &c.* [Let him obtain grace for this people as did Aaron in the tabernacle, Elisha at the river, Zachariah in the temple. Let him be as Peter in the key[s of the kingdom], as Paul in Christian doctrine, etc.][12] The ceremony invoked Charles's sacramental view of kingship, his fervent adherence to orderly hierarchy in church and state.

Subject and object cohered in the coronation of Charles I. The various objects and acts of the coronation embodied Charles's own piety and sense of protocol. While examining the power of Elizabethan pageantry, Richard McCoy comments that the "Stuarts' contempt for popular pageantry, along with their ecclesiastical conservatism and ideas of rule by divine right, eroded rather than enhanced their authority during the course of the seventeenth century."[13] McCoy's astute observation is worth noting, although Charles's coronation was, by all accounts, well received. Nonetheless, the very unity and coherence of the rites sowed the seeds of possible trouble: Charles's detachment from the people, his obsessive sense of decorum, and his attachment to high ritual and ecclesiastical ceremony could be perceived as hearkening back, not to Anglican tradition, but to Rome.

Rumor and speculation on Cromwell and the crown

Under the Protectorate, the high courtly ceremony of the Caroline era was dispersed and disputed in an emerging public sphere. The crown was not ritually bestowed on Cromwell, but was, rather, a topic of debate throughout the Interregnum, shattering the pieties and mysteries of high Caroline ceremony. Contemporaries constantly linked Cromwell with kings; but without the crown, Cromwellian regality for many served only as a reminder of his usurpation.

The kingship question cannot be confined to 1657–58. Rather, from the time of the regicide, rumors abounded that Cromwell sought the crown. The move into royal palaces and establishment of a protectoral court almost immediately evoked suspicion of a monarchical Cromwell.[14] As early as December 1653, parliament voted that the former royal palaces of St. James, Somerset House, Greenwich House, York, Windsor Castle, and Hampton Court be repurchased for the use of the Lord Protector, and *The Faithful Scout* announced that "White-Hall is preparing for his Highnesse to reside in, and the Old Council Chamber is fitting for His Honourable Council to meet in."[15] By March, official newsbooks were reporting

Cromwell's move into a new residence, while unsympathetic observers saw the impending change of residence as a step toward Cromwellian monarchy. The Venetian envoy, Paulucci, wrote in March 1654 that "to add lustre to his authority [Cromwell] is about to take possession of the former royal palace, which he has had done up for his own convenience . . . So he will henceforth exercise regal sway under the royal roof, leaving out the royal title until he takes a fancy to it."[16] Although he elsewhere noted Cromwell's public piety and humility, the Venetian envoy viewed all such behavior as scheming to gain power and the crown.

Thus, those contemporaries unsympathetic to Cromwell were unmoved by distinctions between Cromwellian and monarchical forms; indeed, they tended to attribute the worst possible motives to the differences. Sir Edward Hyde remarks in March 1654 that Cromwell "makes not that hast was expected into state and lustre, which he findes the Army would not be delighted with, yett will steale into it by degrees."[17] Two months later, in May 1654, Hyde writes again that although Cromwell was "removed and settled with his family in Whitehall," he "yett takes on no other state upon him [than] usinge those romes, which are more richly furnished than ever they were in any King's tyme. He eats not alone, but with very meane persons, any Officers of the army, nor does it appeare when he means to advance his state."[18] Expectations colored perception, and royalist observers tended to explain away non-monarchical behavior and focus on (if only to attack) any Cromwellian links with kingship.

Rumors regarding Cromwell and kingship continued throughout the protectorate. A letter-writer of 18 May 1655 comments that "We have had a great rumour of having a King; it hath been so long in expectation that the people of these parts begin to despair for the benefit that will arise thereby; some are of opinion good, and some bad; but we ought to acquiesce with what God will have, and account that rest."[19] Another observer, Henry Whitmore, notes what he interprets as an increasing regality: "What I formerly wrote to you concerning Cromwells preparation for his coronation (I conceive the coyneinge of money with his own effigies and a great seal of the same with the armes of the three kingdomes uppon the reverse of them is in order to it) I believe to be very true, though it is not generally known, and many are of an other opinion."[20] Although the parliament had officially abolished monarchy, kingship remained alive in oral circulation, diplomatic correspondence, and print.

Similarly, the letters of the Swedish diplomats constantly reassure their sovereign that Cromwell is just on the verge of taking the crown. On 1 June 1655, the Swedish ambassador, Peter Coyet, writes a long analysis of the possible benefits and limitations of Cromwellian kingship, beginning with the observation that "the longer the lord protector sits in the saddle, the securer his seat in it."[21] In Coyet's view, Cromwell "will either try to get the law altered by consent, or (which seems more probable) he will very shortly assume the title of king."[22] The following March, Coyet's replacement, Christer Bonde, reports the widespread assumption "that the protector is anxious to assume the crown; and so I thought it not inadvisable to encourage him to do so, since it would greatly strengthen this government, and consequently make it safer for Y[our] M[ajesty] to link himself to it."[23] Bonde's additional observation, that the English kingship would "greatly strengthen" his own sovereign's government is, however, an important reminder that the letters of foreign ambassadors are as much constructions as the more self-consciously rhetorical arguments of prose, pamphlet, and panegyric. The ambassador gives his own perspective, while shaping the news for the audience to whom he writes. Such letters cannot be taken as proof that Cromwell had become a king in all but name.

Bonde's subsequent letters continue to stress Cromwellian kingship in the context of the benefits for his own king. Hence, he reports on 11 July 1656 that "it seems likely that in the course of this parliament his highness will become king; and if he does there can be no doubt that he will collaborate with Y[our] M[ajesty] in the closest possible fashion."[24] And again on 8 August, he writes that "as far as I could gather from my Lord Lambert, there is now no general disinclination to his highness's becoming king. All the principal nobility in the country desire it; and if it comes about it is not to be doubted that as his authority and security increase he will follow his principal inclination and desire, and link himself closely to Y[our] M[ajesty]."[25] But in recounting wide support for Cromwellian kingship, Bonde made the mistake of assuming that perceptions of Cromwell cohered with Cromwell's own views.

Print interventions

Printed texts actively intervened on the issue of Cromwell and kingship. The war of print especially heated up in the summer of 1656 in anticipation of the upcoming parliament that many believed would offer Cromwell the crown.[26] Such texts debated major constitutional issues on a scale unimaginable under the earlier monarchs. Significantly, arguments that Cromwell should be, or already was, king took the same popular printed form as republican arguments against the crown. These printed texts directed their appeal to the public as active and discerning readers in questions of state.

But they also aimed at a very specific and powerful reader: Cromwell himself.

Two republican texts in the summer and autumn of 1656 foregrounded the process of interpretation to show how Cromwell should be "read" and how he himself should "read." Having earlier both aligned and dissociated Cromwell and Caesar, Marchamont Nedham in June 1656 depicted in *The Excellencie of a Free-State* a new threat in that form of tyranny that professes liberty.[27] Now even the republican hero Brutus himself, to whom John Milton (Nedham's friend) had compared Cromwell in his *Defensio Secunda*, was problematic. Brutus had sacrificed his own sons, but he also made way for the reinscription of monarchy under another form. The Roman people endured ten tyrants instead of one, the people having been seduced with merely the shadow of liberty. Nedham thus reiterated the need for the people to understand liberty, to set up a successive government and not to allow rule into the hands of one man.

The essays in *The Excellencie of a Free-State* were written and published earlier (in *Politicus* in 1651–52), but as a speech act in 1656 they had very different valences. The absent presence throughout is the figure of Oliver Cromwell. In the earlier *Mercurius Politicus* editorals, the threat to liberty was the Rump Parliament and hence the decemvirs who replaced the Tarquins. But, as Blair Worden has shown, subtle alterations before the (re)publication in 1656 pointed the finger at Cromwell.[28]

At the end of *The Excellencie of a Free-State*, Nedham resurrects the image of Caesar as Machiavel, with clear implications for England's present ruler. Hence, he cites *The Prince*, ostensibly so that "you may the better know, and avoid the impious Impostors."[29] Machiavelli in *The Prince* has "made a most unhappy Description of the Wiles that have been used by those Jugglers; and thereby left a Lesson upon Record, which hath been practised ever since by all the State Rooks in *Christendom*" (p. 234). Although he promises to cite Machiavelli verbatim, Nedham will also make "two or three Inferences thereupon, for the practice of the people" (p. 234).

Nedham's "Inferences," after a long citation of Machiavelli's most infamous advice, reflect transparently upon Cromwell and contain an implicit injunction to political judgment if not action:

> If a Prince cannot, and ought not to keep his faith given, when the observance thereof turnes to disadvantage, and the occasions that made him promise, are past; then it is the Interest of the people, never to trust any Princes, nor ingagements and promises of men in power, but ever to preserve a power within themselves, either to reject them, or to hold them to the performance whether they will or no. (p. 241)

Nedham thus uses Machiavelli to sharpen judgment in the immediate political circumstances. A judging and discerning people must hold their leaders accountable, making a "narrow search ever into the men, and their pretences and necessities, whether they be fained or not" (p. 242). If indeed they discover deceit, that the ruler has feigned religion and liberty but sought power only for himself, "then they deserve to be slaves, that will be deceived any longer" (p. 242).

Such issues debated in print went well beyond the traditional advice to a king.[30] If Nedham boldly urged the people to dissociate themselves from a deceitful ruler (i.e., Cromwell), James Harrington with equal daring presented in *The Commonwealth of Oceana* a Cromwell figure, Lord Archon, who voluntarily relinquishes his power.[31] Delayed in press, Harrington's tract was not published until after the new parliament was in session. The tract's agrarian model of republicanism is important in the history of political theory, but it also specifically intervened in constructions of Cromwell by holding up the Lord Protector's own professed self-image and showing the natural consequences of that image if genuine: abdication of power. Although the speeches of Lord Archon were quite possibly written to satirize Cromwell's dissolution of the Rump Parliament in April 1653, Harrington's tract, like Nedham's, had new relevance in 1656.[32] Hence, Harrington's Lord Archon, having set up the Commonwealth on a stable footing, hands power back:

> Nevertheless whereas Christianity, though it forbid violent hands, consisteth no less in self-denial than any other religion, he resolved that all carnal concupiscence should die in the place, to which end, that no manner of food might be left unto ambition, he entered into the senate with an unanimous applause and, having spoken of his government as Lycurgus did when he assembled the people, abdicated the magistry of Archon.[33]

The Archon's abdication is a true "self-denial" that coheres with Cromwell's words but contrasts with his ambitious-seeming behavior.

The ensuing action in *Oceana* differs from both Cromwell's conduct and the responses that he evoked. In *Oceana*, the senators protest and weep at the loss of their esteemed leader:

> The senate, as stricken with astonishment, continued silent, men upon so sudden an accident being altogether unprovided of what to say; till the Archon withdrawing and being almost at the door, divers of the knights flew from their places, offering as it were to lay violent hands on him; while he escaping left the senate with the tears in their eyes of children that had lost their father. (pp. 245–46)

If indeed the original subtext was Cromwell's dissolution of the Rump, Harrington's rewriting is laden with irony. In April 1653, the offered violence was from Cromwell himself and the only tears were his own. A manuscript account written just before Cromwell's dismissal of the Rump characterizes him as having "teares at will": "hee not long since protested to the House with weeping eyes, that he would as willingly hazard his life against any whatever that should professe themselves their Enemys, as he had don against those that were publique Enemys to the Commonwealth; but most of them know he hath teares at will, & can dispense with any Oath or Protestation without troubling his conscience."[34] The writer quite prophetically adds that "its hoped they will provide for their owne safety."[35]

Finally, Cromwell insisted that he had not desired power, that he had "hoped to have had leave to have retired to a private life."[36] But his alter ego, Lord Archon, actually retires: "to rid himself of all farther importunity, [he] retired unto a country house of his, being remote and very private, in so much that no man could tell for some time what was become of him" (p. 246). If in the figure of the Archon Harrington held up to Cromwell his own professed image, it was in rebuke and warning, not in praise. Opposing the developing sentiment to crown Cromwell, Harrington boldly and emphatically asserted his republican ideals, including an admonition to Cromwell to use his power to establish a republic and not to hearken after monarchy.

But other texts urged Cromwell to take the crown. Shortly before Harrington's tract, *The Unparalleld Monarch* (September 1656) entered the debate with praise of Cromwell as having all the virtues of an uncrowned king. The text is constructed in itself as a kind of prose icon: long periodic sentences with parallelism, careful patterns of repetition, doublets, anaphora, antithesis, and balance. Echoing earlier panegyric, especially by Waller, the text elaborately constructs the unity for which it argues. Despite its title, the text is structured by a series of verbal and logical parallels: antithesis and symmetry embody the central paradox of the argument, that Cromwell is more kingly than a king. Yet far from demonstrating Cromwell's *de facto* kingship, the text shows an anxious reaction against opposing voices: most threateningly, the opposition of Cromwell himself. We shall see that rather than consolidating Cromwellian regality the text is, to use Stanley Fish's term, a self-consuming artifact.[37]

The address "To the Reader" that opens *The Unparalleld Monarch* makes a plea for unity and obedience in the face of disunity and discontent:

> If we consider what a general forward and ready pronenesse there is in the hearts of most to exasperation and jealousie, what a number of malicious dissenters, what swarms of malecontents, underminers, and

> most abominable seducers there are both at home & abroad, certainly
> we have no little reason to unite & stick close to our Caesar, to speak,
> write, and act for him, to reserve our hearts for his cause, our hands for
> his weapons, our eyes and eares for his sentinels, and our bodies for his
> bulworks.[38]

The cumulative force of the long periodic sentence conveys the power of
the opposition to Cromwell, underscoring the need to "unite & stick close
to our Caesar." Balancing the opening anaphoric repetition (what a
general, what a number, what swarms), the latter part of the sentence
offers a plan for unity in carefully paralleled infinitives and symmetrical
order. As the numbers and types of opponents to Cromwell increase in
each succeeding clause (from dissenters to malcontents, underminers *and*
seducers) the countering actions also multiply first in themselves (unite
and stick close; speak, write, and act) and then in a proliferation of objects
to be reserved (hearts, hands, eyes, ears, and bodies). Parallel phrase and
clause build to the rhetorical climax and logical conclusion of support for
Cromwell. Significantly, the author here adduces Caesar as an apt type of
Cromwell, signalling the imperial courtly style by allusion as well as by
form.

   Yet, although *The Unparalleld Monarch* continues for more than a hundred
elaborate pages, the author insists throughout that Cromwell's regality is
self-sufficient and self-evident, that he needs no supplementary text. In "To
the Reader," the author professes to offer not a logical argument but an
image that in itself conveys Cromwell's regality: "I have not made it my
business to enthrone him by Argument, or to justifie his most happy instal-
ment by necessity and reason; I would only give you a sight of his head and
arms, and if I could do that handsomely and to the life, it could not be
denied but they were made purposely for our Crown and Scepter" (Sig.
A9v). Here and throughout, the author argues that no argument need be
made, that Cromwell's regality is self-evident, that argument is eschewed in
favor of an icon. But the argument that no argument need be made is conveyed in carefully structured prose: parallel clauses and doublets building
up with cumulative force to the diadem. Despite the denial of an authorial
hand, the text makes Cromwell himself into an object of art.

   The author forwards the argument that Cromwell is unparalleled by
elaborating various kinds of parallels: symmetries, analogues, and balanced
antitheses. *The Unparalleld Monarch* represents Cromwell as bringing unity
and concord in polished and symmetrical prose that itself evinces both
potential linguistic chaos and imposed order:

> It was indeed a very blessed and remarkable day in which he entred the
> *Throne*, whence a deliverance sprung from amidst the chaos and bowels
> of confusion and mischief; it proved fatal to *Error*, the wicked Rival to
> *Truth*, and was destructive to *Anarchy*, which is the opposite to Unity,
> and an utter enemy to all Tranquillity and Peace. (pp. 28–29)

Doubled adjectives and nouns (blessed and remarkable; chaos and bowels;
confusion and mischief; tranquility and peace) again serve to heighten and
elaborate meaning. Stylistic as well as thematic balance occurs between the
blessings of Cromwellian rule and the evils which preceded him. But those
disorders and errors remain in the text, however controlled and balanced,
continuing to threaten.

Hence, much of the text's celebration of Cromwellian unity actually
details its opposite. The author focuses on the malignancy and malice that
have prevented Cromwell from receiving a crown: "There is even at this day
a Stoical and base Melancholy Malignancy, a resolved and inexpugnable
malice, a kind of toad-like envy and swelling, or else certainly all the *People*
of this *Nation* would long since have been crowning this *Prince*, every man
had been flying to him with a Crown, He had had heaps of Crowns on his
head" (p. 50). Alliteration as well as parallelism build rhetorically to the
"heaps of Crowns" for Cromwell. The malice of Cromwell's opponents bal-
ances rhetorically against the imagined crowning.

Yet the real stumbling-block to Cromwellian kingship is not the people or
other monarchs but Cromwell himself. Hence the final verse panegyric,
closely modelled on Waller's mellifluous verse, directly urges Cromwell to
take the crown: "Crownes are for *Hero's*, and the wise alone / In factious
states do best become the Throne" (Sig. 17v). The conquest and piety that
the author has praised throughout become a rationale for the crown:

> After so great success so great Renown,
> Did we not give and you accept a Crown,
> Both were ungrateful in the vilest sence;
> You to your Vertues, we to Providence.   (Sig. 17v–r)

Here the author even more directly imitates Waller's polished end-stopped
couplets, with their skillful versification and varied parallelism. But now,
unlike Waller's *A Panegyric*, *The Unparalleld Monarch* addresses Cromwell
directly and openly advocates the crown. The control and compression of
the form evinces the stability for which it argues: *if* Cromwell will accept the
crown.

That "if" is far from certain. The verse panegyric discloses that Cromwell
himself opposes the regality for which *The Unparalleld Monarch* argues.

Further, in insisting that Cromwell is innately a king, that he needs no externals, the text calls into question its own status. If Cromwell is so obviously a king, he does not need the supplement of this rhetorical printed text. Indeed, he does not need the very crown for which the text explicitly argues. Far from confirming Cromwellian kingship, *The Unparalleld Monarch* deconstructs its own argument.

"I cannot undertake this government with the title of king"

The second inauguration was preceded not only by texts arguing that Cromwell should or should not take the crown, but by Cromwell's refusal. Cromwell's views on kingship have been termed "opaque," and his decision to reject the crown has been seen as a long struggle, resolved only after a confrontation with dissenting army officers in Hyde Park, or after defeat in Hispaniola had darkened his vision of providence.[39] Perhaps influenced by widespread and reiterated satire on Cromwell as a Machiavel, both his own contemporaries and later scholars have had trouble believing that he did not want the crown. But the evidence points to a persistent refusal. Observers such as Bulstrode Whitelocke, who alleged that as early as 1653 Cromwell asked "What if a man should take it upon himself to be king?" must be taken with due caution. Although widely cited to link Cromwell and the crown, Whitelocke's comments appear in a Restoration-era text, when Whitelocke had every reason to claim that he had defended the crown for the Stuarts.[40] Nonetheless, the most conclusive evidence must be sought in Cromwell's own words and actions. Offered the crown by parliament in the spring of 1657, Cromwell said no.

Cromwell's recorded comments during the "kingship crisis" consistently and clearly oppose kingship. Such opposition was recorded even by unsympathetic observers who attributed it to dubious motives. Hence Hyde comments on 16 December 1656: "I saw a letter that puts me in Doubt whether Cromwell intendes yet to change his Name or not, or if he does whether it will be at the Sollicitation or soe much as with the Consent of his Assembly, which it seemes are not so entirely his."[41] John Evelyn asserts on 22 March 1657: "The Protector *Oliver*, now affecting *King-ship*, is petition'd to take the Title on him, by all his new-made sycophant Lords &c: but dares not for feare of the *Phanatics*, not thoroughly purged out of his rebell army."[42] And a correspondent of Edward Hyde's writes on 10 April: "I saw one Letter, but give no great Credit to it, that sayes Cromwell will Refuse the title of king, but will accept all the Power that's offered him."[43] The author nonetheless recounts a quite vivid report of Cromwell's plain-spoken refusal: "They say that speaking of the title of king, he said, he was now an old man, and Car'd not for wearing a feather in his Cappe."[44] Yet this observer remains skeptical: "I can not Alter my old opinion, that this change is not at all for our Advantage, & if he does not suddenly find some disturbance from his owne People, but hath a little more time given him to settle himself, I feare others will see too much Reason to be of the same opinion too."[45] This clear refusal becomes opaque only in the perceptions and reactions of others.

Cromwell's own self-representation was never monarchical. Rather, his pointed self-deprecation contrasts with protectoral panegyric. As he reiterates his opposition to the crown, in his distinctive style of paralleled and subordinate clauses, Cromwell characteristically subordinates himself:

> I am a man standing in the place I am in, which place I undertook not so much out of the hope of doing any good, as out of a desire to prevent mischief and evil, which I did see was imminent upon the nation. I saw we were running headlong into confusion and disorder, and would necessarily run into blood, and I was passive to those that desired me to undertake the place that now I have.[46]

Employing passive verb forms to avoid asserting his own will, Cromwell underscores his own submission, past and present. Similarly, he describes his role as merely "a good constable to keep the peace of the parish."[47] Cromwell defines the Protectorship as a place or office, constructing himself as passive rather than active.

Some elements of the Humble Petition and Advice clearly appealed to Cromwell, but the parliament initially insisted that he accept or reject the whole: including the crown. In December 1656, after the single house of parliament had sentenced the radical James Nayler to be bored through the tongue, whipped, and pilloried for his blasphemous ride into Bristol in an imitation of Christ, Cromwell publicly fretted over the potential threat to religious liberty. Without a balance or check to the single house of parliament, the case of James Nayler, he told the army officers, "might happen to be your own case."[48] Hence, Cromwell supported the addition of a second house to parliament, as well as the new power of the Protector to name his successor and to place curbs on the power of the council.

But Cromwell's opposition to the title of king was unwavering. He insisted that God himself had blasted the title:

> Truly the providence of God has laid this title aside providentially. *De facto* it is laid as aside and this not by sudden humour or passion; but it has been the issue of a great deliberation as ever was in a nation. It has been the issue of ten or twelve years' civil war, wherein much blood has been shed . . . And God has seemed providentially not only to strike at the family but at the name. And as I said before, *de facto* it is blotted out, it is a thing cast out by Act of Parliament, it's a thing has been kept out to this day.[49]

Cromwell's speeches during the kingship crisis have been adduced as a model of obfuscation, but the cumulative and repetitive style here has one major effect: of diminishing his own agency. Repetitions and parallels build rhetorically as well as logically to the conclusion that the crown is blotted out; Cromwell loses his own will in the will and actions of the Long Parliament and of God. Repeated terms and phrases – "laid aside," "providence," "providentially," "it has been the issue," "*de facto*" – accumulate logical and rhetorical force, concentrated on the casting out of the crown.

In sense and syntax, Cromwell subordinates his own refusal of the crown to the divine action that precedes it:

> I beseech you think not I bring it as an argument to prove anything, or to make any comparison. I have no such thoughts. God hath seemed to deal so. He hath not only dealt so with the persons and the family, but he hath blasted the title. And you know, when a man comes *a parte post* to reflect and to see that this is done and laid in the dust, I can make no conclusion but this . . . I would not seek to set up that that providence hath destroyed and laid in the dust, and I would not build Jericho again.[50]

Each of Cromwell's sentences echoes and expands the preceding one, with the exception of his interjection of himself in the act of denying that he is interjecting himself (don't think I'm arguing anything). The cumulative parallels not only build rhetorically to the rejection of the title of king, but they show that it has already been rejected: by God himself. Yet such public humility was countered, rather than reproduced, in the printed texts and public ceremony.

In the weeks that preceded Cromwell's final answer, even those closest to him seemed to believe that he would accept the crown.[51] Hence, Henry Cromwell's father-in-law, Sir Francis Russell, writes on 27 April 1657 that "your father beginnes to come out of the cloudes, and it appeares to us that he will take the kingly power upon him."[52] Similarly, Major-General William Jephson informs Henry on 21 April that although Oliver took exception to particular points in the Petition and Advice, "wee made our selves believe . . . that if satisfaction were given in the particulars, the Things in the Petition beeing so desirable, and settlement a thing of soe absolute necessitye, that hee should hardlye know how to deny it with all its appurtenances."[53] This was, he adds, "as visible in their faces, as their noses."[54]

Yet these same friends record Cromwell's unequivocal rejection of the crown. Many express their surprise at Cromwell's refusal and, in doing so, clearly view his decision as firm, not as a ploy to become king in all but name. A month later, then, Jephson writes Henry Cromwell that "His Highness' refusall of the Parliaments Petition & Advice hath soe amazed his most reall servants, as I know not what to write or say concerning it; I am sure tis not a discourse fitt for a letter."[55] On 12 May, Major Anthony Morgan similarly reports Cromwell's "deniall to accept ye title." Given the number of contemporaries who alleged that Cromwell refused the crown only for fear of the army, Morgan's letter contains an interesting account (corroborated in a letter from Charles Fleetwood) of the army's intervention in the process, as they petitioned the House not to press Cromwell further to accept the title of king. According to Morgan, "tis said his H[ighness] knew nothing of ye p[etitio]n but wh[en] he heard of it was extream angry cald it a high breach of priviledge & ye greatest injury they could have offered to him next cutting his throat & indeed coming in as it did makes people abroad say he is afraid of his Army."[56] Similarly conclusive is a letter written to Henry Cromwell by his father-in-law, Sir Francis Russell, that describes the dejection of the "kinglings" and the victory of the Army: "The truth is your father hath of late made more wise men fooles than ever; he laughs and is merry but they hang downe theyre heads and are pittyfully out of countenance."[57]

Even those unsympathetic to Cromwell acknowledged that he had wholly declined the crown. Sir Edward Hyde writes with some asperity that "Mr. Cromwell hath absolutely refused to be called kinge, how his Parliament will beare it, after they have appeared such importunate Coxcombs, we shall shortly see."[58] Some royalists were uncertain whether to regard Cromwell's decision as a good or a bad thing: Sir Allen Apsley informs Hyde on 26 May that "wee are devided in opinion whether the refusal of his highness were for the kings advantage or the contrary, the moste wishe hee had accepted it but the most prudent persons I meet with think best of this exception in the sad condition men are now exposed to under the tyranny of such a sworde."[59] Nonetheless even such speculations attest to Cromwell's clearly negative answer.

Printed texts intervened to praise Cromwell for his refusal of the crown. George Wither responded to the news in his aptly named *A Suddain Flash*:

> For to mine ears, when first that news was brought,
> A thousand thoughts *Flusht* in, and this *Flasht* out
> Which I have now thus *Paper'd* up, for thee,
> To bring to minde what *is*, and what *may be*.[60]

As earlier, Wither's verse is deliberately anti-courtly in its prosaic language and irregular rhythms: his use of parallelism ("*Flusht* in" / "*Flasht* out"; "what *is*" / "what *may be*") provides minimal structure for the outpouring that is more in the style of a prophet than a courtier. In a kind of dramatic dialogue, Wither responds with surprise and wonder to Cromwell's decision:

> But, hath he wav'd that *Title*? and, I pray,
> Are you aright inform'd of what you say?
> Did not a *false-report*, your ears abuse?
> A *Crown! a Triple-Crown* doth he refuse?   (p. 2)

Direct questions and homely language convey the accent of speech, heightening the appearance of veracity. Wither's professed astonishment underscores the sacrifice that Cromwell has made: he labels him a *"Miracle of men."* Such a refusal should, Wither insists, negate suspicions of Cromwell:

> If this (as you affirm it is) be true;
> *Friends*; bid henceforth your *jealousies* adue:
> And, let him who mistrusts him any more;
> Suspect his *Honest wife*, to be a Whore.   (p. 2)

As he had in *Vaticium Causuale*, Wither underscores his anti-courtly message with plain diction and homespun examples. But by narrating Cromwell's refusal only indirectly, Wither hedges his bets, giving himself an escape route if Cromwell were to alter his decision at a later stage.[61] In this, Wither's apprehension was not unique. Many contemporaries continued to speculate on when Cromwell would take the crown. And the regal ceremony that followed seemed to contrast with, as much as confirm, Cromwell's rejection of the title of king.

Appropriating royal forms in the second inauguration

Cromwell left no record of his own views on the ceremony that followed his refusal of the crown. But relations between the ruler's views and the displays that produced his image differed dramatically from what we have seen under Charles I. The Caroline coronation was a unified representation of the essence of sacred monarchy, shaped by Charles's own piety and decorum. Spectacle and print worked to figure forth the person and beliefs of the monarch. But the Cromwellian ceremony seemed to react against Cromwell's own refusal, to be yet another intervention in the debate over Cromwell and the crown.

As in the shift from monarchical icon to Cromwellian print image, the Cromwellian inauguration changed the nature and meaning of its monarchical precedent. The second Cromwellian inauguration appropriated and revised monarchical forms, transforming a sacred rite into a civil ceremony. Although Roy Sherwood notes (and discounts) the absence of the anointing and crown, also absent from the Cromwellian ceremony were the bishops, the blessing of the holy oil, the sermon, the mass, most of the prayers, the anthems, and the choir.[62] The ceremony celebrated not a divine ritual, but a newly recognized Commonwealth state.

As with other aspects of Cromwellian representation, the inauguration seems to have been decided upon very late. In a letter of 30 June to Henry Cromwell, Arthur Annesley characterizes "his Highnesse inauguration by the Parliament to the protectorship of this commonwealth" as a "remarkable day," noting that "for so suddain a businesse (for it was not resolved on above three dayes before) it was transacted with much magnificence and order."[63] A contemporary account describes in more detail the second investiture that took place on 26 June in Westminster Hall. In Westminster, an ascent had been built and the "chair of Scotland," traditionally used in coronations, was brought from Westminster Abbey. A table covered in velvet was set before "his Highness," upon which were laid a Bible, sword, and scepter. Members of parliament, the aldermen of the City of London, and other dignitaries sat in specially constructed seats, built "scaffold-wise, like a *theatrum.*" Cromwell arrived "richly dressed, habited with a costly mantle of estate, lined with ermine, and girt with a sword of great value"; preceding him, the Earl of Warwick bore the Commonwealth sword, and the Lord Mayor, Tichborne, carried the sword of the City of London.[64]

The ceremony that followed both drew upon and revised the monarchical coronation. The theatrical and visual were by no means absent. After the heralds had commanded silence, the Speaker of the House took the place formerly held by the Archbishop of Canterbury. The Speaker presented Cromwell with "a rich and costly robe of purple velvet, lined with ermines; a Bible, ornamented with bosses and clasps, richly gilt; a rich and costly sword; and a sceptre of massy gold."[65] Each of these items symbolized an aspect of Cromwellian civil power. Hence, the Speaker extolled the "Robe of Purple" as "an emblem of magistracy [that] imports righteousness and justice," while the Bible is "a book of books, and doth contain both precepts and examples for good government."[66] The scepter was most clearly monarchical, although its weight here was "for you to be a staff to the weak and poor," while the sword was "not a military but a civil sword . . . not to defend yourself only, but your people also."[67]

As in coronation ceremonies, Cromwell then took an oath. While the royal oath promised to preserve the peace and defend the church, to uphold just laws and abrogate the unjust, and to dispense justice to all without favor, the protectoral vow, printed in *Mercurius Politicus*, was to "uphold and maintain the true Reformed Protestant Christian Religion, in the purity thereof" and to "endeavor, as chief Magistrate of these Three Nations, the maintenance and preservation of the Peace and Safety, and just Rights and Priviledges of the People thereof."[68] The oath recognized an office and state, rather than a person.

The Cromwellian ceremony had the public appeal, but not the private and sacramental side, of the Caroline rite. The ceremony had no "private" anointing, no sanctification by bishops, no sermon, and no communion. The recognition and acclamation at the end, then, was of a different kind of power: "the heralds, by loud sound of trumpet, proclaimed his Highness Oliver Cromwell, Protector of England, Scotland, and Ireland . . . commanding and requiring all persons to yield him due obedience."[69] *Mercurius Politicus* reports that the announcement met with popular applause: "the People made several great Acclamations with loud Shouts, *God save the Lord Protector*."[70] The form of the acclamation echoed monarchical precedent, but what was recognized was not a king.

Nonetheless, *Mercurius Politicus* at times used regal language to describe the proceedings, reporting that Cromwell was presented with "a Robe of Purple Velvet, lined with Ermine, being the habit anciently used at the solemn Investiture of Princes," and that "His Highness [was] standing thus adorned in Princely State, according to his merit and dignity."[71] The splendor and magnificence that belonged to monarchical coronations also marked this event, according to *Mercurius Politicus*, "the whole being managed with state and magnificence, suitable to so high and happy a Solemnity."[72]

A Further Narrative of the Passages of the Times reproduced a tiny etching of the affair that shows both links with and differences from monarchical precedent (fig. 21). In the etching, the Speaker of the parliament presents

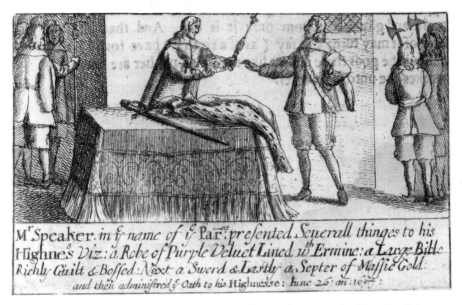

Figure 21 Etching of second protectoral installation, from *A Further Narrative of the Passages of the Times* (1657).

Cromwell, dressed like a courtier, with a Bible and a fleur-de-lis-topped scepter. A "Robe of Purple Velvet Lined wth Ermine" and "a sword" rest on the table between them. While the caption indicates that there should also be "a Scepter of Massie Gold," it is not depicted. Significantly, the tiny image contrasts sharply in size, detail, and pictured magnificence with Hollar's later engraving of the coronation of Charles II in Westminster Abbey. The very form in which the installation was circulated attested to difference from the sacred monarchical rite.

Contemporaries also noted the lack of the crown. Describing the scene in London as "a solemn day of rejoicing," one letter-writer thus narrated the inauguration itself:

> His Highness was sworn royal Protector in Westminster Hall before the judges, the Parliament and all the great officers of State; and had all the formalities as all the Kings had but a Crown; I left out the Lord Mayor and the council of the city of London who were there; and the Parliament afterwards adjourned till January, but presented him a new Instrument of Government that he swore unto; and first presented him with a robe, a Bible, sceptre, and sword; but the crown was wanting.[73]

For this observer, although Cromwell had become a "royal" Protector, the absence of the crown was still telling.

At least one contemporary viewed the second inauguration as an important and successful compromise between republicanism and monarchy. A correspondent of Hyde's wrote on 30 June that "there is at present a generall tranquillity in this Nation, the Protector pleased with his new Investiture & augmented power."[74] Those in favor of a Cromwellian monarchy, according to this account, saw the inauguration as close enough: "His owne party (whom they call Royaliste) satisfyed that they have advanct him in despight of all opposition to Soveraigne authority not doubting to prevayle in the next Assembly or at farthest next Parliament for Coronation." But opponents to Cromwellian kingship were equally satisfied, having "no lesse cause of triumph in their owne opinion that they have had it in their power to give Block to the Major part of the House, to affright his favourites and startle even the Protector Himself." A truce had been achieved, and "they are all now seemingly reconciled."[75]

Nonetheless, James Fraser, whose account of the inauguration we briefly viewed earlier, discloses that some tensions remained. The jubilant scene that Fraser describes as following the ceremony, "bells ringing bonefires burning and all demonstrations of joy that could be contrived," indicates public approval or at least cooperation.[76] But Fraser himself withholds belief, commenting bitterly that "the Idol of the times being set up Baal & Dagon must be bowed to, all must die that do not homage to this Diana. This riseing Sun must be worshipped. This new Translation of Kingly Government into a Commonwelth & of Monarchy into a state must be adored!"[77] Although he views Cromwell as being in "as great State as ever a King of England was," Fraser does not think of him as a king. Yet his account makes clear that kingship remained a volatile issue in both panegyric and satire. Fraser recounts "a desperat Satyr reflecting upon [Cromwell's] Originall & presaging his end" that also addresses the question of Cromwell as king.[78] The satire derides Cromwell as "his High nose Lord Protraitor" and asserts in exceptionally lame meter a cynical view of the kingship controversy: "I do beleeve he will not take the name of King for why / It's farr below him all men knowes, no King was e're so high."[79] Fraser's account shows how contested and variable the image of Cromwell remained. Tensions remained, too, between the publicly humble figure at the center and the lavish panegyric and display of the late Protectorate.

The crowning of Cromwell in print

One printed text mediated the tension between Cromwell's own plain-spoken refusal and the appropriation of monarchical spectacle by arguing that Cromwell's very refusal of the crown qualified him to receive it. Staging a triumph in print, *Anglia Rediviva: Or, England Revived. An Heroick Poem* supplied the central symbol missing in the coronation spectacle: a crown. But by making Cromwellian kingship the people's choice, the poem both argued for and radically transformed monarchy. In courtly and polished verse evoking Waller's *A Panegyric*, *Anglia Rediviva* recounts a classical triumph, complete with arches and culminating in Cromwell's coronation: but now the printed text fully replaces the public ceremony.

This coronation, then, while closely modelled on accounts of the classical triumphs of earlier Tudor and Stuart monarchs, takes place only in print. The author writes, "If things happen as I have Imagined them, I am both Poet and Prophet too: If not, I am a Poet onely, who has more liberty than the Historographer and his likelihood (most commonly) is more worth than tothers Truth."[80] In the opening lines of the poem itself, the parliament meets and *"All opinat with general Consent / For King again, and Kingly Government"* (p. 1). The balanced lines of the verse embody the balance attained with the return to monarchy. The author espouses the republican value of liberty, but insists that such is to be found in a monarchy:

> As for the Peoples Angel, Liberty
> And Fiend, Oppression and Tyranny
> They err, suppose this found with Kings alone
> Proudly and sternly seated on their Throne.   (p. 7)

The initial spondee ("They err") stresses the misconception about kingship, as does the trochaic "Proudly" and the parallelism and alliteration ("Proudly," "sternly seated"). Sound underscores sense in this smooth and polished verse.

Indeed, the poem argues against republican views as much as it argues for Cromwellian kingship: "For Times are chang'd, and Common-wealths no more / In such high reputation, as before / When *Romain* Citizens to *Kings* gave Law, / And Common-wealths their Kingdoms kept in awe" (p. 10). Rather, the well-crafted verse points to a well-crafted state, restored to monarchy:

> All generally *Oliver* for *King* do choose,
>   He modestly the Kingdome does refuse,
> Untill in forc't, his Shoulders he bows down
>   To th' Royall Roabs, and Head unto the Crown.   (p. 9, irreg.)

The use of enjambment propels Oliver's movement to royal robes and crown. The rhyme words are key terms: "choose" / "refuse"; "down" / "Crown." The poem represents Cromwell's coronation not as an elevation,

but an act of submission and devotion: Oliver, rather than the people,
"bows down."

Yet the very act of choosing transforms the monarchical coronation.
Here, rather than heredity or divine-right kingship, the people choose
Cromwell, and he assents to their choice. Elective monarchy was not
unheard of as a constitutional arrangement, and some accounts, including
Milton's *The Tenure of Kings and Magistrates*, suggested that the British mon-
archy had been elective in origin. Nonetheless, the poem's portrayal of
Cromwellian kingship challenges the assumptions and actual practices of
British monarchy: positing its origin in the public voice and the free choice
of the leader. Allegedly, heaven chooses and the people confirm that choice:

> Tis Heaven elects that man for King, not we
> Pointing as t'were with th' finger this is he:
> To which so clear election of Heaven,
> Long since we all our suffrages have given.   (p. 12)

But dramatic present tense and the people's own words overshadow heavenly choice; the dialogue between the people and Cromwell replaces both
the solemn and sacred monarchical coronation and the Cromwellian civil
ceremony.

Like the printed satires of the late 1640s, *Anglia Rediviva* employs the dramatic present tense to reveal Cromwell's inner thoughts. But in this text,
rather unmasking his Machiavellian ambition, the dramatic mode discloses
Cromwellian modesty and humility. Cromwell initially refuses the crown
for fear of seeming ambitious:

> No, no, (quoth he) 't shall ne're be said that I
> Ambitious was of Soveraignty:
> Nor shall the People ever say agen,
> That I had Conquerd for my self, not them.   (p. 17)

As he declares himself "Resolv'd to live and dye with this Renown, / Tis glo-
riouser to win, than wear the Crown" (p. 17), Cromwell's unaffected and
uncourtly speech evinces in itself his lack of ambition. Yet in this account
such modesty precisely qualifies him for the crown.

At the center of *Anglia Rediviva*, Cromwell takes both royal robes and
crown, not from a bishop or the Speaker of Parliament, but from the repre-
sentatives of the people:

> From whom, then, by their hands deliver'd him,
> He did accept the Royall Diadem:
> At which the numerous multitude aloud,
> With voices heaven, as they the earth did croud.   (p. 19).

The polished verse itself, employing zeugma and skillfully varied meter and caesurae, shows the order and balance of the newly confirmed monarchy.

In its reconfiguration of the process of coronation, *Anglia Rediviva* goes well beyond the hybrid nature of the second protectoral inauguration. Yet far from the sacred rituals of divine-right kingship or even the hierarchical Cromwellian ceremony, the poem gives a major role in choosing and crowning Cromwell to the people: "And who now doubts whe're he be King or no / The people generally have proclaimed so?" (p. 20). The poem directs an active public to see, judge, and concur in making Cromwell a king. Yet that very appeal changes the form of the monarchy for which it argues.

What impact did Cromwell have upon the struggle over his own image? We have seen that the representations of Cromwell were largely produced in a political context not controlled by the court. Clearly some of the images reacted against Cromwell rather than represented his own views. But it is worth looking at the court itself to see what figure Cromwell made there.

"He went plain and grave in his habit": Cromwellian self-presentation

Scholarly accounts have almost uniformly focused on the monarchical aspects of the Cromwellian court.[81] But James Fraser again provides us with a vivid eyewitness account of Cromwell at court that quite strikingly reflects Cromwell's own plain-stated views of himself. The figure that Fraser describes is neither lavish nor monarchical.[82] Having described Cromwell's "tall & Statly" stature, his "Constitution Sanguin a reed in his face, a high Roman nose & a fierce & Sparkling eye," Fraser turns to Cromwell's manner of dress: "as to his habit & cloaths, he was no friend to falshows, nor the prodigall vaingloriousnes of Garbs, he went plain and grave in his habit, more like a Senatore than a Souldiour."[83] Ironically, Cromwell's studious lack of fashion became fashionable: "in Imitation of him, gaudy fashions & costly garbs were laid asid in England."[84] Fraser also attested to Cromwellian piety: "I have often seen him, att Sermon and Devotion and most in the Chappel Royall and in the Kings seat glased about with Cristall . . . indeed I have not seen a more reverent composed hearer and carefull to attend the worship."[85] Although Cromwell used great ceremony with foreign ambassadors and upon state occasions, his mode of dress and behavior at court remained strikingly plain.

Such piety and plainness, as we have seen, elicited skepticism and attack, including charges of Machiavellianism. But what positive impact did it have on Cromwell's image in the late Protectorate? Although many of the verbal and visual images of Cromwell originated outside the court, in 1657 he sat for a final portrait by Edward Mascall. As under the monarchs, painting was a medium over which Cromwell could exercise some control, and upon which he could imprint his own style. Given the pervasive rumors of kingship, the Mascall portrait is a important artifact of late Cromwellian representation. Had he abandoned piety and simplicity? Was he in fact represented as a king in all but name?

Significantly, then, the Mascall portrait depicts the sharply delineated features of an older Cromwell, wearing a plain collar, dark fur, and a simple if elegant cloak (fig. 22). Cromwell's hair has thinned and his cheeks are sagging. Unlike the timeless and unchanging sphere of monarchical iconography, mythologized and remote, the effects of time and age upon Cromwell are clear. Indeed, the portrait seems more in the line of Rembrandt and the Protestant Dutch than the Italian Catholic baroque. Cromwell's head emerges in relief from a dark background, and he wears a dark cloak and plain collar. His appearance resembles that of a Dutch burgher.

This final portrait is as striking, even startling, for what is absent as for what is represented. No external symbols of office, authority, or power frame the starkly posed single figure. No memorials of martial and imperial achievements and renown appear. No rich and ornate clothing attests to Cromwell's enhanced status. No written inscription guides the viewer and elevates the subject. Not even a Cromwellian coat of arms, often seen in engravings of the period, appears. In this late portrait we find no signs of royalty, nor indeed of pomp. Cromwell's final portrait was the most puritan and plain style of all.

Constructions of Cromwell under the late Protectorate were more fraught and varied than has been recognized. Speculation about impending kingship culminated with parliament's actual offer of the crown to Cromwell in 1657. But Cromwell's refusal of the crown was incorporated into, even countered by, a second inauguration that drew upon and transformed the sacred monarchical rite into a civic and public ceremony. By the time of the second protectoral installation in June 1657, there seemed to be more support for, or at least more cooperation with, the regime than had been demonstrated in the 1654 triumphal entry. The appeal to the public, however, was double-edged. Cromwell's contemporaries both attacked and supported him to the extent that he looked like a king. The crucial aesthetic and political balance that Cromwell maintained in the final years of his life between republicanism and monarchism was, however, negated when, in death, he was given the crown that he had refused in life.

Figure 22 Edward Mascall, *Oliver Cromwell* (1657).

Five

"I saw him dead": Cromwell's death and funeral

On 3 September 1658, only days after the death of his beloved daughter, Elizabeth, and on the anniversary of his victories at Dunbar and Worcester, Cromwell died, succumbing to natural causes that probably included fever, gallstones, and blood poisoning.[1] Upon Oliver's death, his son Richard was immediately proclaimed Protector, and the royalist uprising that many had expected did not occur. Oliver, who in life had resisted the crown, was displayed in effigy at Somerset House and buried in Westminster Abbey, like a king. What do early reactions to his death show about the protectoral image in 1658? How did the Cromwellian obsequies draw upon and refashion the funeral of James I? Do the monarchical obsequies confirm that Cromwell had become a king in all but name? How did funeral elegies both incorporate and challenge the regality?

Recent literary studies of monarchical spectacle in early modern England have not included such appropriations as the Cromwellian funeral, while historians, less interested in representations, have assumed or argued that the funeral reflected a changed constitutional state.[2] But once again ceremony alone does not tell the full story. Rather, print supplemented and crucially reworked the display. Attention to printed texts surrounding the death and funeral of Cromwell reveals that images other than kingship remained available: that not only was the public ceremony contested by opponents of the Protectorate, but in praising the dead Protector, elegists kept alive a concept of the state that did not inhere in the body of the king. Indeed, the very forms of popular print and the appeal directed to a discerning public underscored assumptions of the Commonwealth at the point of its seeming demise: the people made the king.

I begin this chapter with the obsequies of James I that were specifically imitated for the Cromwellian lying-in-state and funeral. Early

mixed reactions to Cromwell's death gave way to the heroic and monarchical ceremonies. But the posthumous coronation provoked opposition and
reaction as much as popular acclaim. In their elegies on the Protector,
Thomas Sprat, John Dryden, and Andrew Marvell strove to modify the
extravagance of the display more in keeping with Cromwell's own modest
and martial style, as royalist and republican opponents alike attacked what
they saw as a new idolatry. Cromwell as prince veered dangerously close to
the Machiavel, and, with the fall of Richard's Protectorate in May 1659, a
flurry of tracts reintroduced Cromwell as Machiavel, now in hell, and
increasingly contrasted with the martyr-king, Charles I. The monarchical
obsequies for Oliver were, ironically, the first step in a process that revived
the martyr-king and helped to pave the way for the restoration of his son.

Monarchical precedent: the funeral of James I

The funeral of James I was the closest royal antecedent to the Cromwellian
funeral, and contemporary sources indicate that the Jacobean rites were
indeed consulted and imitated by the Protectoral Council.[3] The executed
Charles I was, of course, not given a royal funeral or even a funeral service,
but simply buried in Henry VIII's vault at Windsor. Yet Charles had put his
own imprint on the funeral rites of his father: the obsequies for James
showed increased ceremonialism and the relegitimation of the image associated with the later Caroline church. Indeed, James's funeral might be
understood as a court masque writ large, with the image of the divine-right
king at the center: first, James, then his son.[4] The Cromwellian appropriation, however, was far more participatory, changing the forms and meaning
of the spectacle.

Contrary to precedent, Charles himself served as chief mourner at his
father's funeral. The Venetian envoy, Zuane Pesaro, pointed to Charles's
own input in the ceremony: "it was doubtful whether his Majesty would
take part personally . . . Difficulties arose, but finally the king decided to pay
this last tribute of respect to his father's memory in person."[5] Pesaro noted
that such involvement was unusual: "the king followed in his place and it
was especially remarked that since William the Conqueror the king had
only thrice been present at the funeral celebrations."[6] Charles's participation put the king at the center of the ceremony, as he put himself at the
center of the masques.

The obsequies themselves reflected enhanced Laudian ritual more than
they reflected Jacobean moderation in church and state. After embalming,

the body of James I was twice taken in procession, first by night to Denmark House and later to Westminster Abbey.[7] Most striking and innovative in the obsequies (and imitated for Cromwell) was the use in the lying-in-state at Denmark House of a life-sized and life-like effigy.[8] A contemporary manuscript records the magnificent display of the effigy as it lay upon a coffin containing the actual body, in a room richly hung with black velvet and with the royal escutcheon upon a cloth of gold. The effigy, "in his robes of estate and Royall diadem," remained thus until the funeral, as "the service continewed in all points as if his Majestie had byn lyveinge."[9] The Venetian envoy similarly notes that "after arranging the house where the remains of the late king are laid, they put life-like figures there, and they observe the customary vigil, thirty to forty noblemen and cavaliers being always present day and night."[10] In other words, lavish ceremony and service continued not to the living king, but to his image.

More than a month later, the funeral procession bore James's body and a second effigy to Westminster Abbey. The procession was both elaborate and spectacular. John Chamberlain described the funeral as "the greatest indeed that ever was knowne in England," noting that black mourning had been distributed "for above 9000 persons."[11] Sir Simonds D'Ewes wrote that "the first mourner set out from Somerset House about 10 of the clock in the morning, and the last came not to Westminster till about 4 in the afternoon, – and no marvel, seeing the number of the mourners was near upon eight thousand."[12] The cohesive and unified image-making of the funeral, effigy, hearse, and ceremonial procession continued at the Abbey with a sermon by Bishop Williams that endowed James with the manifold virtues of Solomon. Contemporaries remarked upon the cost of this grand show, which Chamberlain put at above £50,000.[13] In sheer numbers and expense, the display showed the power and majesty of divine-right monarchy.

Contemporaries also noted the splendor and magnificence of the funeral hearse. The Venetian envoy observed that the "great bed of mourning" was "much esteemed for its architecture and decoration."[14] Similarly, Chamberlain praised the hearse as "the fairest and best fashioned that hath ben seen, wherin Inigo Jones the survayor did his part."[15] As the work of Inigo Jones, the hearse thus showed another link with Stuart masques. But on the public stage, the order and decorum of the masque could not be preserved. Chamberlain explained that the late arrival at the Abbey, combined with a two-hour sermon, meant that "it was very late before the offering and all other ceremonies were ended; in summe all was performed with great magnificence, but the order was very confused and disorderly."[16] The wide participation both affirmed the hierarchical order and threatened to disrupt it.

Examination of the funeral obsequies of James I shows that it was less an abstract commemoration than a purposeful deployment of power in the service of hereditary right. The spectacle produced a unified and resplendent image of James, but that image was deployed to enhance his son and heir, Charles. Hence, Bishop John Williams ended *Great Britaine's Solomon* by reflecting on the funeral effigy, not to argue for the medieval and mystical notion of the king's two bodies, but to appropriate the image for the hereditary succession. "God hath provided," he explained, "another Statue yet to adorne the Exequies of our late Soveraigne."[17] He referred not to the "Artificiall Representation within the Hearse, for this shews no more then his outward Body; or rather the Bodie of his Bodie, his Cloathes and Ornaments" (p. 75). Rather, Williams pointed to "that Statue which (beyond all former Presidents of Pietie) walk't on foot this day after the Hearse . . . A Breathing Statue of all his vertues," the new king, Charles (p. 76).

Elegies on James also effected a transfer of power in iconic terms. Hence, John Taylor's *A Living Sadnes, In Duty consecrated to the Immortall memory of our late Deceased albe-loved Soveraigne Lord* (1625) depicts the inherent virtues of both monarchs in conventional sun imagery:

> Though duteous *Sorrow* bids us not forget
> This clowde of *Death*, wherein our *Sunne* did set,
> His *Sonnes* resplendent Majestie did rise,
> Loadstone and Loadstarre to our hearts and eyes:
> He cheeres our drooping spirits, he frees our feares,
> And (like the *Sunne*) dryes up our dewey Teares.[18]

Here, however, Taylor punned on the traditionally monarchical sun imagery, as the son replaced the sun. Skillful versification, balance, and parallelism embody the hierarchy and order with which the true heir succeeds to the throne. The heat of the sun / son dries the dewy tears of speaker and reader alike. The verse is polished and courtly, decorous even, in describing grief.

Thomas Heywood's *A Funerall Elegie* similarly puns on sun / son in verse that both describes the visual, iconic symbols of kingship and constitutes a kind of verbal icon in its order, polish, and stateliness:

> *Charles James* succeeds King James in his true Right,
> In Majestie, Globe, Scepter, Sword, and Crowne.
> A Royall *Sonne*, to give great Kingdomes light,
> After his *Fathers* set, and going downe.[19]

The kings did not have to carry out any specific action but were praised simply for the life-giving virtues of their royal nature.

Given the extent to which the symbolic ceremonial forms were used to define and enhance a distinctively Caroline view of monarchy, the Cromwellian borrowing from the funeral of James I was not only an aesthetic imitation: it was a seizure of power. Contested in life, Cromwell's image was even more unstable in death. The Council drew upon Jacobean rites to stabilize the contested forms and legitimate the regime. But the Stuart precedent used to justify the transition from Oliver to Richard also reminded some viewers that Cromwellian power was a usurpation of the true monarchical line.

Early reactions to Cromwell's death

From the beginning, Cromwell's death was an event interpreted and given meaning in print. Reactions appeared in addresses, sermons, elegies, panegyric, and satire, as well as in the more material forms of the effigies, funeral procession, and funeral monument. In the official account in *Mercurius Politicus*, Marchamont Nedham recalled that 3 September had already been to Cromwell "a day of Triumphs and Thanksgiving for the memorable Victories of Dunbar and Worcester":

> Thus it hath proved to him to be a day of Triumph indeed, there being much of Providence in it, that after so glorious Crowns of Victory placed on his head by God on this day, having neglected an Earthly Crown, he should now go to receive the Crown of Everlasting life.[20]

Nedham's long periodic sentence embodies the delays that it describes, as Cromwell moves through his earthly life on his way to a heavenly crown. Nedham repeats and plays upon the various kinds of crowns associated with Cromwell: earthly crowns shift to eternal as the martial victor achieves a triumph in the heavenly sphere.

Formal and ceremonial proclamation of Richard was supplemented by addresses in print. The Venetian envoy wrote that the succession of Richard was proclaimed "by trumpet before the President of the Council, various councillors, the mayor and aldermen of the city, in the presence of troops of horse and companies of foot, in the usual places of London and Westminster."[21] The envoy attested to the public appearance of goodwill toward Richard: "there was a great crowd and a good deal of applause from the people, with all the pomp and ceremony usual on such occasions."[22]

Addresses to Richard poured in from corporations, cities, the army, and elsewhere, indicating a widespread acceptance by the gentry of the peaceful succession. Uniformly lavish in "comparing Oliver Protector (so called) to Moses, David, and Elijah, and saying that he was the great asserter of the Liberties of Gods people," the addresses seemed to one later skeptic to have been "hatched at court by the late Secretary Thurloe and the old Malignant pamphletter . . . Nedham."[23] Whether or not they were hatched at court, such texts were more than descriptive; they also did cultural and political work by employing biblical language to naturalize and defend the succession.

Likewise, sermons drew upon the legitimation of biblical type. In *The Protectors Protection*, a sermon published in October 1658, Samuel Slater lauded Oliver as an English Moses who "when he had fought the Nations Battels, carried us thorow the wilderness, preserved us from the rage and fury of our enemies, and brought us within sight of the promised Land, gave up the ghost, laid down his *leading-staff* and his life together, with whose fall the Nation was shaken."[24] As in the addresses, Slater employed the figure of Moses to support the accession of Richard to the office of Lord Protector: "*Moses*, it is true, is dead, but we have a *Joshua* succeeding him, let us pray, that what the other happily *begun*, this may more happily *finish*, and bring the accomplishment of all your *right-bred* hopes" (p. 58). In sermons upon Cromwell's death, Moses and Joshua exemplified succession by appointment and merit, not simply by heredity.[25]

Despite the momentary quiescence of both royalists and republicans, however, tensions remained. If official printed responses lamented the death of Oliver, manuscript accounts showed much more skepticism. John Evelyn was curt and cryptic: "*Sept* 3. Died that archrebell *Oliver Cromewell*, cal'd Protector."[26] Ralph Josselin, who had long had misgivings about the Lord Protector, wrote: "Cromwell died, people not much minding it."[27] A manuscript satire dated 3 September alleged that Cromwell's ambition had caused him to be cut off by the true monarch, Death:

> Here is Deaths chair of state. Our Governour
>   She did prevent ambitious of his power
> For tho I hardly dare style him a king
>   Her Titles as the Queen, the Nations ring
> And while the people cry with flattring breath
>   Save the Protector, some cry long live Death.[28]

Framed by the evocation of a personified Death, the speaker's seemingly guileless account destabilizes the ceremonies of mourning. Similarly, a royalist letter-writer disclosed the discontent that lay beneath the appearance of assent to Richard's succession. Writing that Richard had been declared successor, and "this whole day has been spent in the pageantry of such solemnities as the occasion required," the author nonetheless hoped for imminent change:

> All men's hearts (allmost quite dead before) are of a sudden wonderfully revived to an expectation of some great change, and good men are the more encouraged to hope that the effects of so alltogether an unexpected providence will be much good to the Kingdome, as observinge that God himselfe seems to have undertaken the worke, havinge thus seasonably removed the great obstructor of our happyness by his owne hand.[29]

The author urged immediate action: "Oh! for gods sake, my Lord, as you tender the happinesse of that good King, and the wellfare of bleeding kingdomes, lett not delayes loose the benefitt of such an happy juncture." In his view, Richard was ill-suited to his new position, "an ape on horseback," and the time was ripe to overthrow Cromwellian rule.

Amid the contested forms, albeit also the peaceful succession, the Protectoral Council acted decisively to imprint a particular image upon Oliver: that of king. Preparations for an elaborate lying-in-state and funeral were soon under way. In early October, one contemporary wrote of "an effigies of wax" that had been made to represent the late Protector. Further, "black velvet" was being bought all over London to adorn Whitehall and Somerset House: this writer, however, disparaged the solemn ceremonial trappings as hollow and vain: "because men cannot mourn enough for the death of His Highness, the stones and walls are taught to do it."[30] Oliver would remain as contested in death as he had been in life.

Cromwell's dependence upon Providence and his habitual resistance to planning ahead left the arrangements for his funeral completely in the hands of a new Council eager to legitimize itself and prone to do so in the most traditional form possible: a monarchical funeral. The Venetian envoy wrote in late September that "at Whitehall they are now preparing for the funeral of the late Protector, which will take place in four or five weeks time, with extraordinary pomp and magnificence. They are consulting ancient books to see what was done by the kings on such occasions, and say that it will be more splendid than ever before."[31] Later, the envoy pointed to conscious adaptation of the rites for James I: "it was decided to follow the forms observed at the burial of King James; but this will be much greater, for that did not cost more than 30,000£ sterling, whereas this will run to some 100,000, the cloth alone coming to nearly 40,000£, 30,000 yards having been provided, besides many other things required, which cost a lot."[32] Although estimates of the cost ranged widely, the envoy's assertion of the Jacobean model for the funeral is confirmed by striking resemblances in form and ritual.

As contemporaries speculated over why the funeral was being delayed, Cromwell's body itself was buried privately, as James's had been. On 11 November 1658, Lady Hobart wrote that "My Lord protector's body was Bered last night at one o'clock very privittly, & tis thought that will be [no] show at tall: the army doe bluster a letill: god send us pes for I dred a combustion."[33] Despite Lady Hobart's skepticism, there was indeed a show: like James, Cromwell was commemorated by a life-sized effigy that lay in state at Somerset House. The Venetian envoy wrote that "Somerset House has been prepared for the lying-in-state of the late Protector, where he will remain until the day of the funeral, which is not yet fixed. The body was brought from Whitehall privately the other night, accompanied only by his Highness's servants. There it lies in extraordinary pomp."[34] But did the ceremony celebrate, as Sherwood argues, Cromwellian kingship?[35] Did the effigy reflect what Ernst Kantorowicz has influentially described as the king's two bodies, the glory and immortality of kingship, despite the death of the mortal body of the king?[36] The answers to such questions shed light both on the shifting production of a Cromwellian image and on the dynamics and forms of the monarchical power that preceded and followed it. Closer examination reveals a more complex, if not confused, representation, with an interplay of public ceremony, printed and manuscript texts, government directive, and popular reaction.

"Like a king": Oliver's funeral obsequies

Like James I, Cromwell was represented in effigy in a formal lying-in-state. The effigy itself was "curiously made to the life according to the best skill of the Artist in that Imployed vizt Mr Symons."[37] Thomas Simon, who had earlier designed Cromwellian medals and coins, was now employed to construct the head of the effigy, the body of wood having been carved by one "Mr. Phillips beinge carver to the house & surveyor."[38]

The official newsbook account in Nedham's *Mercurius Politicus* (14–21 October) interpreted the display as a ceremony of honor befitting princes:

> On Monday the 18 instant, the Representation of the person of his late Highness in Effigie will be exposed to publick view at Somerset-house upon a bed of State vested with his Robe of Estate, a Scepter placed in

one hand, a Globe in the other, and a Crown laid on a Velvet Cushion a
little above the head, after the antient and most becoming Ceremony of
the preceding Princes of this Nation upon the like occasion; which point
of Honor is the more due to his memory, by how much he advanced the
honor of our Country by his incomparable Actions, beyond the
example of any that swayed the Scepter of his land before him.[39]

The elaborate parallels of the language here reflect the elaborate ceremony
that commemorated Cromwell with multiple objects and symbols: robe,
scepter, globe, and crown. Although the display in itself mimicked the monarchical lying-in-state, the mode of reporting had changed; the newsbook
now made the account widely available, directing its appeal to a broad
public and praising Cromwell for having advanced not his own honor but
the honor of his country.

The official newsbook account thus circulated even more widely the
well-attended display of the effigy. Nedham describes how the people
approached the room holding the effigy through three antechambers hung
with black; the Cromwellian arms was now crowned with the imperial
crown, and upon each cloth of estate was also "a large Majesty-Escocheon
fairly painted and gilt upon Taffity."[40] In the fourth room was the prone
effigy, reproduced in a contemporary engraving (fig. 23). Again, *Mercurius
Politicus* described the display in detail:

> The Effigies it self [was] apparelled in a rich Suit of uncut Velvet, being
> robed first in a Kirtle Robe of Purple Velvet, laced with a rich gold lace,
> and furr'd with Ermins; upon the Kirtle is the Royal large Robe of the
> like Purple Velvet laced, and fur'd with Ermins, with rich strings, and
> tassels of gold; his Kirtle is girt with a rich Embroidered Belt, in which is
> a fair Sword richly gilt, and hatcht with gold hanging by the side of the
> Effigies.[41]

Repeated adjectives evoke monarchy: "rich," "Royal," "Purple," "gold."
The purple velvet, gold lace, and ermine constituted the sartorial splendor
of majesty; completing the image were the timeless symbols of rule, the
scepter "representing Government" in the right hand of the effigy, and
the globe "representing Principality" in the left.[42] While the effigy wore
"the Cap of Regality of Purple Velvet, furr'd with Ermins," on a chair of
estate just behind stood the imperial crown itself.[43]

Although the effigy was initially left lying on a bed covered with black
velvet, after a certain amount of time had elapsed it was raised to an
upright position and the crown was placed upon its head. Another contemporary engraving, made shortly after the funeral, depicted the upright and

Figure 23 Effigy of Oliver Cromwell, lying-in-state, from *Some Farther Intelligence of the Affairs of England* (1658).

crowned effigy (fig. 24).[44] Whether the implications of this ceremony were understood by many observers is unclear. In *Salt upon Salt*, George Wither quite correctly pointed out that this was a Roman Catholic rite, representing the soul's having passed through purgatory. But a more typical observer may have been Roger Burgoyne, who in a letter of 11 November noted the change with great interest but without speculating on its symbolism: "We are all a whist, no newes stirring but that the old Protector is now gott upon his leggs againe in Sumersett House, but when he shall be translated to the rest of the Gods at Westminster I cannot tell. Pray, doe you come and see."[45]

Pamphlets published just after the funeral, such as *The True Manner of the most Magnificent Conveyance of His Highnesse Effigies*, also circulated the lying-in-state in print. Although *The True Manner* reported "multitudes of all sorts of people coming dayly to behold [the effigy]," it disseminated the display more widely in print.[46] And the "Representation of him in Summerset House by particular Order of the Lords of the Council" (p. 3) repeated the

Figure 24 Upright effigy of Oliver Cromwell (1658).

details from the newsbook regarding both the lying-in-state and the funeral procession.

"King" Oliver appeared most formally in the funeral procession that took place on 23 November 1658. That the event was expected, from the beginning, to be grand and popular is attested by the petition of the Westminster Abbey officers to the Governors of Westminster asserting their right to erect (and charge for the privilege of using) scaffolds for viewing the funeral. The petition explicitly calls upon royal precedent, as the officers argue that "it hath bin always the right of the late Deane and Chapter of West[minster] and their usual Custom against the Coronation Day, going to Parliament, or funerall of any king, queene, prince, or peere of England, to permitt the said Officers at their owne Cost and Charges, to erect Scaffolds upon the ground neere the Church yard wall leading from the Conduit to the West pale of the said Church."[47] What has occasioned the petition is that "the ffunerall of his Late Deceased Highnes Drawing neere," some parishioners of St. Margarets Westminster have "presumed to farme out the said ground to some of their fellow parishioners for the use aforesaid pretendinge that the profitts arising thereby shall go to the use of the poore of the said parish."[48] The dispute, the resolution of which is unrecorded, clearly links the Cromwellian funeral with earlier monarchical ritual.

The Cromwellian funeral procession was a complete iconic display, drawing upon the full visual resources of monarchical ceremony.[49] Both sympathetic and skeptical observers noted the solemnity, splendor, and regality of the display. Peter Mundy describes the elaborate procession of mourners, the banners, standards, and streamers, and the silver and gold trumpets, intermixed with drums. Even the horses of state were lavishly caparisoned with rich coverings and black plumes; Cromwell's own horse wore red velvet, richly embroidered with gold and silver. At the center of the display was the effigy of Oliver, "beeing placed in a stately chariot adorned with [e]scutcheons, armes, banneretts, etts., drawne with six horses covered downe to the ground with blacke velvet and blacke plumes" as the solemn procession passed down "streets beeing railed and lynde with redcoates (souldiers) from Somersethouse to Westminster Abbey."[50]

Sir Edward Dering, who observed the procession from a place at the end of the Banqueting House at Whitehall, added further details of the effigy: "upon ye bed lay not ye body, for that was buried before, but the effigies of ye protector, made I take it in wood, but carved & coloured like him & drest in ye same clothes he wore at his daughter Franciss wedding [but] over it a robe of purple velvet, lined with ermine and a crowne upon his head."[51] The Venetian envoy similarly notes the "pomp and state" of the funeral procession: "the effigy of the late Protector, his actual body having been buried privately many weeks ago, was followed on foot from Somerset House to Westminster Church. It was borne on a car, wearing a crown on its head and holding the sceptre and orb in its hands, with every other token of royalty, and drawn by six magnificent horses superbly caparisoned."[52] The magnificent effigy both emulated and went beyond monarchical precedent.

Various eyewitnesses attested to the popularity of the spectacle. Dering noted that "there were very good numbers of mourners & many horses involved & attendance of Ambassadors on foot."[53] The Venetian envoy recorded both the great numbers of people and the fear of disturbances: "a huge crowd of people gathered to watch the ceremony, and divers companies of infantry and many troops of horse were dispersed about at all the corners of the city, for safety's sake and to prevent any disturbances which might arise."[54] *Mercurius Politicus* reported "many thousands of people being Spectators."[55] In numbers alone, the crowd was impressive, attesting to the increased popularity and acceptance of Cromwellian spectacle at the point of his death, and, paradoxically, only when he had assumed the traditional trappings of a king.

The ceremonies within Westminster were less widely viewed, but again were available in print. Arriving at Westminster, the gentleman of the protectoral household carried the effigy in a "magnificent manner" up to the east end of the Abbey and placed it "in that Noble Structure which was raised there on purpose to receive it; where it is to remain for some time, exposed to publick view."[56] A payment ledger for "Worke bespoke provided and done for the standing hearse at Westminster Abbey" reveals details of the elaborate display, including such items as "26 greate sheilds a yard deepe Imbossed att 30 sh[illings] a peece," "5 dozen of Badges beinge his highness Creast Imbossed att 24 sh[illings] a dozen," "Three dozen of Escroules beinge mottos sutable to his Highness meritt att 30 sh[illings] a dozen," "10 dozen Escochons wrought on Taffaty with fine Gould and Silver att 7 [pounds] 10 sh[illings] a dozen," and "one greate Banner of the white Lyon at 6 [pounds]."[57] Such magnificent accoutrements suited the monarchical ceremonies, however ill-suited they were to Cromwell's own self-negating style.

Other contemporaries attested to the splendor of the catafalque for the Lord Protector, which was, in fact, modelled on the one designed by Inigo Jones for the effigy of James I.[58] Peter Mundy writes that "at the Abbey, the effigies was placed in a triumphant, ritch and artificall monument in Henry the Seventh['s] Chappell . . . where it lies in a magnificent manner and shall remaine for a certain tyme to be seene."[59] And the Venetian envoy reports that the effigy "now lies in state in the church in a prominent position, exposed to view for a certain time."[60] The display was perceived as not only instructive but profitable, causing a dispute between the Westminster Abbey bellringers and monument-keepers, both of whom wished, in the words of the bellringers' petition, to be appointed "to protect & attend his Highness . . . Hearse & to keep the same from harme and damage."[61]

Material monument and printed word together attested to Cromwell's power and enhanced stature. *Mercurius Politicus* concludes: "This is the last ceremony of honor, and less could not be performed to the Memory of him, to whom posterity will pay (when envy is laid asleep by time) more honor then we are able to express."[62] Ceremony, effigy, and funeral hearse clearly imitated previous monarchical forms.

Oppositional images

The crowned effigy and funeral hearse most fully constructed Cromwell as king. But when one moves from the official accounts of the obsequies to private texts, a different picture emerges that calls into question the adequacy or even efficacy of the lavish spectacle. Rather than simply inspiring awe and obedience, the monarchical display stirred up opposition from royalists and republicans alike. If Edmund Ludlow's later account can be believed, there was a good deal of disaffection even at the lying-in-state in Somerset House: "This folly and profusion so far provoked the people that they threw dirt in the night on [Cromwell's] escutcheon that was placed over the great gate of Somerset-house."[63] John Evelyn was similarly unimpressed with Oliver's funeral. Despite the regal trappings, "*Oliver* lying in Effigie in royal robes, & Crown'd with a Crown, scepter, & *Mund*, like a King," he found it "the joyfullest funerall that ever I saw, for there was none that Cried, but dogs, which the souldiers hooted away with a barbarous noise; drinking, & taking *Tabacco* in the streetes as they went."[64] Again, the display failed to convince.

The appearance of regality, combined with delays caused by a fight between ambassadors over precedence and other "disorders," confirmed for some observers that Cromwell was only a mock-king. For one contemporary letter-writer, "our long exspectations weere on tewsday last satisfied, though the little performance answered them not. *parturiunt montes nascetur ridiculus mus* [mountains labor, a ridiculous mouse is born]."[65] This writer scoffed at the official printed account of the funeral: "The gazett will informe you of the particulars, but not of any thinge therein disorderly carried."[66] Such disorders as "the long demur after the first mourners ere the rest followed" persuaded him that "they weare but novices in the garbs of majesty who were the maister controwlers and contrivers therein."[67] To underscore the false regality, the writer pointed to an ironic addition to the funeral of the former brewer: "And a sow accidently gott gruntinge in amongst the chiefe mourners, some said he expected there would be a dole of graines, and would have his share."[68] The trap-pings of monarchy, without the real presence, revealed the hollowness of the show. In this account, at least, the funeral not only failed to convince but the very display was counter-productive, disclosing a true lack of status and legitimacy: "Indeed one might easily smell from whence they came, for true Royalty cloathed in sacke cloth would have made a braver shew then this did with all the cost bestowed upon it."[69]

Others responded to what they saw as the idolatry of the funeral proces-sion, not failing to note the irony of such an idolatrous spectacle being set up for Cromwell the iconoclast. Quaker Edward Burrough was scandalized by the "dead invented Image of Wood or wax, arrayed and decked with some foolish inventions" made for him "who was once a great Instrument in the hand of the Lord to break down many Idolatrous Images and grie-vous Idols."[70] Like Burrough, George Wither in *Salt upon Salt* (1658) also alleged that "we are already drawing very nigh / To *Superstitions*, and *Idolatrie*."[71] Wither claimed that "*Spectators* Jeeringly do say, / *It is a very costly Puppet-Play*" (p. 18). The poet found it scandalous that "HE, who vilifide / Not long ago, the *vanitie* and *pride* / Of former *Princes*" (p. 19) should now be buried with "more vain pomps" than any English king.

The success of the monarchical spectacle – its apparent appeal to the people – was also its vulnerability. The French ambassador, M. de Bourdeaux, reported in December 1658 that objections to the funeral were immediate and that they took, significantly, the form of print: "On that day great numbers of printed papers were distributed, inveighing no less against the vanity and expense of the funeral, than against the validity of all the acts done in England since the dissolution of the Long Parliament; and now all persons express their sentiments with great freedom."[72] The burial of Cromwell as a monarch stirred up precisely the opposition it was designed to forestall. Cromwellian supporters had both to answer this opposition and to incorporate (or counter) the new regality in elegies that grappled with the meaning and impact of Cromwell's character and rule.

Elegies on Cromwell

Various elegies on Cromwell, many of which were published after the mon-archical funeral, showed new representational issues and tensions.[73] Elegies by Thomas Sprat, John Dryden, and Edmund Waller were published together in January 1658, the time of the new protectoral parliament, when republican agitation increased. These elegies have been consistently disparaged and dismissed as aesthetic failures linked with the uncertainties and impending political failure of the Protectorate.[74] But the elegies are a more complex and successful summing of Cromwell's life and character than has been recognized. Although Sprat and Waller incorporate increased regality, both Dryden and Marvell reassert action and piety more in keeping with Cromwell's own plain style.

Thomas Sprat (1635–1713) was at the time a student at Wadham College, Oxford, who would go on to be Bishop of Rochester and Dean of Westminster. Sprat's *To the Happie Memory of the most Renowned Prince* evokes the battles of the civil wars and the early republic, denying Cromwell's desire for a crown in terms much like those we have seen throughout the Protectorate:

> Thou fought'st not to be high or great,
>   Not for a Scepter or a Crown,
>   Or Ermyne, Purple, or the Throne;
>   But as the Vestal heat
>   Thy Fire was kindled from above alone.[75]

Although directly addressed to Cromwell, the verse is objective and observant in tone, not exclamatory, or, it might be noted, particularly grief-stricken. But the argument takes a crucial turn. Because Cromwell had not sought the crown, he deserved the regality he at last received:

> 'Tis true, thou wast not born unto a Crown,
>   Thy Scepter's not thy Fathers, but thy own.
>   Thy purple was not made at once in haste,
>   But, after many other colours past,
>   It took the deepest Princely Dye at last.   (p. 16)

Although it uses simple, even plain language, Sprat's elegy endows Cromwell with full royal regalia, reflecting the unequivocal kingship of his funeral.

Waller's elegy on Cromwell, *Upon the Late Storm, And of the Death of His Highness Ensuing the Same*, is even more hyperbolic and imperial. Describing the storm that occurred on the night of Cromwell's death, for instance, Waller employs the pathetic fallacy of nature mourning that is more conventionally associated with monarchy:

> We must resign! Heaven his great soul does claim
> In storms, as loud as his immortal fame;
> His dying groans, his last breath, shakes our isle,
> And trees uncut fall for his funeral pile;

> About his palace their broad roots are tossed
> Into the air. So Romulus was lost!
> New Rome in such a tempest missed her king,
> And from obeying fell to worshipping.   (lines 1–8)[76]

Waller's characteristically crafted lines – end-stopped couplets, parallel-isms, strong caesurae – control the grief that they describe, although such run-on lines as "tossed / Into the air" imitate its propelling force. Waller not only parallels Cromwell with Romulus but evokes the deification of Romulus upon his death.

As he had in his earlier *Panegyric*, Waller shows Cromwell as active and martial:

> From civil broils he did us disengage,
> Found nobler objects for our martial rage;
> And, with wise conduct, to his country showed
> Their ancient way of conquering abroad.
> Ungrateful then! if we no tears allow
> To him, that gave us peace and empire too.   (lines 23–28)

Balanced lines imitate the order achieved by Cromwell, builder of empire. Strong verbs ("disengage," "showed") are emphasized by their position as rhyme words. But the elegy becomes monarchic, as Waller associates Cromwell with the fellow-princes who mourn his death: "Princes, that feared him, grieve, concerned to see / No pitch of glory from the grave is free" (lines 29–30).

As with his earlier panegyric, Waller's elegy evoked protests in print and manuscript.[77] Wither castigated the hyperbole and excess of Waller's verses in *Salt upon Salt*:

> These are *Wits* bubbles, blown up with a Quill,
> Which *watrie-Circles*, with *weak-Air* doth fill;
> Or, like a *squib*, which fires, and cracks, and flies,
> And, makes a *noise*, that little signifies.   (p. 5)

Wither's deliberately rough rhythms, abrupt caesurae, and exaggerated alliteration ("*Wits*" / "*watrie*" / "*weak*"; "bubbles" / "blown"; "fill" / "fires" / "flies") mock both the substance and style of Waller's verse. Other responses remained in manuscript. "On Waller's Poem on the Death of the Protector" bluntly attacked both the poet and his allegedly heroic subject:

> So sang the poet who for thirst of fame
> To show his witt hath ravished his shame

> Oliver's dead that hellish imp of Mars
> Whence is his nose sure in the divells arse
> O bury him not but let him ly
> A copy to draw divells by.[78]

This quite vicious verse ridicules Waller's well-known wit. The author also rewrites Waller's subject, making Cromwell not terrifying but debased and demonic. The term "imp" and the nose and arse imagery recall the satires of the early republic. Another manuscript verse, William Godolphin's "Mr. Wallers Poem on the late Storme at the death of his Highnesse construed," similarly undermined Waller's subject, the heroic Cromwell, by separating him from Roman heroes and even from humanity: "In battle Hercules won the lyons skin, / But our fierce Tyrant had the beast within."[79] Employing Waller's own distinctive balance and antithesis against him, Godolphin transformed the admiring princes of the elegy: "Tyrants that lov'd him greivd, concernd to see, / There must be punishment for cruelty."[80] He likewise burlesqued Waller's final lines through judicious substitution: "Unworthy then if we base tears allow / To him that gave us warrs & ruin too."[81] Such satire inverted the panegyric to overturn the inversions of Cromwellian usurpation.

A more qualified response to Cromwell's death than Waller's is found in Dryden's *Heroique Stanzas to the Glorious Memory of Cromwell*.[82] Dryden (1631–1700) was cousin and clerk to the Lord Chamberlain, Sir Gilbert Pickering, who had arranged Cromwell's funeral, and he is listed as marching in the funeral procession with John Milton and Andrew Marvell as "Secretarys of ye ffrench & Latin Toungs."[83] *Heroique Stanzas* was Dryden's first major poem, although, like Waller, he would later celebrate the king's return in effusive verse. Dryden's elegy, unlike the other elegies, has received some critical acclaim, but specifically because it is seen as emotionally detached, cautious, or remote in its attitude toward Cromwell.[84] Yet I would argue that the qualifications and "muted" tones of the poem that critics have taken to indicate ambivalence toward Cromwell in fact reflect Cromwell's own activism and plain style.

From its beginning *in medias res*, the *Heroique Stanzas* praises an activist Cromwell in language and form that imitates such action:

> And now 'tis time; for their Officious haste,
> Who would before have born him to the sky,
> Like *eager Romans* ere all Rites were past
> Did let too soon the *sacred Eagle* fly.   (lines 1–4)

Although Dryden eschews the precipitate action of the earlier elegists, and his opening stanzas consist largely of disclaimers, the form itself (multiple dependent clauses, run-on lines) impels the verse forward to its conclusion: praising Cromwell.

Dryden depicts himself as a figure in action, questioning, striving to depict Cromwell:

> How shall I then begin, or where conclude
> To draw a *Fame* so truly *Circular*?
> For in a round what order can be shew'd,
> Where all the parts so *equall perfect* are?   (lines 17–20)

Unlike Waller's exclamatory verse or even Sprat's objective proclamation, Dryden begins his portrait of Cromwell in the interrogative, foregrounding his own role as artist in constructing or shaping the image. While James Winn has pointed out a possible allusion to the paintings in-the-round of Cromwell by Samuel Cooper and Peter Lely here, it is important to note that "fame" is not a visual quality.[85] Dryden offers not a set icon but a figure who shifts and moves throughout.

Similarly, Dryden replaces traditional royalist iconography with a new Cromwellian activism. As with the earlier poetic images of Cromwell by Marvell, Fisher, and others, Dryden presents an active figure, changing and in motion:

> Swift and resistlesse through the Land he past
> Like that bold *Greek* who did the East subdue;
> And made to battails such Heroick haste
> As if on wings of victory he flew.   (lines 49–52)

Dryden, like Waller, carefully crafts his verse: but he envisions an activist, not a monarchical Cromwell. Careful placement of words underscores the movement: hence the initial position of "Swift" and all verbs as rhyme words. Indeed, Dryden's Cromwell takes on epic proportions, as he strews conquests "Thick as the *Galaxy* with starr's is sown" (line 56).

Dryden quite directly contrasts this activist Cromwell with the passive martyr-king of the *Eikon Basilike*, the famous frontispiece of which showed a palm pulled down by weights: "His *Palmes* though under weights they did not stand, / Still thriv'd; no *Winter* could his *Laurells* fade" (lines 57–58). Finally, Dryden depicts heaven itself as reflecting Cromwell's own simplicity and plainness: "Heav'n in his Portraict shew'd a Workman's hand / And drew it perfect yet without a shade" (lines 59–60). Even the divine artist paints Cromwell within time and history, not striving for the flattering shadows of monarchical iconography.

Dryden's Cromwell continues to triumph, even in death. The conclusion of the poem avoids the monarchical effigy by imagining, rather, an urn in which Cromwell's ashes rest, while "His Name a great example stands to show / How strangely high endeavours may be blest, / Where *Piety* and *valour* joyntly goe" (lines 146–48). Dryden adroitly achieves the balance of his final ending, looking and not looking, not because Cromwell does not have a crown (as with *The Unparalleled Monarch*), but because he does.

Marvell's much-criticized *A Poem upon the Death of O. C.* challenges the monarchical funeral ceremony and effigy even more boldly than does Dryden's elegy.[86] Marvell replaces the elaborate and regal funeral with a focus on the private and domestic Cromwell. To the extent that the poem gives an image of Cromwell, it is an anti-icon: looking not at Cromwell's regal effigy but at his corpse.

As in *The First Anniversary*, Marvell again thematizes viewing, and, rather than simply constructing an image, he shows the reader how to see. He sets out the providential nature of Cromwell's peaceful death, in rebuke to the people who "blame the last *Act*, like *Spectators* vain, / Unless the *Prince* whom they applaud be slain" (lines 9–10).[87] Again, Marvell focuses on misperceptions, underscoring the pride and futility of the viewers by the inversion of adjective and noun ("*Spectators* vain"). Like the "lusty sailors," the foreign princes, and the "*Chammish* Issue" who misinterpreted Cromwell's earlier accident, the people now misinterpret his death.

Marvell thus argues for the appropriateness of a peaceful death for Cromwell, bringer of peace through war. Cromwell died not in battle but of "*Love* and *Grief*," after the death of his daughter, Elizabeth. She, not the regal effigy, is his true image:

> Like polish'd Mirrours, so his steely Brest
> Had ev'ry figure of her woes exprest;
> And with the damp of her last Gasps obscur'd,
> Had drawn such staines as were not to be cur'd.
> Fate could not either reach with single stroke,
> But the dear Image fled the Mirrour broke.   (lines 73–78)

Marvell constructs an elaborate analogy, with Cromwell as mirror to Elizabeth, yet the language remains simple and plain: largely monosyllabic. Marvell's Cromwell is first and foremost a private figure, a father not of his country, but of his favorite daughter: "For he no duty by his height excus'd,

/ Nor though a *Prince* to be a *Man* refus'd" (lines 83–84). Such a view replaces the public and artificial image with a strikingly personal and private moment.

Marvell's stress on the natural and private continues with the natural images he uses to describe Cromwell's grief. Cromwell grieves as "the sad Root pines in secret under ground" (line 56) or like a vine deprived of a dear branch that "unto the Grief succeeds, / And through the Wound its vital humour bleeds" (lines 95–96). Marvell subordinates Cromwell's martial conquests to his piety and the personal ties of family and friendship:

> If he Eliza lov'd to that degree,
> (Though who more worthy to be lov'd than she?)
> If so indulgent to his own, how deare
> To him the children of the Highest were?   (lines 209–12)

In a succession of images, Marvell presents an active Cromwell enjoying the hunt or spending his days "in warre, in counsell, or in pray'r, and praise" (line 240).

The stress on nature and the natural in *A Poem upon the Death of O. C.* culminates in a stark and startling image of Cromwell's corpse itself:

> I saw him dead, a leaden slumber lyes,
> And mortal sleep over those wakefull eyes:
> Those gentle rays under the lids were fled,
> Which through his looks that piercing sweetnesse shed;
> That port which so majestique was and strong,
> Loose and depriv'd of vigour, stretch'd along:
> All wither'd, all discolour'd, pale and wan,
> How much another thing, no more that man?   (lines 247–54)

The opening stressed monosyllables – "I saw him dead" – convey starkly the personal moment. Balanced antitheses strive to contain the paradoxes of the dead Cromwell, but the emotion nonetheless spills over in run-on lines that do not come to a complete stop until the final question. The oxymorons of piercing sweetness and sleep on wakeful eyes move to antithesis between lines: following the description of a majestic Cromwell are two lines on his pale and withered corpse.

The stark image of the corpse reverberates throughout *A Poem upon the Death of O.C.*, like a *memento mori* inscribed upon a tomb. If the passage recalls literary tradition – *Quantum mutatus ab illo Hectore* – it also reflects a powerful and intensely private grief.[88] As in his earlier Cromwell poems, Marvell again chooses between images and then thematizes viewing, showing the activist reader what and how to see.

Although no visual image is as stark and graphic as Marvell's depiction of the corpse itself, the realism is to some degree captured in Cromwell's death mask (fig. 25). The death mask reveals Cromwell's features quite faithfully. From this mask the more idealized regal effigy was made, transforming the stark natural image into the undying and timeless splendor of monarchical iconography. Marvell reminds us not only of the death mask, but of the corpse underneath.

Marvell breaks the decorum of the form to echo the breakdown in emotion; the tone becomes exclamatory and the meter is disjointed through frequent caesurae and exclamation points: "Oh! humane glory, vaine, oh! death, oh! wings, / Oh! worthlesse world! oh transitory things!" (lines 255–56). But Marvell then employs paradoxes to transform the dead Cromwell:

> Yet dwelt that greatnesse in his shape decay'd,
> That still though dead, greater than death he lay'd;
> And in his alter'd face you something faigne
> That threatens death, he yet will live again.   (lines 257–60)

In compressed and newly controlled verse, Marvell moves from antitheses within lines (greatness in decay; dead yet greater than death) to antitheses between lines: Cromwell's face is altered, but he may live again. Marvell again draws upon a natural image to depict Cromwell's increased stature in death. Like the "sacred oak" that appears greater when fallen, Cromwell's fame will live on, indeed will grow: "So shall his praise to after times encrease, / When truth shall be allow'd, and faction cease" (lines 271–72). The verse ends not with violent emotion but with balance and control, reflecting the order that comes with truth and the cessation of faction.

Significantly, the oak was also used in a death medal of Cromwell (fig. 26). The reverse of the medal depicts a healthy oak tree beside the stump of another, possibly representing Richard and Oliver, respectively. Around the border is inscribed "NON DEFITIENT OLIVA SEP 3 1658." Marvell, then, was unusual but not unique in his representation. Rather, he made choices among multiple and opposed images, reasserting a martial and wholly human Cromwell in sharp contrast to the funeral pomp.

"His late Mosaical Highness": images of Oliver in Richard's Protectorate

Although Marvell reasserted the martial Cromwell, regal images of Cromwell continued through the brief remainder of Richard Cromwell's

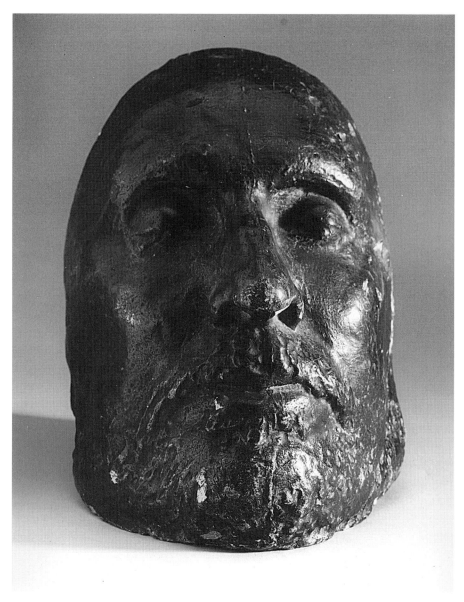

Figure 25 Cromwell's death mask (1658).

reign. Engravings of the effigies lying and standing in state were reproduced in 1658 and 1659.[89] In another late engraving, Cromwell wears his
habitual plain falling collar, beneath robes of state (fig. 27). This engraving is
notable in that Oliver himself, not the more generic visage of the effigy,
appears. The image shows Cromwell in the form of regal authority that he
rejected in life.

Figure 26 Death medal of Cromwell (1658).

Oliver was also fully monarchical in a late panegyric that marked an important transition between the posthumous panegyric and the satire that followed. Henry Dawbeny's *History & Policie Re-viewed*, inopportunely published in April 1659 just shortly before Richard's Protectorate fell, uses the figure of Moses to praise Oliver, who has become a divine-right monarch. Yet with the monarchical Cromwell came the shadow of his alter ego, the Machiavel.[90]

Dawbeny signals his awareness of disputed views over Cromwell and tries to obviate objections from the "envenom'd Party, that shoote out your Arrows, even bitter words, against the precious Memory of his late Mosaical Highnesse."[91] During the civil war years and the early republic, the figure of Moses had been used to justify revolution: now Dawbeny employs the same figure to legitimate a princely Oliver. Yet this long prose icon, like *The Unparalleld Monarch* that it in some ways resembles, does not epitomize or confirm Cromwellian regality. Rather, it shows anxiety and tensions, as Dawbeny's princely Oliver evokes his opposite: the Machiavel.

Dawbeny proceeds by accumulation and embellishment, the copiousness and accumulation of his style reflecting the manifold virtues of his subject. Above all, Dawbeny praises Cromwell as both pious and favored by providence. Dawbeny instances Moses, who was "by the extraordinary

OLLeuer Lord Protector of y Commonwealth of Eng :
Scot and Ir: & hebegan his Gouerment y 16 of December
1653 died September y 3 and buried at westminster .

Figure 27 Posthumous engraving of a regal Cromwell (1658).

indulgence and favour of Heaven, attended with a glorious felicity, in all his
undertakings" (p. 106). But Cromwell enjoys heaven's favor even more fully:
"Now the greatest favourit of fortune, or properly speaking, the dearest
Darling of Divine Providence, that ever the Christian World produced, was
this most excellent person, his late most Serene Highnesse" (pp. 107–08).
Alliteration, hyperbole, and embellishment here and throughout help to
create a prose icon. Yet the evocation of Lady Fortune recalls Machiavelli's
advice in *The Prince* on how to master that lady, and Machiavelli had himself
adduced Moses as one important example of wiliness and craft.

By making his Moses / Cromwell a prince, Dawbeny is open to charges of Machiavellianism, charges he highlights throughout by his constant anxious denials. Dawbeny repeatedly insists on how "contrary to *Machiavillian* doctrine" or how much tending to the "confusion of all *Machiavillians*" (p. 123) the example of Moses / Cromwell proves, as "His Mosaical Highnesse" is content to follow "his old Master *Moses*, rather than Mr. *Machiavel*" (p. 154). Dawbeny's repeated denials, however, serve to keep the subject in the foreground, as he continually contrasts Cromwell and Machiavelli:

> Now, by this onely it is plain, that our first and second *Moses* have clearly been of a quite contrary Religion to *Machiavel*, before cited and all his Crew, who would have a Prince, or Statesman, practise Religion, onely according to the necessity of their affairs, and to learn how they may sometimes be wicked, that is, to make shew of Religion, and honesty, so far forth as may serve their turns; but in very deed, to be compleat knaves. (p. 187)

Moses, however, "a wiser man sure, than a million of Machiavels" understood that God reproves and condemns false religion. Indeed, Dawbeny argues, Cromwell soared above all policy whatsoever, armed only with "Piety and Religion":

> This high towering Eagle, as we have seen, winged onely with Piety, and Religion, from the very first time that he was called forth into action, to this very day, could never be found (as aforesaid) beating of his wings, in those lower Regions of the air, conversing with those pitiful humane policies, but borne, I say alwayes, upon those heavenly wings aforesaid. (p. 193)

Such piety and religion were "a piece of divine Policy indeed, and fetcht doubtlesse from the Gates of the City of God" (p. 198). Dawbeny reiterates, then, that Cromwell partakes not of earthly and Machiavellian craft but of heavenly and divine policy: its defining opposite.

Not surprisingly, Dawbeny's tract evoked precisely the image he aimed to avoid: piety merged with policy. In *England's Worthies* (1660), William Winstanley scoffs at Dawbeny's "prodigious enterprise" of comparing Cromwell to Moses: "his pen is too palpably fraught with flattery, yet not without unparalleld subtilty; he having like the little Indian Gentleman, in the short jacket, pickt the vermin out of *Nic. Machiavels* head for his use . . . *Machiavel* never so disguising himself with the vizard of Religion, that he appears to be an arranter devil then the *Florentine*."[92] "Certain I am," Winstanley concludes, "that I never read a book that more pleased or displeased me" (p. 560).

Dawbeny's late tract confirmed what opposition to the monarchical funeral had already suggested: that imbuing Oliver with the full trappings of monarchy was a risky way of bolstering the regime of his son. The funeral itself, far from solidifying Richard's power, provoked opposition from royalist and republican alike. When the regime actually fell, the funeral served as exemplum to stigmatize the entire Protectorate as an illegitimate hankering after monarchy.

The Machiavel and the martyr-king: Oliver and Charles I in summer 1659

If the Machiavel was the uncanny shadow of the pious Moses under the Protectorate, after the fall of Richard's government in May 1659, crafty Cromwell himself reappeared. Or, rather, he came back with a vengeance. The many tracts in which a Machiavellian Cromwell confesses his ambition and hypocrisy seem overdetermined, anxious to construct the Machiavel in order to destroy the image of a pious Cromwell. Piety was now the shadow of policy.

By June 1659, Secretary Nicholas described the entire Cromwell family as having descended into infamy: "Olivers crowne (tho' once speciously guilt) is now soe full of reproach and thornes that none of his descendants or friends dare touch or avow it; but the monster is now understood by every pamphletter."[93] On 24 June, a letter to Nicholas alluded to the lavish funeral that had left Richard heavily in debt: "Richard is vendible here with an oules head pictured and many other circumstances of contempt, and confyned to his chamber for feare of streete bayliesses. Henry of Ireland hath laied down the cudgells there . . All that family are already in the kennell, the dirission of porters and ballad mongers."[94] As in the 1640s and early 1650s, popular print once again satirized and attacked Oliver.

Attacks on Oliver also took more material form. In early June, *The Weekly Post* reported the destruction of Cromwell's funeral monument in Westminster Abbey: "The stately and magnificent Monument of the late Lord Protector, set up at the upper end of the Chancel in the Abbey at *Westminster*, is taken down by Order of the Council of State."[95] The effaced symbols of Cromwellian power and rule were replaced with a written inscription on the wall that disclosed his true villainy: "*Great in policy, but matchless in Tyranny*," while "publick sale [was] made of the Crown, Sceptre and other of the Royal ornaments after they were broken."[96] The magnificent regality deteriorated into squabbles over profits from taking down the hearse.[97]

Printed texts likewise replaced the image of the regal funeral with the image of Cromwell in hell.[98] As in the early years of the Interregnum, royalist satire reappeared in popular forms to attack Cromwell for being an upstart and a Machiavel. Such texts preserved the mystique of divine-right kingship by presenting not the king himself, but his enemies. But the results, as we saw in the satires of the late 1640s, were complex. Satiric attacks paradoxically kept Cromwell alive and well in the public sphere.

The World in a Maize, Or, Olivers Ghost (May 1659) stages a dialogue between Oliver and Richard that reintroduces the topic of Charles's martyrdom, although Charles himself does not appear. A woodcut on the title page gives a new image of Oliver: not kingly, classicized, or heroic (fig. 28). Rather, Oliver is a ghost who wears a winding-sheet and carries a flambeau in his left hand. The moon in the upper-right corner indicates that this is a nocturnal ghost, emerging not from heaven but from hell. Oliver disturbs his son Richard by coming to inquire the news of recent events. In the dialogue that follows, Richard describes his own misgivings about his office: for "honour is but a bawble, / And to keep it is but a trouble."[99] But in this he is not his father's son. Oliver confesses to having been "both a Pollitician and a Machivillan" (p. 5). Yet even this confession does not plumb the depths of Cromwellian villainy, and a Hamlet-like Richard tries to ascertain whether this is indeed his father's ghost by questioning him about his role in the regicide:

> R[ICHARD]. If you be my father's Ghost answer me this,
> Who cut off the man that did not amiss.
> O[LIVER]. That Riddle, if I be not mistaken is concerning the *Jews*,
>   putting Christ to death that had no sin, or guile found in him.
> R[ICHARD]. Sure thou art not my Fathers Gost that cannot unfold this
>   Riddle. (p. 6)

Although Charles I does not appear in *The World in a Maize*, the text attests to his innocence. And, Cromwell's mistaken assumption that his son refers to Christ himself reminds the reader of the Christic Charles in earlier royalist elegies. Yet, as in the earlier satires, the textual effects are complex, even paradoxical: Charles's innocence is recalled by and through Cromwell, who dominates the stage / page.

An ensuing series of tracts in summer 1659 staged conversations between Cromwell as Machiavel and Charles as martyr-king. *A Dialogue Betwixt the*

Figure 28 Title page with woodcut ghost of Cromwell, from
The World in a Maize (1659).

Ghosts of Charls the I, Late King of England: and Oliver, The late Usurping Protector (June 1659) presents both a dialogue and a visual image of Cromwell's ghost and the ghost of Charles I (fig. 29). The image of Cromwell is identical to that in *The World in a Maize* described above. Charles dresses in a winding-sheet and carries a flambeau in his left hand, although this ghost looks less like Charles than the other ghost (with its distinctive nose) looks like Cromwell. Cromwell disturbs the rest of Charles, as one "who now would fain be at rest himself, but cannot."[100] Rather, Cromwell's conscience torments him, leading him to confess to Charles his "ambitious and damnable Plots, to ruine you and yours, and to set my self in your stead" (p. 5). Cromwell confesses to manipulating events from the time of the first civil war: "It was I that laid the plot to draw your Subjects obedience from you, under pretence of Religion and Liberty; It was I that after we had Routed your Army in the Fields, jugled you into the Isle of *Wight*" (p. 5). In the act of demonizing Cromwell, the text accords him tremendous power and influence.

In *A New Conference Between the Ghosts of King Charles and Oliver Cromwell* (June 1659), the ghost of Cromwell again disturbs the "dust, at Rest now some years" of Charles I.[101] Cromwell responds to the king's charge of a "base Hypocritical Temper" almost with glee: "Oh Sir! I did no other then Imitate most of our Rank, which, according to our Creed, viz. *Nicholas Machiavell's* Prince, who saith, *A Prince or Tyrant ought never to want good Pretences, to colour the worst of Actions with*" (p. 2). That Cromwell, to Charles's surprise, can in fact now rank himself among princes confirms him as a Machiavel. Oliver readily admits his misbehavior: "I made a shift to gain the Supremacy; and because the Nation was under age, I made my self their *Protector*; and would have made my self *King*, but that I durst not accept of the Title, because I had a Hand in your death; the which the People all knew: therefore I could not find a colourable pretence" (p. 2). His blackly comic summary of the kingship crisis reveals not only his own ambition, but the hypocrisy of the army officers, who "had somewhat tender Consciences, in regard I had not a Crown for every one of them to harden their Consciences with" (p. 2). Yet Cromwell's pretended conscience has ironically become real. When the king questions "Didst thou not come out of the World by the Rope or the Ax or by the hand of some *Felton* or other?," Cromwell replies: "No; but I came by the Immediate hand of God, who never suffered that worm of Conscience to die within me, but it still lay Gnawing and Tormenting of me, brought an unusual Feaver upon me, that dryed up all my blood, that at my departure not one drop almost was left

Figure 29 Ghosts of Charles I and Oliver Cromwell, woodcut and title page of
A Dialogue Betwixt the Ghosts (1659).

24

A
DIALOGUE
Betwixt the
GHOSTS
OF
CHARLS the I,
Late *King* of *England* :
AND
OLIVER
The late Usurping *PROTECTOR.*

LONDON,
Printed in the year, 1659. *June 9.*

Figure 29 (*cont.*)

within me" (p. 3). Yet thanks in large part to the tract that satirizes him, Cromwell does not depart but remains alive and well: in print.

A month later, *The Court Career, Death Shaddow'd to life* (July 1659) similarly juxtaposed the martyr-king and his conniving nemesis. The visual images themselves on the title-page have changed (fig. 30). In this crudely sketched if emphatic woodcut, Charles's ghost now wears a crown (ornamented with crosses and jewels) as well as a winding-sheet, and he carries a flambeau in his right hand. A nimbus of light surrounds Charles's head, and he stands in a classicized chamber that features three columns and an arch that suggest heaven. Cromwell also wears a winding-sheet and carries a flambeau in his right hand. Tongues of fire play about his body, and he is clearly underground; the presence of these two features almost certainly represents the cave of hell.

Meeting up with the king, Cromwell represents his illicit reign and subsequent death as full of torment: "Furies without me; fears and frights within me constantly encountred me: horror, horror; despaire and horror, my sole disconsolate comforts at my departure."[102] As in the royalist satires around the time of the regicide, Cromwell confesses his ambition and duplicity, "for howsoever I pretended or formerly dis-avowed, a Diadem was my aim" (p. 7), since "ambition had rais'd such a flame in my thoughts, as my only *Note* was a *Crown*, a *Crown*; neither did my ambition admit a period, till my breath expired" (p. 9). The tract holds up as a warning Cromwellian misdeeds and their punishment.

Nonetheless, *The Court Career* also entertains, as Cromwell the former brewer describes his frolics at, for instance, his daughters' weddings: "*Nol* himself knew then how to lay aside his staff o' state. No Page nor Lacquey in the Lobby could play the Tom-boy more nimbly nor actively; for throwing of cushions, ruffling young wenches, snatching Allamodian favours, scrambling of junkets, bowzing of bride-possets" (p. 8). Cromwell the brewer now takes up his trade in hell:

> O Huntington, Huntington, little didst thou dream
> That NOL should by *Charon* launch o're the *Stygian* stream:
> Or become such a *Brewer* where he now remains,
> As to furnish all *Tartary* with Ale and Grains!   (p. 15)

Cromwell expresses the lesson he has learned in part in brewing terms: "Thus men divin'd; and this have I found: *That I should pass o're the Stygian Lake, / And as I had brew'd, so might I bake*" (pp. 24–25). Yet the brewer in hell shows an irrepressible, carnivalesque side not fully contained by the satire.

Figure 30 Charles I in heaven and Oliver Cromwell in hell, from
The Court Career (1659).

Similarly, Cromwell the Machiavel breaks out of the confines of the satire to amuse and entertain the reader of *The Court Career*. When Charles questions how "such a Head-piece, in comparison of whom, *Machiavel* might be justly accounted a *Novice*," could end up in "the hideous horror of an infernal *Tartary*," Cromwell falls back into pious cant: "In answer, it was PROVIDENCE; a *change* not by my *choice*. But my hope was, before I *descended* to it, to make it mine own, and erect a *New Court* of *Justice* in it, as I had formerly done in other countries" (p. 26). His ambition continues even in hell.

Although Cromwell recounts a Faustian vision of horror and believes that he has become "a spectacle to Angels in my suffering, and a reproach to men in their censuring" (p. 10), *The Court Career* is not simply tragic or monitory. Rather, the tract depicts a Cromwell who remains energetic and scheming. Indeed, Cromwell exits laughing, as the recollection of how he enjoyed the Royal Exchequer "makes [him] grin and laugh beyond measure amidst [his] suffering" (p. 28). Setting out to blacken Cromwell and idealize the martyr-king, the tract at the same time gives Cromwell new life and vitality in print.

The summer of 1659 was a transitional point both politically and iconographically. Over the next nine months, forms of government would be abruptly cast and recast, as the army variously recalled and turned out the Rump Parliament. In December 1659 General George Monck began his march southward from Scotland, ending with an entry into London, and ultimately the recall of the full parliament, new elections, and an overwhelming move to restore the Stuart monarchy.[103] From the fall of Richard's Protectorate, the ideological and iconographical groundwork was laid, as a series of ephemeral tracts, commenting on immediate changes and events, produced Charles as martyr and Cromwell as Machiavel and brewer. The printed image of the martyr-king undoubtedly helped to legitimate and enhance his son, about to be restored to the British crown. But popular print also kept Cromwell alive as a key figure in the public imagination. Producing Cromwell in the unpredictable medium of print, royalists unleashed rather than contained him as a populist figure. If the martyr-king had haunted the Commonwealth and Protectorate, old Noll would continue to have an impact in the reign of Charles II.

Six

Ceremony, print, and punishment in the early Restoration

In May 1660, Charles II returned to an apparently jubilant nation.[1] But although widespread recrimination and bloodshed did not follow, Cromwell was by no means left to rest in peace. How and with what effects was Cromwell attacked in print after the Restoration? How did the anti-ceremony of exhuming both demonize and publicize Cromwell? In what ways did representations of Charles II respond to Cromwellian forms of power? How did the figure of Cromwell continue to shape political culture? Did the revolution in print and emerging public opinion that we have been tracing in Interregnum England continue?

The return of the Stuart monarchy brought both political change and, as recent scholars have perceptively argued, representational crisis.[2] The traditional view of the early Restoration as a secularized, neo-classical, and firmly monarchical age has been questioned and complicated in recent studies by an emphasis on continuing forms of resistance and dissent, and on religious and political language inherited from the 1640s and 1650s.[3] Other studies have pointed to new Carolean forms of public display or argued that Charles II was the first monarch to employ the resources of print.[4] To the extent that Cromwell has figured in these studies, however, it has been largely as a negative force, the target of either persisting republican sentiment or of royalist satire that effectively stigmatized and erased him.[5] Accounts of the 1660s have not attended to the ways in which Charles II was forced to engage with Cromwellian forms or in which Cromwell continued to have an impact in the public sphere.

The early Restoration evokes many of the same issues in political culture that we explored in chapter 1: but it is a return with some significant differences. While the pressures of civil war pushed the royalists into print, by 1660 Charles II recognized the exigencies of print and the public. But images of the new king did not stand alone. Supporters of Charles II not only employed print to legitimate the returning monarch; they also relaunched an aggressive assault on Oliver Cromwell. But in doing so they reconstructed Cromwell as a figure in the public sphere. Exhumed in body and in print, Cromwell again took life in a popular, comic mode. Blackly humorous printed texts did not so much contain as unleash Cromwell, keeping him alive in the public imagination and setting the stage for his eventual recuperation.

The return of Charles II

On 29 May 1660, Charles II returned to a scene of extravagant joy and celebration. John Evelyn captures the excitement of the moment as he describes Charles's entry into London "with a Triumph of above 20000 horse & foote, brandishing their swords and shouting with unexpressable joy."[6] Evelyn recounts the lavish staging of the entry: "The wayes straw'd with flowers, the bells ringing, the streetes hung with Tapissry, fountaines running with wine."[7] The magnificent procession had its counterpart in a crowd equally impressive in its numbers: "the Mayor, Aldermen, all the Companies in their liver[ie]s, Chaines of Gold, banners; Lords & nobles, Cloth of Silver, gold vellvet every body clad in, the windos & balconies all set with Ladys, Trumpets, Musick, & [myriads] of people flocking the streetes."[8] A keen observer, Evelyn also attests to his own joy: "I stood in the strand, & beheld it, & blessed God."[9]

Charles was indeed a master of public ceremony, as the Venetian envoy describes him, "raising his eyes to the windows looking at all, raising his hat to all and consoling all who with loud shouts and a tremendous noise acclaimed the return of this great prince so abounding in virtues and distinguished qualities of every sort."[10] The envoy goes on to make clear that Charles remained very much in public view: "so far he has been allowed no rest, showing himself at every moment to the people who press impetuously forward to offer their devotion to their sovereign. He takes all his meals in public and by his royal presence affords his people the utmost consolation and enjoyment."[11] The public display and, in turn, participation of the populace in ceremonies and celebration marking the return of Charles II seemed an utter repudiation of the previous regime.

Yet the very means by which Charles was reinstated showed the ongoing influence of the Interregnum period. No longer aloof, monarchy was in (if not of) the public sphere. Charles's triumphal entry into London reappropriated for the monarchy the ceremonial triumph so effectively used by

Cromwell. But an outpouring of printed verse also welcomed back the new monarch, publicizing and disseminating the display.[12]

These verses imbue Charles II with both the sanctitude of his martyred father and the martial heroism formerly linked with Cromwell. Rachel Devon's *Exultationis Carmen* combines the martial figure with the martyr, as she welcomes Charles both as "Milde *Cæsar*, born of Heav'nly Race" and as "The living Image of our Martyr'd King, / For us His People freely suffering."[13] *To the King, upon his Majesties Happy Return* similarly combines the saintly and the martial as it praises Charles's "nobler Conquest" over hearts and minds:

> You might possess by Armies, and by Fleets,
> All where the Sun doth rise, or where he sets;
> But You a nobler Conquest have design'd,
> The placing Limits to Your greater Minde:
> And may those highest Titles never cease,
> *A King of Greatest Pow'r, and Greatest Peace.*[14]

Other panegyrics revisit actual scenes of military defeat (most notably at Worcester) to transform martial defeat into spiritual victory.[15] Henry Beeston's *A Poem to His most Excellent Majesty* re-envisions defeat as fortitude and patience, which in turn become a new kind of heroism:

> But had *You Conquer'd, You* had been *subdu'd,*
> Lost *Your* peculiar part of *Fortitude,*
> *Your Patience*; which *You* may singly own,
> Since none (but *You*) *suffer'd* into a *Throne.*
> This was *Your* way; old *Heroes* cannot *share,*
> E'en let *them* pass for *Barreters* in *War.*[16]

Such a new kind of heroism allows Charles to recuperate the public ceremony of triumph, as Beeston goes on to exult: "And where's the *Roman*, or the *Greek Parade*, / Can *march* with *Glorious Tuesdays Cavalcade*?" (p. 7).

Carolean panegyric does not so much ignore or erase Cromwell as appropriate and revise distinctively Cromwellian martial forms to legitimate the Stuart king. Alex Brome's *A Congratulatory Poem* praises Charles for a new kind of victory through suffering, as he by "patient suffering did subdue / The *Traytors* fury, and the *Traytors* too."[17] Brome explicitly contrasts Charles's new kind of heroism with the illicit victories of Cromwell:

> No more that proud *Usurper* now shall boast,
> His partial *Conquests*, which more *Money* cost,
> And *Blood* than they were worth, no more remember,
> His thrice auspicious third day of *September.*   (pp. 6–7)

Yet, once again, the effects of popular royalist print prove complex, even paradoxical, as, in the process of insisting on Cromwell's absence, the text in fact recalls him.

Charles II not only recuperated the Cromwellian martial mode, but also combined it (at least initially) with the piety and aura of the martyr-king. An undated engraving reworked the famous frontispiece of *Eikon Basilike* to show not a kneeling but an upright king, full of regal splendor and reaching for the crown (fig. 31). By recalling the *Eikon Basilike*, the engraving imbues Charles II with the sanctity of his martyred father. But this Stuart king stands upright, dressed in armor under the ermine robe, and he holds a sword upon which is inscribed *"Fidei Defensor."* Charles's new role was to defend, not to die for, the faith.

Other texts recalled the Van Dyck martial images that had most recently been used by Cromwell. William Walwyn's *God Save the King, or a Sermon of Thanksgiving for His Majesties Happy Return to the Throne*, depicts Charles II wearing both the bejeweled Stuart crown and the full plate armor of Van Dyck portraiture (fig. 32).[18] Small crowns in the background remind the viewer of the three kingdoms over which this divinely anointed monarch reigns, and an inscription underscores the regality. Unlike his martyred father, Charles could also assume a martial appearance.

The printed text of *God Save the King*, however, draws upon the power and force of martyrdom to legitimate the new king. In the Epistle Dedicatory, Walwyn writes that "you have here also another *Eikon Basilike*, or true *Pourtraicture* of His Sacred Majesty" (Sig. A1r). Walwyn's choice of biblical text combines divine right with popular acclamation: *"I Samuel 10.24: And all the people shouted, and said, God save the King"* (p. 1). If the frontispiece to *God Save the King* shows a martial image, the sermon itself makes clear the king's suffering and sanctity: "Witness his patience and tolerancie, under his almost insufferable afflictions and contumelies, who having the free profer of Forein Princes Ayd, and Assistance for his Restitution, He chose rather to want his Crowns than to Swim to his Throne in the Blood of his Subjects" (p. 23). Charles, Walwyn continues, preferred "to be received with our Conduits running with *Wine*, than with our Channels running with *Blood*: and with *Bonfires* in our Streets, than with the *Conflagrations* of our Towns and Cities" (p. 23). Walwyn's sermon underscores the divine providence that has returned Charles to the throne.

Images of Charles II thus strikingly combined the regal (always tenuous for Cromwell) and the martial (after 1646, tenuous for Charles I). And, unlike his father, Charles II was widely represented in popular print from

Figure 31 Charles II, reaching for crown (*c.*1660).

Charles y second, by y grace of God, King
of England, Scotland, France, & Ireland. Defender
of the Faith. &c:

Figure 32 Charles II in armor, wearing crown, from William Walwyn, *God Save the King* (1660).

the beginning of his reign. Yet the circulation of images of Charles II in popular print also tended to desacralize the royal person and hence render royal authority problematic.[19] Royalist texts again turned to demonizing the enemies of Stuart monarchy.

"The effigy of the tyrant Oliver Cromwell": early attacks

In the celebrations of the return of the Stuart monarch in May 1660, Cromwell was not forgotten, but displayed in print, as puppet, as effigy, and, finally, in person. By placing the blame for the regicide and its aftermath on Cromwell, royalists found a convenient scapegoat and target of attack, and many writers avoided the issue of their own compliance and accommodation with the Cromwellian regime. But acts of destruction were paradoxically constructive, and acts of forgetting were acts of remembering.[20] Even acts of abuse once again produced Cromwell as a figure in the public sphere.

Such abuse, first of all, took material form in the production and destruction of Cromwellian effigies. Thomas Rugge writes of Charles's May 1660 entry into London: "The joy was that night ended . . . with bonfiers; in Westminster a very great fiere made, and on the top of the fier they put old Oliver Cromwell and his wife in sables, theire pictures lifely made like them in life, which was burnt in the fire, and State armes."[21] Later, the celebrants replaced Cromwell's image with the figure of Charles II, "flying into the aire they were to be seene, Charles the Second, the Kings armes."[22] The Venetian resident also observed the symbiotic conjunction of celebration and desecration upon the entry of the king into London: "for three days and three nights they have lighted bonfires and made merry, burning effigies of Cromwell and other rebels with much abuse."[23] But in attempting to destroy the memory of Cromwell, such acts also did the opposite: displaying, reminding, and remembering in the very process of erasing the Cromwellian image.

Mercurius Publicus recounted a parodic trial and punishment at Sherborne which again gave Cromwell a central place in ceremonies celebrating the restored king. After a day of jubilation at the proclaiming of Charles II, some "witty Wags" set up a high court of justice which formally indicted the effigies of John Bradshaw and Oliver Cromwell, "prepared and brought thither by a guard of Soldiers," commanding them "to hold up their bloody hands, which for the purpose were besmeared with blood."[24] After being sentenced "to be dragged to the place of Execution, to be there hanged upon two Gibbets of forty feet high, on both sides the States Arms," the effigies "had many a blow with fists, swords, halberts, and pikes which were aimed at the execrable malefactors"; indeed, as they hung upon the gibbets, the effigies were "so hacked and hewed, so gored and shot throw, that in a short time but little remained, besides *Cromwels* Buff Coat and Bloody Scarff, that were worth the burning."[25] Nonetheless, according to this account, the people were not satisfied until "they had made a fire between the Gibbets and burnt all they could get of their Garbage or Garments."[26] Yet this very act of eradication made Cromwell symbolically central to the day's festivities.

Such material abuse – and publicity – continued in the months following the return of Charles. Thomas Rugge writes in June that "in this month the effigies of the Prottector, Oliver Cromwell, was hanged up in a haulter in a window in Whit Hall. It stood for one whole day, but by order from his Majesty, it was taken down."[27] The Venetian envoy corroborates Rugge's account, alleging popular interest and support for this material vengeance: "the effigy of the tyrant Oliver Cromwell, whose name and memory are increasingly cursed by the people, was exposed all day yesterday hung from a window in the court of the palace, with a rope round its neck, abused by all the populace who thronged to see it and who spared no act of contempt and ignominy."[28] Yet even such acts of desecration meant that the visual image of Cromwell remained in public view.

Other kinds of objects ridiculed the former Lord Protector while lauding the Stuart monarchs. Thomas Rugge describes, for instance, a "greate store of tobacco boxes" made at the time which contained the images of Cromwell, Charles I, and Charles II: "[on] the outside of the box lide the late Kinge, [on] the inside of the box lide the present King Charles the Second, and on the inside of the bottome the picture of Oliver Cromwell, leaninge to a post and gallow tree over his heade, and about his neck a haulter tied to the tree, and by him the picture of the devill, wide mouthed."[29] Rugge's reaction discloses how Cromwell's fame continued, albeit as infamy: "so that men in great power (right or wronge goten), are admired, but once fallen from that are the most dispiseable men that are."[30] Such material objects were, of course, intended to denigrate Cromwell. But they also kept Cromwell alive: for further attack but also for possible sympathy and recuperation. And printed texts, to which we now turn, also gave Cromwell new life.

Printed attacks in spring and summer 1660

Popular printed satire in spring and summer of 1660 set out to degrade Cromwell and, conversely, idealize the martyr-king and his newly restored son.³¹ But at the same time such satire made Cromwell a key figure in the public imagination. Royalists themselves sustained the Cromwellian image, albeit in derision. Keeping Cromwell alive in print helped to keep alive alternative political, religious, and aesthetic values, which could eventually be recuperated in a more sympathetic mode.

The month of Charles's return brought an outpouring of popular satiric print. Such texts as *A Parly between the Ghosts of the Late Protector and the King of Sweden* (May 1660) restaged the regicide in comic mode, as a rebellion in hell. But the effects of such texts were complex, as the satire rewrote the tragic past, yet at the same time unleashed the very figure it attempted to contain. An unrepentant Cromwell in *A Parly between the Ghosts* is as outrageous – and entertaining – as ever. As the King of Sweden (Cromwell's real-life ally) arrives in hell, the Protector is well settled in, "taking Tobacco in the great Divells own Closet."³² Nonetheless, he responds to the occasion with the same blatant hypocrisy that presumably stood him in such good stead on earth: putting on "his Godly-Speech-making-Countenance, and with a sorrowful aspect [he] went forth to meet his Brother of *Sweden*" (p. 5).

Colloquial prose and droll simile convey the energy, vitality, and high spirits with which Cromwell continues to persevere in wrongdoing: even in hell. When Cromwell meets the King of Sweden, "they hugg'd one another as the Devil hugg'd the Fryar" (p. 5); as he hears the news of events on earth, in particular of the loss of the Protectorate, Cromwell freely insults his own offspring: "Would I had wrung off their Necks, when they were first Kitten'd. I am sure I was a Cock of the game, and did my best to get Cocks of the game; but my Wife it seems was a Dunghil Hen" (p. 8). But when at the end of the tale of their mutual woes, "the King of *Sweden* and the *Protector* cry'd like two Pigs" (p. 9), Cromwell himself is skewered with a barnyard simile.

A Parly between the Ghosts reduces the regicide from tragedy to farce as Cromwell "whose Pate was full of Crotchets" cooks up a new plot, then employs all the rhetorical tricks of a Machiavel to gain support: "laying his Hand upon his Breast, and Weeping most bitterly, he vow'd solemnly . . . that for his part he sought not his own ends at all, but only the good of Humane kind, who as he saw dayly, groan'd under the sad Oppression and Tyranny of that proud Usurper *Sathan*" (p. 12). Far removed from the intricacies of political theory and high debate, the text colorfully reduces Machiavelli himself to a hawker in hell, "a great statesman once, now he cryes Ink and Penns" (p. 14). Caught in the act of rebellion and punished, Cromwell is made morally and physically ludicrous: "chained before the

General pissing place next the Court Door, with a strict charge, that nobody that made water thereabouts, should pisse any where, but against some part of his body" (p. 19). Yet Cromwell remains unrepentant to the end, swearing "by the Lord he knew nothing of the businesse" and threatening, as always, to break out of the confines of hell: and of satire.

Other popular satire during the month of the king's return likewise gave a new afterlife to Cromwell. *A Third Conference between O. Cromwell and Hugh Peters* (May 1660) offers a Cromwell who vaunts his former "toying and tickling" with Mrs. Lambert and boasts of having planned the regicide: "Thou knowest in thy Conscience (*Peters*) that there was none that had so great an hand in procuring his death as thee and I."[33] Cromwell freely acknowledges his Machiavellianism: "Thou knowest how closely I pursued the example of *Clopius* the Roman Tribune, and the Counsel of *Machiavel* ever to pretend Religion and Providence for a Warrant for my villanies" (p. 6). And he takes pride in his most recent infernal accomplishments: "Tis very true, Peters, that Hypocrisie & jugling thou speakest of, is that which carried me with so much honour out of the world, into the highest favour of my Infernal Soveraign" (p. 6). If Cromwell is a moral exemplar against wrongdoing, his vitality and obvious enjoyment complicate the point.

A Third Conference allows Cromwell and his prime accomplice not only to speak but to sing for themselves, as the work concludes with a dance to a song composed and sung by Cromwell:

> By Ruine and Blood
> My Power once stood,
> Which no body can deny, Boyes!
>   to murder the King
> And Misery bring,
> What Instrument had you, but I, Boyes.
> To live by the Spoile was my joy and delight;
> And he that may get a Crown, will he not fight?   (p. 11)

Despite their perfidy, the singing and dancing figures of Cromwell and Peters control the printed page / stage, entertaining and amusing their audience in a long tradition of stage Vices and Machiavels. As such, the very printed text that sets out to excoriate Cromwell revivifies and publicizes him.

The Case is Altered; or, Dreadful news from Hell (August 1660) likewise presents a lively and exuberant Oliver in the very process of mocking him in word and image. In the frontispiece to this text, the heads of Oliver and Elizabeth Cromwell appear (fig. 33). Cromwell wears a high-crowned hat

Figure 33 Woodcut heads of Oliver and Elizabeth Cromwell, from *The Case is Altered* (1660).

with three feathers stuck into the band and his characteristic plain, falling collar. Elizabeth wears a simple black hood and a bead or pearl necklace.

In the text of *The Case is Altered*, Oliver readily admits his ambition and wrongdoing. However, he does so in a colloquial and homely manner that is more comic than threatening. Back from the grave, Oliver reassures a startled Elizabeth that it is indeed he: "Thy Lord, sweet heart, and Queen *Joan*, the Old Dragon late Lord Protector."[34] Oliver comes to hear what has happened "since I departed my late reprobate vale of Tyranny," inquiring in particular after "my dear Imps, the two Princes *Richard* and *Henry*" (p. 6). When Elizabeth laments that Richard "knew no more how to govern than did a dog," Oliver soothingly agrees: "Aye thou sayst true, *Jug*, he had more mind to his Dogs and his Haucks, then he had to be a Tyrannical Protector, like me" (p. 8). But Oliver also seeks more company in hell, where he continues his plotting, now against the devil himself. Despite the title that promises "Dreadful news from hell" and its opprobrious labelling of "that grand Tyrant and Traytor *Oliver Cromwell*," *The Case is Altered* entertains and amuses as much as it functions as a moral exemplum.

Other texts in the summer of 1660 more broadly survey recent history to place the blame for the regicide and its aftermath firmly and fully on Cromwell. But, in doing so, such texts give Cromwell a political power and prominence not found in the complex and shifting realities of the previous decade. The publicizing of Cromwell is visual as well as printed. *The Devils Cabinet Councell Discovered* (July 1660) links Cromwell with the devil and hell, transforming his former exalted position. In a frontispiece to the work, the devil leads a council meeting around a large table, with Cromwell seated on his left (fig. 34). All of the earthly councilmen wear cloaks, sugarloaf hats, and simple tunics over plain, falling collars. Two female devils hold up a banner with the title of the scene, above which is suspended the arms of the Commonwealth. The text explains the civil wars, regicide, and Commonwealth with reference to Cromwell and his machinations. Rewriting the 1640s and 1650s to assign responsibility for all events to Cromwell himself, the satire makes Cromwell a more powerful and influential figure in print than he was in historical reality.

Other satiric texts similarly give the dominant role to Cromwell, in part by recalling (albeit in derision) the heroic Robert Walker portrait. The frontispiece of *Cromwell's Bloody Slaughter-house* foregrounds Cromwell, with Charles appearing only in miniature in the background (fig. 35). *Cromwell's Bloody Slaughter-house* was probably written shortly after the king's death by John Gauden (1605–62), a Presbyterian clergyman and eventual Anglican

Figure 34 Cromwell's council in hell, frontispiece to *The Devils Cabinet Councell Discovered* (1660).

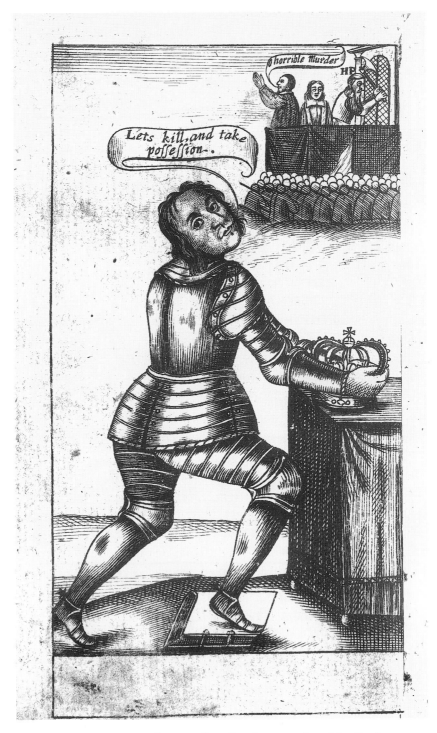

Figure 35 Engraving of Cromwell stealing the crown, from John Gauden,
Cromwell's Bloody Slaughter-house (1660).

bishop now better known as the ghost-writer of *Eikon Basilike*. While *Eikon Basilike* constructed an image of Charles as pious martyr-king, *Cromwell's Bloody Slaughter-house* does the obverse, vilifying Charles's opponents as "cursed Cains," "murtherers of the Father of your Countrey," "impudent Ravishers both of Church and State," "Monsters of Men," "putid Apostates," "execrable Saints," "shameless Sinners," and "trayterous Tyrants": and all this in only one of more than one hundred impassioned pages.[35]

Cromwell, in fact, does not feature by name in the written text of *Cromwell's Bloody Slaughter-house*, but the title and engraving make him the central target of attack. The engraving appropriates the heroic Walker portrait, but here Cromwell's body is strikingly turned, with his back to the viewer and his head at a noticeably odd angle. The stealth of this position is appropriate to Cromwell's theft of the ornate crown. At the same time, he tramples a clasped book, quite possibly a Bible, beneath his feet, underscoring the sacrilegious nature of his actions.

This engraving, like *The Royall Oake of Brittayne*, links Cromwell with Ahab and the murder of Naboth for his vineyard: "Lets kill and take possession." Finally, in the background is the execution of Charles himself, with a clergyman (Juxon) protesting from the scaffold, "O horrible Murder," and a masked executioner with axe raised. The background scene makes clear the contemporary application of the biblical allusion. Cromwell grasps the crown with his hands at the precise moment that the king is beheaded.

Yet if Cromwellian appropriations of Caroline forms recalled the absent king, did satiric renditions of the Robert Walker portrait also recall the heroic Cromwell? Histories of reading show that readers appropriated texts for their own purposes, often at variance with the ends for which they were intended. We shall see that court records continue to reveal lingering sympathy for Cromwell and that the martial Cromwell will reappear as a positive figure after disillusionment with the restored monarchy sets in.

Ironically, the concern to demonize Cromwell made him a key figure even in texts that celebrated the return of the king. *The Subjects Joy for the Kings Restoration*, a masque published in 1660 by clergyman Anthony Sadler (1630–80), gave center-stage to Cromwell in both word and image. In the 1650s, Sadler had been rejected by Cromwell's Triers; even after the Restoration, he was no model clergyman but was charged, variously, with libel, disorderly practice, failure to hold divine services, and debauchery. But Sadler put his biblical knowledge to good use in this (almost certainly unacted) masque that celebrated the return of Charles II by constructing Cromwell as an arch-traitor and villain.

Hence, the engraved frontispiece of *The Subjects Joy* features not Charles II but Cromwell, albeit satirically (fig. 36). The figure of Cromwell beneath the word "Jeroboam" immediately recalls the Walker portrait and its subsequent imitations, although Cromwell is presented full length, and we see his left side, not his right. Cromwell holds the Wheel of Fortune (upon which is inscribed the traditional "Regno, Regnabo, Sis Sine regno, Regna[vi]sti") with another figure. This figure is a chimera, a synthesis of Dame Fortune (the traditional bearer of the Wheel) and a devil. The resulting monstrosity retains the gender (indicated by the drooping right breast) and fabled forelock of Dame Fortune, but grafted onto a demon that sports a cat's head, bat's wings, and a goat's legs and tail. Psalms 52:7 is written upon the oval frame that encloses this unholy pair: "Loe this is the man that tooke not god for his strength but trusted unto the multitude of his riches and strengthen'd himselfe in his wickedness." Such a condemnation of the once mighty Cromwell would have seemed quite fitting in 1660.

Yet, like the appropriation of the Caroline forms, the use of heroic Cromwellian portraiture might also recall its more positive origins. And, in the very process of denigrating and scapegoating Cromwell, royalist satire gives him a key role in the unpredictable medium of print. Once more given a voice in dramatic dialogues and plays, an energetic and conniving Cromwell (like the Vice, Machiavel, and Richard III figures to whom he is compared) threatens to steal the show. At the same time, attacks on Cromwell move from his image to his very person.

The disinterment of Cromwell

On 30 January 1661, the anniversary of the execution of Charles I, the bodies of Oliver Cromwell, Henry Ireton, and John Bradshaw were exhumed from their graves in Westminster Abbey, dragged to Tyburn on hurdles, and hanged before a crowd of thousands. At sunset, the bodies were taken down, decapitated, and buried in a pit under Tyburn, while the heads were placed on spikes atop Westminster Hall. Why the quite literal overkill? How do we read the semiotics of this macabre ceremony? Did the exhumation seal the repudiation of Cromwell and of republican ideals? What role did print play in relation to the ceremony? The disinterment of Cromwell was intended as a solemn display of justice and punishment. But, exhumed from the grave, Cromwell was once again up and about in the public sphere. Interpreted and disseminated in printed satire, the ceremony of exhumation lost its solemn juridical import and became part of a blackly comic mode.

Figure 36 Cromwell as Jeroboam from Anthony Sadler, *The Subjects Joy* (1660).

The anniversary and first formal commemoration of the death of the martyr-king was marked by fasting and sermons "to implore the Divine blessing on this nation to prevent similar horrid spectacles," and the day was kept in all three kingdoms "in an exemplary manner."[36] But this "exemplary manner" included the punishment of Charles's now dead enemies, "Parliament having decreed that the bodies of Cromwell, Brascio [Bradshaw], Ireton and Pride should be disinterred, hanged and buried under the gallows."[37]

Royalist accounts allege that the ceremony had the full approval of the people. Thomas Rugge writes that "Oliver Cromwels vault beeing broke open, the people crowed very much to see him, who gave sixpence a peece for to see him."[38] The Venetian resident claims that the spectacle of exhumation and hanging was carried out "before a great crowd amid the universal approval of the city and of all the people."[39] Secretary Nicholas asserts that the corpses, "being dragged on sledges to Tyburn, remained hung on the gibbet, in the view of thousands, attracted by so marvellous an act of justice."[40]

Certainly for some observers the rite of exhumation served to reinforce hierarchy in church and state. John Evelyn's response to viewing the "Carkasses of that arch-rebell *Cromewell*, *Bradshaw* the Judge who condemn'd his Majestie & *Ireton*, sonn in law to the Usurper, draged out of their superbe tombs (in Westminster among the Kings) to *Tyburne*, & hanged on the Gallows there from 9 in the morning til 6 at night" was a pious affirmation of proper order: "looke back at November 22: 1658, & be astonish'd – *And [fear] God, & honor the King, but meddle not with them who are given to change.*"[41] For Evelyn, then, the exhumation was not only an undoing of the trial and execution of Charles I, but an astonishing reversal of the pride and pomp with which Cromwell had been buried a few short years before. But precisely what moral, if any, others drew from the ceremony is unclear.

Some accounts spoke of no moral at all. Eyewitness Samuel Sainthill, a Spanish merchant, dwells, rather, on the grotesque, parodic nature of the ceremony. Sainthill writes dispassionately of the decayed state of the bodies: Cromwell's "in green cerecloth, very fresh embalmed," while "Ireton having been buried long, hung like a dried rat, yet corrupted about the fundament. Bradshaw, in his winding sheet, the fingers of his right hand and his nose perished, having wet the sheet through; the rest very perfect, insomuch that I knew his face, when the hangman, after cutting his head off, held it up."[42] He also describes the final mutilation and disposal of the bodies in a hole under the gallows, "Cromwell had eight cuts, Ireton four, being seare cloths, and their heads were set up on the South-end of Westminster Hall."[43] Yet the ceremony seems less a solemn display than a carnivalesque and potentially anarchic rite, as Sainthill adds that "of [Bradshaw's] toes, I had five or six in my hand, which the prentices had cut off."[44]

Dissenting voices were also available, albeit not yet in print. Samuel Pepys saw the order for the exhumation as excessive: "[it] do trouble me that a man of so great courage as [Cromwell] was should have that dishonour, though otherwise he might deserve it enough."[45] Further, as with the funeral of Cromwell, the display of the corpse was not enough on its own. The exhumation became an object for print. Satiric broadsheet, ballad, and pamphlet jeered at Cromwell and his companions, fully deploying a carnival laughter with its abusive language and mocking parody. And, once disinterred in body, Cromwell again became a public figure. As we saw in our analysis of the late 1640s, comic satire could be double-edged: the popular printed texts of the early Restoration resurrected the very figure they were intended to destroy, and Cromwell's opponents were the ones who, more than any covert sympathizers, kept him alive in the public sphere.

Some texts described or recounted the juridical ceremonies without giving a speaking role to Cromwell. But even these texts transformed the solemn display through black comedy and humor, ballad and song. *The last Farewell of three bould Traytors* deployed the grotesque body as a sign of moral transgression: deceit, cunning, and treason. The verse also reintroduced the crafty Cromwell:

> Who did not hear of *Olivers* Nose,
>   with a fa, la, la, la, la, lero.
> It was of the largest size as I suppose,
>   with a fa, la, &c.
> O he was excellent cunning and *wise*,
> And Craftily fooled the people with *lies*,
> And thought by his wit to surmount the *skies*,
>   with a fa, &c.[46]

The lively doggerel recounts how Oliver progresses "from a Captain unto a Lord Generall, / And then a Protector at last of all." But falling "mighty sick" and dying, Cromwell rests in a tomb until Monck "brought in our King and the Traytors knapt," including "a tyrant under ground wrapt." Ironically, Cromwell's bright nose gives away his burial place to those wishing to dig him up: "looking into the Valt round, / *Olivers* Nose they quickly found." Dragged off to Tyburn to be hanged and beheaded,

Cromwell, Bradshaw, and Ireton become part of a carnivalesque feast for
the devil:

> Cromwel, Bradshaw, and Ireton, farewel,
>   with a fa, &c
> A mess under Tiburn for the Devil of hell,
>   with a fa, &c
> From Tyburn they e're bid adieu,
> And there is an end of a stincking crew,
> I wish all may to their king prove true,
>   with a fa la la la la lero.

Despite the reaffirmation of hierarchy ("Vivat Rex"), *The last Farewell of
three bould Traytors* complicates precisely such order, employing a popular
and blackly comic form that directs its appeal to as wide an audience as possible.

Other satiric texts allow the three dead men to speak for themselves, as
their ghosts reunite at Tyburn. *A New Meeting of the Ghosts at Tyburn* (March
1661) focuses on the execution of Charles I and on how the regicides have
now gotten their just deserts. But as the tract opens, Oliver shows the lively
energy that characterized the satires of the late 1640s: "Why how now my
Mirmidons, what's the reason we cannot lye quiet in our Graves?"[47] Oliver
acknowledges his guilt: "Did we ever think to be call'd to so strict an
Account for our murdering of so good a KING, and so many of his Honest
Subjects; but now alas, we find the dire effects of our blood and Villany,
crying out loud for Justice against us at a High Court of Justice indeed" (p.
3). Yet in the very process of confessing, Cromwell takes center-stage, domi-
nating the scene and relegating the image of the martyr-king (however
poignant) to the margins.

Although the other ghosts similarly speak and confess, they do so primarily to blame Cromwell, who thus remains the key figure. Hence Bradshaw
curses Cromwell: "Wo worth the time that I beheld thy bloody face, or
hearkened to thy alluring tongue, with which (and hope of preferment) I
was at first drawn to that bloody and most horrid fact, of murdering my
KING" (p. 4). Ireton exults in the time when "our Words and Swords was
Laws, and that we were King-killers and hang'd and banish'd every one that
did but speak against us or our Tyrannical doings" (p. 5). He nonetheless recognizes the justice of their macabre punishment, telling Oliver: "it was very
fit that our rotten Carcasses should be hang'd together (although dead) that
had been the cause of hanging and murdering so many innocent persons,

whose blood we now find, to our sorrow, crying so loud against us for vengeance" (p. 5). Pride similarly holds Cromwell responsible: "I am sure it was
long of your delusions, and our father the devill (that now pays us our
wages) to perswade me to murder my King, and to affront him to his face,
while he was alive, who is so glorious and happy, now we are tormented" (p.
6). Rewriting the history of regicide, the satire makes Cromwell an all-pow-
erful figure.

Print also supplied – and undermined – the traditional scaffold confession, unleashing the subversive and carnivalesque element perhaps always
implicit in the solemn display of punishment.[48] *The Speeches of Oliver
Cromwell, Henry Ireton, and John Bradshaw* (February 1661) burlesques the
genre of scaffold confession.[49] The lively and enterprising figure of
Cromwell again complicates the satiric attack. In his speech at the gallows,
Cromwell disingenuously comments that "It being a thing commonly
expected at this place to speak something; I shall not break that good old
custome (although I must needs confesse, I have broken all else that lay in
my power)."[50] The irrepressible brewer is back, as Cromwell cheerfully
admits: "I was the Son of a *Brewer* in the Isle of *Elie*, which I need not to have
told you, for it is visibly to be seen in my *Nose*, being the colour of his
Copper" (p. 4). Cromwell marshalls a long list of vices to prove, paradoxically, that he behaved like a gentleman: "I am loth to say either He [John
Bradshaw] or I were Gentlemen, because many here would be apt to give
me the lye. However, for my part I followed alwaies Gentlemens exercises;
Swearing, Whoreing, Drinking, and other the like commendable qualities,
whilst I was a young man" (p. 4). The ex-brewer employs his red nose for
material gain: "indeed though I have none of the best Faces, I quickly found
'twas well approved of for a Warlike or Ammunition Face having the advantage of a light from my *Nose*, in all dark and Warlike Stratagems (not except-
ing Plundering itself) by which I quickly found a nearer way to get Wealth,
then by Brewing" (p. 4). Cromwell's ensuing account is as comic as it is reprehensible: "For I fell to hopping from a Captaine to a Collonel, and so on till
I got to be a Generall; and now I am fairly hop't hither, what cheats I acted
on God and man, you all too well know, and therefore I need not name
them" (pp. 4–5). Energetic and loquacious, Cromwell engages and entertains as much as he provides a moral lesson for the reader.

Further, printed texts depicted the exhuming as an anti-triumph, challenging but nonetheless recalling the heroic mode so central in earlier
representations of Cromwell. In *Justa Sive Inferiæ Regicidorum*, Cromwell

confesses that his illicit ambition to be king has appropriately led to a triumph at Tyburn:

> Imagination prompt'd me to be King,
> 'Tis easie work, I have it in a string.
> Here's a triumphant Chariot without wheels,
> Not subject to mad Fortunes giddy reels;
> And here's three standing Crowns, whose massy weight
> Will break the neck to this curst politick pate.[51]

Similarly, J. D. Durnovariae's *Short Meditations on . . . the Life and Death of Oliver Cromwell* points out the irony in Cromwell's ambition leading only to the "Trophie" of Tyburn: "But the Corps of him whose aspiring minde could never be satisfied hath now no other Tombe but a Turf under *Tyburn*, and no other Trophie but the Scituation of the common place of Execution circumfering him. *So let all the Kings Enemies perish O God.*"[52] The inversions, then, lead back to restored authority and power, although it is worth noting that such texts recall Cromwell's heroic image in the process of attacking him. Visual texts likewise placed the martial hero at Tyburn. An undated woodcut depicts Cromwell with a devil and hanging tree (fig. 37). The gallows with open noose stands behind Cromwell, while a wolf-headed devil beside him speaks the line "My deare Noll art Come weele nere part company." Visual satire thus inverts Cromwell's heroic status, linking him with the devil and an ignominious end. But in so doing it also reproduces the Robert Walker image, reminding viewers of the very past that it sets out to eradicate.

The frontispiece to James Heath's *Flagellum* (1663) similarly reworked the Robert Walker portrait of Cromwell (see fig. 2) by adding a noose that evoked the exhuming (fig. 38). Heath (1629–64), who had been at The Hague at the court of Charles II, compiled this long derogatory biography of Cromwell as well as *A Briefe Chronicle* of the civil wars and Interregnum. The frontispiece of *Flagellum* shows Cromwell three-quarter length in full armor. But now a cloud overhead turns threatening and dark and a rope descends from the cloud to wind around Cromwell's neck, indicating his eventual fate. The caption underneath the engraving, furthermore, reveals Cromwell to be a moral monster by linking him with the ambitious, traitorous, and cruel Roman, Sejanus.

Heath takes the Latin text beneath the portrait from the famous tenth satire of Juvenal, a graphic description of the downfall of Sejanus. The inscription changes only the names:

Figure 37 Woodcut of Cromwell and the gallows (*c.* 1661).

Cromwellus ducitur Unco
Spectandus, gaudent omnes quae labra quis Illi
Vultus erat – nunquam mihi credis amavi
Hunc Hominem – Inv[isus] sat[is].[53]

["Cromwell is dragged by the hook to be viewed as a spectacle; everyone rejoices: what lips, what a gaze he had! Believe me, never did I love
this man – He was hated enough."]

Sejanus had risen to power under the Roman emperor Tiberius, in part by
murdering Tiberius' own son, Drusus. Having encouraged Tiberius himself
to withdraw to the island of Capri, Sejanus grew cruel and tremendously
powerful until Tiberius, alerted by his sister-in-law Antonia, accused
Sejanus of treason and ordered his execution. The destruction of Sejanus

Figure 38 Satiric frontispiece of Oliver Cromwell from James Heath, *Flagellum* (1663).

was swift and remarkable, followed by a blood-bath of his adherents. According to Juvenal, statues of Sejanus were torn down, with the heads melted to make pipkins, pitchers, frying-pans, and slop-pails. After his execution, Sejanus' corpse was dragged through the streets by an *uncus* (hook). This custom (the hook was normally attached to a chariot) was an expression of "public justice" (i.e. mob violence) external to Roman legal machinery, process, and statute.[54]

Heath's selection of these satiric lines is telling. He links Cromwell with Sejanus as examples of posthumous mockery. Even more strikingly, the two figures are linked as upstarts of no noble blood who presume to rule, and in both situations the fickle urban populace chooses to distance itself from a high political figure once admired. Juvenal's brutal and sarcastic language heightens the repudiation.

Heath's own text reveals the deceptive nature of Cromwell's seemingly heroic portrait. In his preface to the reader, Heath explains that he writes to expose "that poyson of *Asps* under [Cromwell's] Lips," as an "antidote," to those "suck'd in by that *Pestilent Air* of his pious pretences" (Sig. A4v). Cromwell's very success, Heath argues, discloses his evil: "Now the *destructivenesse* of these *Chymeras* and *Whimsies* of Piety, that *austere Sanctimony* under which we laboured, could never better be *discovered*, then by the *divine permission* of this mans arrival and *ascent* to the Supreme power, thereby giving the world a Specimen of the *deep mischief* of pretended and morose *Holynesse*" (Sig. A5). Heath's printed and visual image counters the martial image of Oliver Cromwell. Yet in the very process of this attack, Heath evokes that heroic image. As such, the text produces Cromwell as a figure in the public sphere and keeps alive the possibility of his eventual vindication.

Even after the ceremony and subsequent print renditions of the exhumation, attacks on – and thus publicizing of – Cromwell continued. Desecrated in print, visual image, and effigy, the Cromwellian image had a place in the celebrations surrounding the coronation of Charles II.[55] Throughout the 1660s, printed texts continued to ridicule Cromwell as a devil, Machiavel, brewer, and mock-king.[56] Restoration drama obsessively recounted the downfall of tyrants and usurpers, reflecting transparently on Cromwell.[57] Cromwell provided a convenient scapegoat on whom to place all the blame for the regicide and the years of Interregnum. Yet the effects of such texts, as we have seen, were complex and ambivalent. By rewriting the 1640s and 1650s to assign all responsibility to Cromwell, such texts made him a more powerful and influential figure in print than he was in historical reality. And they also kept him alive in the public imagination.

The very hysteria of the attacks on Cromwell in Restoration England suggests that such repudiation is not the whole story.[58] On the contrary, it suggests that those in power felt that alternative values and forms of government in church and state retained some lingering appeal: as did Cromwell himself. Lucy Hutchinson's *Memoirs of Colonel Hutchinson*, largely hostile to the Protectorate, nonetheless makes a remarkable concession to Cromwell: "His wife and children were setting up for principallity, which suited no better with any of them than scarlett on the Ape; only, to speak the truth of himselfe, he had much naturall greatnesse in him, and well became the place he usurp'd."[59] Lucy Hutchinson was not the only observer to recall Cromwell's "natural greatness," especially as the euphoria over the return of Charles II rapidly diminished.

Court records in the early 1660s attest to ongoing sympathy for Cromwell. On 20 May 1660, the eve of the triumphal entry of Charles II into London, Richard Abbott of Brighton was charged with the following seditious words: "A King! if I had but one batt in my belly, I would give it to keep the King out, for Cromwell ruled better than ever the King will."[60] On 9 April 1662, George Taylor was arraigned at York Castle for saying, "It was a good day when the King's head was cutt off. There hath beene noe peace like as was in Oliver the Protector's time. It is a pitty but that all Kings' heads should bee cutt off."[61] In November 1663, James Parker was charged at York Castle with saying, "I served Oliver seaven yeeres as a souldier and if any one will put up the finger on the accompt that Oliver did ingage, I will doe as much as I have done. As for the kinge, I am not beholding to him. I care not a fart for him."[62] Although somewhat less graphic, James Wright of Darnton in the county of Durham was similarly charged in July 1664 with "giving ill languages, saying he valued none of the king's officers, and that Oliver Cromwell was a better man than the king."[63] Court records show that popular sentiment for the Lord Protector continued.

Diaries confirm this sentiment. In February 1667, Pepys recounts that "at dinner we talked of Cromwell, all saying he was a brave fellow and did owe his crown he got to himself as any man that got one."[64] A few months later, Pepys muses that "it is strange how . . . everybody doth nowadays reflect upon Oliver and commend him, so brave things he did and made all the neighbour princes fear him; while here a prince, come in with all the love and prayers and good liking of his people, and have given greater signs of loyalty and willingness to serve him with their estates than ever was done by any people, hath lost all so soon."[65] Pepys attests to the increasing sympathetic recuperation of Cromwell and of the plain-style martial mode.

It is true that the positive memory of Cromwell kept alive in these accounts is that of an heroic Cromwell, occluding to some extent the godly dimension of his personality. As with the memory of the Machiavellian Cromwell, then, the recuperation of Cromwell was molded to values more fitting to the Restoration period. The martial Cromwell was perhaps remembered – strategically or not – at the cost of more threatening politics, whether radical sectarianism or an alternative republican heritage. Yet once in the public sphere, the figure of Cromwell might well break out of such ideological confines, evoking a range of precedents from the past: and possibilities for the future.

Afterword

In the four hundred years since his birth, Oliver Cromwell has meant many things to many people. Yet there has also been an ongoing tendency to assimilate him to monarchy, to see the cultural and political changes of the republic steadily and inexorably erased in the courtly forms of (especially) the late Protectorate.

The shifting popular print images of Cromwell that I have been tracing from the time that he first became a public figure through the period of his power to his death and eventual disinterment tell a different story. Rather than simply imitating monarchy, Cromwellian print transformed Caroline ceremony and portrait in a newly emergent public sphere. Upon his return, Charles II was forced to respond to cultural and political change, and attempts to denigrate and erase alternatives paradoxically gave Cromwell a new afterlife.

Exploring a wide range of original and often startling texts – manuscript, print ephemera, canonical literature, paintings, engravings, and medals – this study has shown that readers and viewers responded in diverse ways to Cromwell, and that their responses and representations had at best a fraught relation with Cromwell's own views. This very contest and dispersion of initiative marked a crucial difference from monarchical forms. Paradoxically, Cromwell first became a public figure not in parliamentary texts, but in royalist satires that created the very populist figure they feared. The early republic drew upon and revised monarchical ceremony, portrait, and panegyric in celebration not only of the state, but of those who served the state, most notably the Lord General Cromwell. As Lord Protector, Cromwell participated in civic ceremony, including an entry into London and two inaugurations. But print and a politically informed public altered monarchical precedent, and non-monarchical forms remained available, even in the second Protectorate. Cromwell himself remained plain and non-regal in manner. He refused the crown in 1657, and the monarchical funeral obsequies defied rather than embodied his own views and wishes. Reflecting Cromwell's own puritanism and self-denial, canonical writers such as John Milton, Andrew Marvell, and John Dryden – along with the (now) lesser-known Payne Fisher, George Wither, and Marchamont Nedham – helped to produce a new syncretic and anti-formalist aesthetic that showed ideological and cultural change.

Such changes were part of the legacy for Charles II. In 1660, monarchical ceremony appealed to a much broader audience. The courtly world of Van Dyck portraiture and the Caroline masque opened up into London as theater, and print disseminated the display to an even wider public. The exorcising of Cromwell in Carolean England was only apparent. The popular forms by which Cromwell was attacked kept him alive and attested paradoxically to his ongoing impact.

Although my story ends with the ceremony of disinterment and the print and manuscript texts that react to this display, the ghost of Oliver Cromwell lived on. At moments of crisis and change from the Popish Plot and Exclusion Crisis to the "Glorious" Revolution to Jacobite uprisings and intrigue well into the eighteenth century, Cromwell reappeared in print and manuscript satire. Such texts were meant, of course, to hold Cromwell up as a warning against rebellion and sedition. Yet when placed upon the page / stage, an energetic and humorous Cromwell once again threatened to run away with the show, and the very texts that set out to stigmatize and erase Cromwell kept him alive in the public imagination.

Finally, the intensity and persistence of such attacks on Cromwell suggests that alternative practices and forms in church and state continued to seem threatening – and hence continued to have some appeal. Although intended to do the opposite, the satiric figure of Oliver's ghost embodied and carried on one distinctive strand of the mid-seventeenth-century challenge to established ecclesiastical and monarchical forms. And that ghost has had a long afterlife indeed.

Notes

Introduction

1 James Fraser, "Triennial Travels. Part First Containing a Succinct and Breefe Narration of the Journay and Voyage of Master James Fraser through Scotland, England, and France . . . from June 1657 to June 1658." Aberdeen University Library, Special Collections and Archives, MS. 2538 / 1, folio 32v. I would like to thank Joad Raymond for drawing my attention to this manuscript and facilitating my access to it. See also Raymond's "An Eye-Witness to King Cromwell."

2 *Ibid.*

3 *Ibid.*

4 *Ibid.*, folio 34r.

5 *Ibid.*, folio 34r-v.

6 *Ibid.*, folio 34v.

7 *Ibid.*

8 *Ibid.*

9 *Ibid.*

10 *Ibid.*

11 Many of my printed texts are drawn from the valuable Thomason Tract collection of more than 23,000 pamphlets from 1641 to 1660. See Lois Spencer, "The Professional and Literary Connections of George Thomason," and her "The Politics of George Thomason." For the dating of the tracts in relation to the events they describe, see the recent debate between Stephen Greenberg, "Dating Civil War Pamphlets" and his "The Thomason Collection," and Michael Mendle, "The Thomason Collection."

12 Valuable surveys of mid-seventeenth-century Britain include G. E. Aylmer, *Rebellion or Revolution? England 1640–1660*; Ivan Roots, *Commonwealth and Protectorate*; Austin Woolrych, *England without a King, 1649–1660*; Ronald Hutton, *The British Republic, 1649–1660*; Derek Hirst, *Authority and Conflict: England 1603–1658*; and John Morrill, ed., *Revolution and Restoration: England in the 1650s*. On Oliver Cromwell, see especially John Morrill, ed., *Oliver Cromwell and the English Revolution*, and David Smith's useful collection of documents in *Oliver Cromwell: Politics and Religion in the English Revolution, 1640–1658*. Among the best of many biographies are Christopher Hill, *God's Englishman*; Barry Coward, *Oliver Cromwell*; and Peter Gaunt, *Oliver Cromwell*. The most accessible and complete edition of Cromwell's writings is W. C. Abbott's

massive *The Writings and Speeches of Oliver Cromwell*, although see the caveats in John Morrill, "Textualizing and Contextualizing Cromwell."

13 On Elizabeth, see especially John King, *Tudor Royal Iconography*; Susan Frye, *Elizabeth I*; and Wendy Wall, *The Imprint of Gender*; on James, see Jonathan Goldberg, *James I and the Politics of Literature*; on Charles I, see Kevin Sharpe, *Criticism and Compliment* and *The Personal Rule of Charles I*, pp. 222–35; and Thomas N. Corns, ed., *The Royal Image: Representations of Charles I*; on Charles II, see Paula Backscheider, *Spectacular Politics*; and Harold Weber, *Paper Bullets*. Peter Burke, *The Fabrication of Louis XIV*, similarly explores the iconography of a French monarch in the early modern period.

14 Ruth Nevo's early *The Dial of Virtue*, pp. 74–137, explored the tension between virtue and fortune in Cromwellian literature. More recently, Roger Pooley, "The Poets' Cromwell," surveys a range of high and low poetry, while Jean LeDrew Metcalfe, "The Politics of Panegyric: Poetic Representations of Oliver Cromwell," analyzes some canonical texts. Gerald MacLean, *Time's Witness*, pp. 219–55, discusses Cromwellian heroic modes in his study of the poetics of legitimation and opposition. Dale B. J. Randall's *Winter Fruit: English Drama 1642–1660* treats dramatic representations of Cromwell in his survey of Interregnum drama. Susan Wiseman, *Drama and Politics in the English Civil War*, attends to dramatic satire on Cromwell as part of a royalist versus republican aesthetic. Nigel Smith, *Literature and Revolution*, includes texts on Cromwell under rubrics of genre. David Norbrook, *Writing the English Republic*, investigates republican reactions to and representations of Cromwell. Three dissertations have usefully focused on various aspects of Cromwellian representation: see Michael Seymour, "Pro-Government Propaganda in Interregnum England, 1649–1660"; Bruce Lawson, "Providentialism and Machiavellianism in the Poetry, Prose, and Pulpit Oratory about Oliver Cromwell"; and Vivienne Stevens Johnson, "Images of Power: Oliver Cromwell in Seventeenth Century Writings."

15 In their early study, *English Art, 1625–1714*, Margaret Whinney and Oliver Millar critiqued Robert Walker, an early painter of Cromwell, for showing "the most slavish dependence on Van Dyck by an English painter," p. 76. Later art historians echo this sentiment. Ellis Waterhouse, *Painting in Britain, 1530–1790*, p. 53, points out the dependence of parliamentary portraiture on Van Dyck, adding that "there would, on grounds of style, be more reason to surmise that Walker, the much inferior counterpart to the Royalist Dobson on the Parliamentary side, may have actually been a pupil of Van Dyck." William Gaunt, *Court Painting in England from Tudor to Victorian Times*, p. 133, describes Walker as "an artist of not more than moderate capacity but a sedulous imitator of Van Dyck." More extensive and positive are David Piper, "The Contemporary Portraits of Oliver Cromwell" and Knoppers, "The Politics of Portraiture: Oliver Cromwell and the Plain Style."

16 John Morrill has a seminal essay on "Cromwell and his Contemporaries" in his edited collection, *Oliver Cromwell and the English Revolution*. In his important series of essays on Cromwell, Blair Worden is concerned in part with representation. See especially Worden, "Oliver Cromwell and the Sin of Achan"; "Andrew Marvell, Oliver Cromwell, and the Horatian Ode"; "Harrington's 'Oceana': Origins and Aftermath, 1651–1660"; and "John Milton and Oliver Cromwell." R. C. Richardson, ed., *Images of Oliver Cromwell*, considers posthumous representations. Roy Sherwood's ground-breaking work on the Cromwellian court in *The Court of Oliver Cromwell* and *Oliver*

Cromwell: King in All But Name leads him to argue that Cromwell was a *de facto* king, a point to which I will return.

17 Classic revisionist studies include Conrad Russell, *The Causes of the English Civil War* and Russell, ed., *The Origins of the English Civil War*. See the useful articulations of the issues in Barry Coward, "Was there an English Revolution?"; Richard Cust and Ann Hughes, eds., *Conflict in Early Stuart England*; and Ann Hughes, *The Causes of the English Civil War*.

18 Two seminal accounts, Roy Strong, *Van Dyck: Charles I on Horseback* and Stephen Orgel, *The Illusion of Power*, argued respectively for the idealized, spiritual meaning of Caroline portraiture and of the court masques; both forms glorified Charles, and both were escapist and unreal, only an "illusion of power." In keeping with this general line of interpretation, Judith Richards, "'His Nowe Majestie' and the English Monarchy," more recently contends that few people outside of royal circles ever saw the Van Dyck images so well known today. On the responses by Malcolm Smuts and Kevin Sharpe, see pp. 21–23.

19 David Norbrook argues for the early emergence and endurance of a republican aesthetic in his magisterial *Writing the English Republic*.

20 See the recent discussions of Interregnum drama in Dale Randall, *Winter Fruit: English Drama 1642–1660*, and, with more concern to recuperate republican aesthetics, Susan Wiseman, *Drama and Politics in the English Civil War*.

21 See Sharon Achinstein, *Milton and the Revolutionary Reader*.

22 See Nigel Smith, *Literature and Revolution in England, 1640–1660*.

23 See, respectively, Sean Kelsey, *Inventing a Republic*, and Kevin Sharpe, "'An Image Doting Rabble': The Failure of Republican Culture in Seventeenth-Century England."

24 Roy Sherwood, *Oliver Cromwell: King in All But Name*, has argued most recently for the former; Barry Coward, *Oliver Cromwell*, posits a reformist impulse to the end.

25 Challenging the court–country divide, see J. C. Robertson, "Caroline Culture: Bridging Court and Country?" and Kevin Sharpe, *Criticism and Compliment*, pp. 1–53. See also the essays in Kevin Sharpe and Peter Lake, eds., *Culture and Politics in Early Stuart England*; and in Susan D. Amussen and Mark A. Kishlansky, eds., *Political Culture and Cultural Politics in Early Modern England*.

26 Smuts, *Court Culture and the Origins of a Royalist Tradition*, p. 254. Nonetheless, in "Public Ceremony and Royal Charisma," Smuts views Charles's failure to reach beyond the court and genres like the masque and Van Dyck portraiture as contributing to the suspicions and misunderstanding among which his royal authority collapsed.

27 Sharpe, *The Personal Rule of Charles I*, p. 223. See also Sharpe's *Criticism and Compliment*, and "The Image of Virtue" in his *Politics and Ideas in Early Stuart England*.

28 On the criticisms implicit in the masques, see the differing perspectives offered by Kevin Sharpe, *Criticism and Compliment*, and Martin Butler, *Theatre and Crisis 1632–1642*; Butler's "Politics and the Masque: *Salmacida Spolia*"; and his "Reform or Reverence? The Politics of the Caroline Masque."

29 Elizabeth Eisenstein's magisterial work, *The Printing Press as an Agent of Change*, most comprehensively explored the effects of print; also wide-ranging is Lucien Febvre and Henri-Jean Martin, *The Coming of the Book*. On issues of print, see also Arthur Marotti,

Manuscript, Print, and the English Renaissance Lyric; Harold Love, *Scribal Publication in Seventeenth-Century England*; Joseph Loewenstein, "The Script in the Marketplace"; Wendy Wall, *The Imprint of Gender*; and Natalie Zemon Davis, "Printing and the People," in her *Society and Culture in Early Modern France*. On popular culture and the history of reading see James Raven, Helen Small, and Naomi Tadmor, eds., *The Practice and Representation of Reading in England*.

30 See the important essay by Ann Baynes Coiro, "Milton and Class Identity: The Publication of *Areopagitica* and the 1645 *Poems*." Also relevant here is Annabel Patterson's ground-breaking *Censorship and Interpretation*.

31 For early (divergent) accounts of the breakdown of censorship, followed by an explosion of print, see F. S. Siebert, *Freedom of the Press in England, 1476–1776*, pp. 165–263; Sheila Lambert, "The Beginning of Printing for the House of Commons, 1640–42"; Christopher Hill, "Censorship and English Literature"; Annabel Patterson, *Censorship and Interpretation*; Anthony Fletcher, *The Outbreak of the English Civil War*, pp. 191–227; and Blair Worden, "Literature and Political Censorship in Early Modern England." More recently, and with particular attention to print and an emergent public sphere, see Lois Potter, *Secret Rites and Secret Writing*, pp. 1–37; Nigel Smith, *Literature and Revolution*, pp. 23–53; Sharon Achinstein, *Milton and the Revolutionary Reader*; Joad Raymond, *The Invention of the Newspaper*; and Dagmar Freist, *Governed by Opinion*.

32 Siebert, *Freedom of the Press in England, 1476–1776*, pp. 231–32. See also Joseph Frank, *The Beginnings of the English Newspaper, 1620–1660*, and William Clyde, *The Struggle for the Freedom of the Press from Caxton to Cromwell*.

33 Feather, *A History of British Publishing*, p. 49.

34 *Ibid.*

35 *Ibid.*

36 On visual as well as verbal texts, see the valuable discussion of visual prints and print-sellers in this period in Alexander Globe, *Peter Stent: London Printseller circa 1642–1665*.

37 David Cressy, *Literacy and the Social Order*; Keith Thomas, "The Meaning of Literacy in Early Modern England"; Margaret Spufford, *Small Books and Pleasant Histories*; Tessa Watt, *Cheap Print and Popular Piety*; and Wyn Ford, "The Problem of Literacy in Early Modern England."

38 Jürgen Habermas, *The Structural Transformation of the Public Sphere*. Although scholars have quarrelled with his dating of the public sphere in England from 1690, Habermas's Whig teleology and assumption of the liberalizing effects of print have been highly influential and little challenged. See, however, the critiques in David Zaret, "Religion, Science, and Printing in the Public Spheres in Seventeenth-Century England"; David Norbrook, "*Areopagitica*, Censorship, and the Early Modern Public Sphere"; and, especially, Steve Pincus, "'Coffee Politicians Does Create': Coffeehouses and Restoration Political Culture."

39 See Roger Chartier, *The Cultural Uses of Print in Early Modern France*, trans. Lydia G. Cochrane; Chartier, ed. *The Culture of Print: Power and Uses of Print in Early Modern Europe*, trans. Lydia G. Cochrane; and Chartier, *The Cultural Origins of the French Revolution*, trans. Lydia G. Cochrane. See also Robert Darnton, "History of Reading."

40 See, for instance, the concise definition of appropriation in Chartier, *The Cultural Uses of Print in Early Modern France*, pp. 6–8.

1   "A Coffin for King Charles, A Crowne for Cromwell": royalist satire and the regicide

1 For example, Lois Potter, *Secret Rites and Secret Writing*, studies royalist forms and the cult of secrecy; Elizabeth Skerpan, *The Rhetoric of Politics in the English Revolution, 1642–1660*, stresses the influence of seventeenth-century rhetorical theory and of rhetorical genres (deliberative, epideictic, and forensic) on four moments of debate; Thomas Corns, *Uncloistered Virtue*, repoliticizes literary texts, with considerable attention to Milton; Nigel Smith, *Literature and Revolution*, traces generic instability and transformation; Sharon Achinstein, *Milton and the Revolutionary Reader*, demonstrates how a newly emergent public sphere informs Milton's appeal to a few worthy readers; Joad Raymond, *The Invention of the Newspaper*, provides a seminal account of newsbooks as a literary and material form in the 1640s; Steven Zwicker, *Lines of Authority*, juxtaposes canonical and non-canonical texts to show the political engagement of mid-century literature; while the essays in Thomas Healy and Jonathan Sawday, eds., *Literature and the English Civil War*, explore a range of topics of debate on literature and history in the civil war.

2 See the discussion of civil war newsbooks in Lois Potter, *Secret Rites and Secret Writing*, pp. 1–37; Nigel Smith, *Literature and Revolution*, pp. 54–70; Joad Raymond, ed., *Making the News*; Raymond, *The Invention of the Newspaper*; C. J. Sommerville, *The News Revolution in England*. On the dissemination of the "news," see also Richard Cust, "News and Politics in Early Seventeenth-Century England." For a range of examples of Cromwell in newsbooks, see *Cromwelliana*.

3 On Cromwell's early years, see the seminal study by John Morrill, "The Making of Oliver Cromwell."

4 See J. S. A. Adamson, "Oliver Cromwell and the Long Parliament."

5 For background, see Clive Holmes, *The Eastern Association in the English Civil War*.

6 Newsbooks and other tracts on Marston Moor in which Cromwell features include *The Parliament Scout* no. 55 (4–11 July 1644); *The Parliament Scout* no. 57 (18–25 July 1644); *A More Exact Relation of the late Battell Neer York*; *Mercurius Civicus* no. 59 (4–11 July 1644); *A Full Relation of the late Victory Obtained*; and *The Kingdomes Weekly Intelligencer* no. 62 (2–9 July 1644); see also C. H. Firth, "Marston Moor."

7 See Clive Holmes, *The Eastern Association in the English Civil War*, pp. 195–219; A. N. B. Cotton, "Cromwell and the Self-Denying Ordinance"; and J. S. Adamson, "Oliver Cromwell and the Long Parliament," pp. 60–66.

8 See the recent discussions of Cleveland in Sharon Achinstein, *Milton and the Revolutionary Reader*, pp. 88–96, and Joad Raymond, *The Invention of the Newspaper*, pp. 221–25.

9 John Cleveland, *The Character of a London Diurnall*, p. 1.

10 *The Oxford Character of the London Diurnall Examined and Answered*, p. 1.

11 *A Full Answer to a Scandalous Pamphlet*, p. 9.

12 Bruno Ryves, *Mercurius Rusticus*, p. 244.

13 See Geoffrey Nuttall, "Was Cromwell an Iconoclast?"; Margaret Aston, *England's Iconoclasts: Volume I, Laws Against Images*, pp. 62–68. Although the very real destruction of the civil war years should not be discounted, the still popular image of Cromwell as iconoclast may be largely drawn from royalist satire. On Cromwell's later image as iconoclast, see J. P. D. Dunbabin, "Oliver Cromwell's Popular Image in Nineteenth-

Century England," and Alan Smith,"The Image of Cromwell in Folklore and Tradition."

14 Independent minister Joshua Sprigge includes a highly positive counter-image of Cromwell in his *Anglia Rediviva. Englands Recovery* (1647), a defense of the Self-Denying Ordinance and the first year of the New Model Army.

15 Edward Dacres had recently published English translations of Machiavelli's *The Discourses* (1636) and *The Prince* (1640). On the influence of Machiavelli in England, see J. G. A. Pocock, *The Machiavellian Moment*; Felix Raab, *The English Face of Machiavelli*; and, more recently, Victoria Kahn, *Machiavellian Rhetoric*. On the Levellers, see G. E. Aylmer, *The Levellers in the English Revolution*. Representative Leveller tracts from this period include John Lilburne, *The Juglers Discovered* (1647); *A Word to Lieut. Gen. Cromwel* (1647); and *The Machivilian Cromwellist* (1648).

16 On the vitality of Interregnum drama, including the stage Machiavel, see discussions in Nigel Smith, *Literature and Revolution*; Dale Randall, *Winter Fruit*; and Susan Wiseman, *Drama and Politics in the English Civil War*.

17 *Craftie Cromwell: or, Oliver ordering our New State. A Tragi-Comedie*, title-page. For previous critical discussion, see Nigel Smith, *Literature and Revolution*, pp. 77–78. Smith suggests John Crouch as the author.

18 *The Second Part of Crafty Crumwell*, p. 2.

19 *Mercurius Elencticus* no. 17 (15–22 March 1648), p. 131.

20 *Mercurius Elencticus* no. 18 (22–29 March 1648), p. 133.

21 See Mikhail Bakhtin's classic statement of the grotesque in his *Rabelais and His World*. Also useful are Wolfgang Kayser, *The Grotesque in Art and Literature*, and Geoffrey Galt Harpham, *On the Grotesque: Strategies of Contradiction in Art and Literature*. On the applicability of the Bakhtinian grotesque to early modern England, see Peter Stallybrass and Allon White, *The Politics and Poetics of Transgression*.

22 *A Case for Nol Cromwells Nose and the Cure of Tom Fairfax's Gout*, p. 6.

23 C. V. Wedgwood provides a full account, including many contemporary documents, in *The Trial of Charles I*.

24 Franco Moretti, "'A Huge Eclipse': Tragic Form and the Deconsecration of Sovereignty."

25 Nancy Klein Maguire, "The Theatrical Mask / Masque of Politics."

26 On these points, I am indebted to Elizabethan Skerpan Wheeler's valuable study, "*Eikon Basilike* and the Rhetoric of Self-Representation."

27 See [John Gauden,] *Eikon Basilike*. Among the many recent scholarly treatments of *Eikon Basilike*, see Richard Helgerson, "Milton Reads the King's Book"; Lois Potter, *Secret Rites and Secret Writing*, pp. 156–84; David Loewenstein, *Milton and the Drama of History*, pp. 51–73; Steven Zwicker, *Lines of Authority*, pp. 37–59; Sharon Achinstein, *Milton and the Revolutionary Reader*, pp. 162–68; Laura Knoppers, *Historicizing Milton*, pp. 13–41; and Laura Blair McKnight, "Crucifixion or Apocalypse? Refiguring the *Eikon Basilike*."

28 See especially Kevin Sharpe, *Criticism and Compliment*, pp. 1–53, and his *The Personal Rule of Charles I*, pp. 222–35.

29 Kevin Sharpe, for instance, speaks of the masques as "political liturgies," *The Personal Rule of Charles I*, p. 230.

30 On the nature and effects of this popular exposure of Charles in print, see especially Joad Raymond, "Popular Representations of Charles I"; Elizabethan Skerpan

Wheeler, *"Eikon Basilike* and the Rhetoric of Self-Representation"; and John Peacock, "The Visual Image of Charles I."

31 I am indebted to Don-John Dugas for identifying the figures of Virtue and Time in this engraving.

32 On ballads, see Hyder Rollins, "The Black-letter Broadside Ballad," and Sharon Achinstein, "Audiences and Authors: Ballads and the Making of English Renaissance Literary Culture."

33 *A Coffin for King Charles, A Crowne for Cromwell, A Pit for the People,* single sheet.

34 See the recent discussions of the play in Nigel Smith, *Literature and Revolution,* pp. 81–84, who suggests that Samuel Sheppard may be the author, and Susan Wiseman, *Drama and Politics in the English Civil War,* pp. 62–69. When the work was expanded and reprinted after the Restoration as *Cromwell's Conspiracy* (1660), Charles did appear in a scaffold scene with Bishop Juxon.

35 *The Famous Tragedie of King Charles I,* p. 7.

36 *Mercurius Elencticus* no. 69 (21–28 February 1649), Sig. Mmmv.

37 *Ibid.*

38 John Crouch, *A Tragi-Comedy called New-Market Fayre,* p. 84.

39 Crouch, *The Second Part of New Market Fayre,* p. 216.

40 Barry Coward, "Was there an English Revolution in the Middle of the Seventeenth Century?" See also the historical and ideological distinctions drawn by Sarah Barber, *Regicide and Republicanism.*

2 Portraiture, print, and the republican heroic

1 Kelsey, *Inventing a Republic.*

2 Sharpe, "An Image Doting Rabble."

3 Abbott, ed., *The Writings and Speeches,* vol. II, p. 37.

4 Art historians on Walker have been, for the most part, brief and unsympathetic. See Margaret Whinney and Oliver Millar, *English Art, 1625–1714,* pp. 76–78; Ellis Waterhouse, *Painting in Britain, 1530–1790,* pp. 53–55; and William Gaunt, *Court Painting in England from Tudor to Victorian Times,* pp. 133–35. For more extended (and sympathetic) accounts, see David Piper, "The Contemporary Portraits of Oliver Cromwell," and Knoppers, "The Politics of Portraiture: Oliver Cromwell and the Plain Style."

5 On Charles I as collector, see Ronald Lightbown, "Charles I and the Tradition of European Princely Collecting" and Arthur MacGregor, "King Charles I: A Renaissance Collector?" Of the many valuable studies of Van Dyck, see Arthur Wheelock, Susan Barnes, and Julius Held, eds., *Anthony van Dyck*; and Christopher Brown, *Van Dyck.* On Van Dyck and Caroline portraiture, see Roy Strong, *Van Dyck: Charles I on Horseback*; Oliver Millar, *Van Dyck in England*; Graham Parry, *The Golden Age Restor'd*; Malcolm Smuts, *Court Culture and the Origins of a Royalist Tradition*; and John Peacock, "The Visual Image of Charles I."

6 The similarity to the Rubens painting was pointed out to me by Don-John Dugas. For reproductions of these works, see Michael Jaffé, *"The Standard Bearer*: Van Dyck's Portrayal of Sir Edmund Verney," 90–106; Frances Huemer, *Corpus Rubenianum Ludwig Burchard I,* pt. XIX, 1, Portraits, plate 52; and Harold Wethey, *The Paintings of Titian,* vol. 2: plates 56 and 57; and vol. 3: plate L-12–VIII.

7 On this point, I am indebted to John Peacock, private communication. Although the Walker has been linked with other Van Dyck paintings, Peacock is the first, to my knowledge, to suggest the link with the Strafford and the precise occasion of the appointment to Ireland. Oliver Millar, *Van Dyck in England*, pp. 67–69, reproduces and discusses the Strafford painting.

8 On Strafford, see the valuable collection of essays, J. F. Merritt, ed., *The Political World of Thomas Wentworth, Earl of Strafford, 1621–1641*.

9 See the portraits reproduced in Piper, "The Contemporary Portraits of Oliver Cromwell," and in Michael Jaffé, "*The Standard Bearer*: Van Dyck's Portrayal of Sir Edmund Verney."

10 British Museum, Additional MS 22,950, folio 41v.

11 Kevin Sharpe, *The Personal Rule of Charles I*, pp. 209–22, describes Charles's reforms at court and his obsession with order and decorum, in contrast to James I. Valerie Cumming, "Great vanity and excesse in Apparell," p. 322, notes that elegant dress was in fact more to be found in the portraiture of Van Dyck than in the eclectic range of royal clothing and furs acquired and sold by Commonwealth officials between 1649 and 1651.

12 David Howarth, *Images of Rule*, pp. 147–48.

13 Van Dyck's *Frederik Hendrik* is reproduced and discussed in Arthur Wheelock, *et al.*, *Anthony van Dyck*, pp. 236–38. This derivation was suggested to me by Don-John Dugas.

14 On Cooper, see Daphne Foskett, *Samuel Cooper, 1609–1672*.

15 Walpole, ed., *Anecdotes*, vol. III, pp. 110–11.

16 *A Modest Narrative of Intelligence* no. 10 (2–9 June 1649), p. 80.

17 *The Man in the Moon* no. 8 (28 May–5 June 1649), p. 73.

18 *Mercurius Elencticus* no. 12 (9–16 July 1649), p. 89.

19 *Ibid.*, p. 93.

20 *The Loyall Subjects Jubilee, or Cromwels Farewell to England*, broadsheet.

21 *A Sad Sigh, with some Heart-Cracking Groanes sent after the Lord Governour*, p. 2.

22 On Cromwell in Ireland, see Toby Barnard, *Cromwellian Ireland*; Patrick Corish, "The Cromwellian Conquest, 1649–1653" and "The Cromwellian Regime, 1650–1660"; and David Stevenson, "Cromwell, Scotland and Ireland."

23 Toby Barnard, "Irish Images of Cromwell," finds that the blackening of Cromwell's reputation in Ireland comes significantly after his own time. For contemporary skepticism, see *A Curse Against Parliament-Ale. With a Blessing to the Juncto; a Thanksgiving to the Councel of State; and a Psalm to Oliver* (October 1649).

24 *The Right Picture of King Oliver from top to toe: That all the World may a false Rebell know*, p. 1.

25 *A Speech or Declaration of the Declared King of Scots*, p. 5.

26 Bodleian Library, Tanner MS 56, folio 208v.

27 *Ibid.*, folio 218a.

28 *Ibid.*

29 Cleanth Brooks, "Marvell's *Horatian Ode*." See also Warren Chernaik, *The Poet's Time*, p. 15; and Barbara Everett, "The Shooting of the Bears."

30 Blair Worden, "Andrew Marvell, Oliver Cromwell, and the Horatian Ode," links the poem with contemporary polemics and newsbooks. Michael Wilding, *Dragon's Teeth*, pp. 114–37, sees Marvell as siding with Cromwell against the more radical Levellers

who now oppose him. David Norbrook, "Marvell's 'Horatian Ode' and the Politics of Genre," argues that Marvell appropriates and overturns a royalist genre to praise Cromwell specifically as the founder of a republic, as part of the revolutionary sublime opposed to the monarchical aesthetic of the beautiful. See also Norbrook, *Writing the English Republic*, pp. 245–71.

31 M. L. Donnelly, "'And still new stopps to various time apply'd': Marvell, Cromwell, and the Problem of Representation at Midcentury," similarly contrasts monarchical iconography and Cromwellian activism in his study of Marvell's later panegyric on Cromwell.

32 Lines 9–12. Cited from *The Poems and Letters of Andrew Marvell*, ed. H. M. Margoliouth, vol. I, pp. 91–94.

33 On the Machiavellian Cromwell, see Joseph Anthony Mazzeo, "Cromwell as Machiavellian Prince in Marvell's 'Horatian Ode'," and Blair Worden, "Andrew Marvell, Oliver Cromwell, and the Horatian Ode."

34 On Cromwell and Scotland, see Ian Gentles, *The New Model Army*; F. D. Dow, *Cromwellian Scotland, 1651–1660*; and David Stevenson, "Cromwell, Scotland and Ireland."

35 Abbott, *The Writings and Speeches*, vol. II, p. 321.

36 *Ibid.*, p. 330.

37 *Ibid.*, p. 391.

38 *Ibid.*

39 On Cromwellian medals, see Henry Henfrey, *Numismata Cromwelliana*, and on medals more generally, see Christopher Eimer, *An Introduction to Commemorative Medals.*

40 *Another Victory in Lancashire Obtained against the Scots*, p. 2.

41 *A Perfect List of all the Victories Obtained by the Lord General Cromwell*, broadsheet.

42 Previous work on Fisher has been valuable but brief and has taken Thomas Manley's translation, *Veni, Vidi, Vici* (discussed below) as a stand-in for Fisher's own neo-Latin text. Ruth Nevo, *The Dial of Virtue*, pp. 82–84, discusses Fisher's poem as panegyric, while Gerald MacLean, *Time's Witness*, pp. 226–33, argues that the work is not panegyric but generically mixed, giving an important role to the Council of State. David Norbrook, *Writing the English Republic*, introduces Fisher as a figure evincing the "way in which the cult of Cromwell could blend into a new monarchism" (p. 231), although he also notes the republican context and genesis of the poem (pp. 233–38).

43 Fisher, *Irenodia Gratulatoria*, Sig. A1v.

44 Thomas Manley, *Veni, Vidi, Vici*, has been taken as a straightforward, if uneven, translation of Fisher. But Manley in fact dilutes Fisher's republicanism and enhances the link between Cromwell and Julius Caesar in his title, his new dedication to Cromwell that includes a lengthy analogy between Cromwell and Caesar, and a translation that mitigates Fisher's sharp language on Caesar.

45 Useful analyses of the sonnet include E. A. J. Honigmann, *Milton's Sonnets*, pp. 144–52; and Anna Nardo, *Milton's Sonnets and the Ideal Community*, pp. 144–52. See also Blair Worden's extended discussion in "John Milton and Oliver Cromwell."

46 On Milton's early republicanism, see the essays in *Milton and Republicanism*, ed. David Armitage, Armand Himy, and Quentin Skinner.

47 Cited from *John Milton: Complete Poems and Major Prose*, ed. Merritt Hughes, pp. 160–61.

48 On this point, see Bruce Lawson, "Fortuna as Political Image in Three Poems on Cromwell."

49 See the varied scholarly interpretations of Cromwell's later ecclesiastical policies in

Blair Worden, "Toleration and the Cromwellian Protectorate"; J. C. Davis, "Cromwell's Religion"; and Anthony Fletcher, "Oliver Cromwell and the Godly Nation."

50 See Blair Worden, "John Milton and Oliver Cromwell."

51 Within the broad parameters of Cromwell pushing for further reform and wanting to preserve liberty, however, scholars have offered varied interpretations of his motivation for the dissolution. Since Cromwell destroyed the bill under debate, absolute certainty may be unattainable. But, in important accounts, Blair Worden, *The Rump Parliament*, pp. 345–84, sees Cromwell as having been persuaded by Thomas Harrison and other "saints" against any elections at all; Austin Woolrych, *Commonwealth to Protectorate*, pp. 68–102, argues that Cromwell acted in the belief that the bill did contain a recruiter clause (by which the Rump would perpetuate itself); and Ian Gentles, *The New Model Army*, pp. 413–39, sees multiple motives including the officers' desire to forestall the accession to power of the ungodly, their acting in self-preservation, and their genuine grievance against the Rump for failing to provide good government and for being dilatory about reform.

52 Kelsey, *Inventing a Republic*, especially pp. 165–89.

53 Bodleian Library, Clarendon MS 47, folio 207r. The verse also appears in Bodleian Library, Rawlinson MS Poet. 246, folio 15; and Bodleian Library, Tanner MS 52, folio 13.

54 *Ibid.*

55 Clarendon MS 45, folios 398v-399r.

3 "Riding in Triumph": ceremony and print in the early Protectorate

1 See David Bergeron, *English Civic Pageantry*. Important recent studies on Elizabeth's entry include Clifford Geertz, "Centers, Kings, and Charisma: Reflections on the Symbolics of Power; Mark Breitenberg, "'. . . the hole matter opened': Iconic Representation and Interpretation in 'The Quenes Majesties Passage'"; Susan Frye, *Elizabeth I*, pp. 22–55; Steven Mullaney, *The Place of the Stage*, pp. 1–25; Malcolm Smuts, "Public Ceremony and Royal Charisma"; Richard McCoy, "'Thou Idol Ceremony': Elizabeth I, *The Henriad*, and the Rites of the English Monarchy"; and Wendy Wall, *The Imprint of Gender*. On James's entry, see Jonathan Goldberg, *James I and the Politics of Literature*, pp. 1–39.

2 *Mercurius Politicus* no. 184 (16–22 December 1653), p. 3053.

3 *Great Brittain's Post* no. 151 (14–21 December 1653), p. 1243.

4 *Severall Proceedings of State Affaires* no. 221 (15–22 December 1653), p. 3500.

5 David Cressy, *Bonfires and Bells*, p. 92.

6 Thurloe, *A Collection of the State Papers*, vol. I, p. 641.

7 *Ibid.*

8 *Calendar of State Papers, Venetian*, 1653–54, p. 165.

9 *Ibid.*

10 *Ibid.*

11 On the fifth monarchists, see Bernard Capp, *The Fifth Monarchy Men*; and P. G. Rogers, *The Fifth-Monarchy Men*. Fifth-monarchist printed texts attacking Cromwell in 1654 include John Rogers, *Mene, Tekel, Perez*; Anna Trapnel, *The Cry of a Stone*; and Trapnel, *Strange and Wonderful Newes from Whitehall*.

12 Thurloe, *A Collection of the State Papers*, vol. I, p. 641.

13 *Calendar of State Papers, Domestic*, 1653–54, p. 304.

14 *Ibid.*, p. 306.

15 See *The Clarke Papers*, ed. C. H. Firth, vol II, p. 244.

16 Abbott, *The Writings and Speeches*, vol. III, p. 456.

17 *Ibid.*

18 On the nature and function of the city elite, see Ian Archer, *The Pursuit of Stability*; Alfred Beaven, *The Aldermen of the City of London*; and George Unwin, *The Gilds and Companies of London*.

19 I draw in this paragraph from Robert Ashton, "Insurgency, Counter-Insurgency and Inaction"; Valerie Pearl, *London and the Outbreak of the Puritan Revolution*, pp. 107–59; and James Loxley, *Royalism and Poetry in the English Civil Wars*, pp. 68–73.

20 Lawrence Price, *Great Britaines Time of Triumph*, title page.

21 John Bond, *King Charles his welcome home*, p. 1.

22 On the Caroline masque, see Steven Orgel, *The Illusion of Power*; Kevin Sharpe, *Criticism and Compliment*, pp. 179–264; Graham Parry, *The Golden Age Restor'd*, pp. 184–203; Malcolm Smuts, *Court Culture and the Origins of a Royalist Tradition*, pp. 245–83; and Thomas N. Corns, "Duke, Prince and King."

23 *Ovatio Carolina*, p. 9.

24 See the useful historical background in Robert Ashton, "Insurgency, Counter-Insurgency and Inaction"; and Valerie Pearl, *London and the Outbreak of the Puritan Revolution*, pp. 107–59

25 *Mercurius Politicus* no. 191 (2–9 February, 1654), p. 3262.

26 *Ibid.*

27 See also Edmund Litsfield's Latin panegyric, *Triambeisis Celsissimi Domini Oliverii Cromwelli*, that praises Cromwell in sun imagery and mythological terms more traditionally associated with monarchy.

28 *Mr. Recorders Speech*, pp. 4–5. The speech was also published in *Mercurius Politicus*.

29 *Mercurius Politicus* no. 192 (9–16 February 1654), p. 3270.

30 Abbott, *The Writings and Speeches*, vol. III, p. 456.

31 Evelyn, *Diary*, vol. III, p. 93.

32 Bodleian Library, Clarendon MS 47, folio 379r.

33 *Ibid.*, folio 379v.

34 *Calendar of State Papers, Venetian*, 1653–54, p. 184.

35 *Ibid.*, p. 186.

36 On portraiture of Tudor and Stuart monarchs, see David Howarth, *Images of Rule*; on Elizabeth, see Andrew Belsey and Catherine Belsey, "Icons of Divinity: Portraits of Elizabeth I." On the Van Dyck Charles, see Roy Strong, *Van Dyck: Charles I on Horseback*; Oliver Millar, *Van Dyck in England*; and John Peacock, "The Visual Image of Charles I."

37 C. H. Collins Baker, *Lely and the Stuart Portrait Painters*, and Oliver Millar, *Sir Peter Lely 1618–80*, provide considerable background on Lely.

38 British Library, Additional MS 23,069, folio 11.

39 In addition to the Latin panegyrics by Payne Fisher and others, Latin satires on Cromwell also appeared: see *Comparatio Inter Claudium Tiberium Principem et Olivarium Cromwellium Protectorem* (1656). On Cromwell and Roman history, see Howard Erskine-Hill, *The Augustan Idea in English Literature*, pp. 194–208; Gerald MacLean, *Time's Witness*, pp. 224–55; David Armitage, "The Cromwellian

Protectorate and the Languages of Empire"; and David Norbrook, *Writing the English Republic*, pp. 299–378. On classicized architecture, see the ground-breaking work by Timothy Mowl and Brian Earnshaw, *Architecture without Kings: The Rise of Puritan Classicism Under Cromwell*.

40 Ralph Josselin, *Diary*, p. 347.

41 Bodleian Library, Clarendon MS 48, folio 227r.

42 Thurloe, *A Collection of the State Papers*, vol. II, p. 614.

43 "The Character of a Protector" was copied down by George Thomason in June 1654. Variants appear in Bodleian Library, Ashmole MS 37, folio 199; Bodleian Library, Rawlinson MS Poet. 26, folio 148v; Bodleian Library Don. MS e. 6, folio 15v; and Bodleian Library, Rawlinson MS Poet. 173, folio 107.

44 On Streater, see Nigel Smith, "Popular Republicanism in the 1650s," and Joad Raymond, "John Streater and *The Grand Politick Informer*."

45 [John Streater,] *A Politick Commentary On the Life of Caius July Caesar*, p. 2.

46 Marvell also uses this metaphor in his *First Anniversary*. On republican connotations of the ship-of-state metaphor, see John Wallace, "Marvell's 'lusty Mate' and the Ship of the Commonwealth."

47 See, for instance, Fisher's comments, pp. 44–45, on Cato and on the *Curii*, including the republican military hero Manius Curius Dentatus.

48 Austin Woolrych, "Milton and Cromwell: 'A Short but Scandalous Night of Interruption?'" presented the classic argument for Milton's eventual disillusionment with Cromwell. Barbara Lewalski concurs in "Milton: Political Beliefs and Polemical Methods." Many of the essays in *Milton and Republicanism,* ed. Armitage, Himy, and Skinner, push Woolrych's argument even further, positing a republican Milton who bitterly repudiated the later Protectorate. In contrast, Robert Fallon, *Milton in Government*, pp. 177–212, argues from Milton's continued activity in the protectoral government that he continued to support Cromwell to the end. My own position, invoking Milton's stress on puritan piety, to some extent mitigates the extreme rejection. For another reminder that Milton also sees Cromwell as puritan saint, see David Loewenstein, "Milton and the Poetics of Defense" and his *Milton and the Drama of History*, pp. 74–81.

49 See especially, Martin Dzelzainis, "Milton's Classical Republicanism"; Blair Worden, "Milton and Marchamont Nedham" and Worden, "John Milton and Oliver Cromwell."

50 Perhaps influenced by Milton, Fisher's *Oratio Anniversaria in diem Inaugurationis Serenissimi nostri Principis Olivari* (1655) places an even greater stress on piety than did his first two panegyrics. Hence he lauds Cromwell as unexcelled not in arms but in piety: "In Exercitu quoad Armorum Disciplinam habuit fortasse pares, sed quoad *Pietatis*, procul dubio neminem" [In the army as far as discipline of arms he had perhaps equals, but as far as piety, without a doubt, nobody] (Sig. A2v).

51 *The Works of John Milton*, ed. Frank Allen Patterson, vol. VIII, p. 202 [Latin original]; *Complete Prose Works of John Milton*, ed. Don Wolfe, vol. IV, p. 662 [English translation]. While I turn to the Columbia *Works* for convenient reference to the Latin, I am citing the more recent English translation in the Yale *Complete Prose*, which I prefer.

52 *The Works of John Milton*, vol. VIII, p. 212; *Complete Prose Works*, vol. IV, pt. 1, p. 667.

53 *The Works of John Milton*, vol. VIII, p. 214–16; *Complete Prose Works*, vol. IV, pt. 1, p. 668.

54 *The Works of John Milton*, vol. VIII, p. 216; *Complete Prose Works*, vol. IV, pt. 1, p. 669.

55 *The Works of John Milton*, vol. VIII, p. 218; *Complete Prose Works*, vol. IV, pt. I, p. 670.

56 *The Works of John Milton*, vol. VIII, p. 226–28; *Complete Prose Works*, vol. IV, pt. I, p. 673–74.

57 *The Works of John Milton*, vol. VIII, pp. 248–50; *Complete Prose Works*, vol. IV, pt. I, p. 684.

58 For a more extensive account of the newsbook coverage and an important demonstration of the interrelations between news and poetry at this time, see Joad Raymond, "The Daily Muse."

59 *The Faithful Scout* no. 199 (29 September–6 October 1654), p. 1574.

60 *Calendar of State Papers, Venetian, 1653–54*, p. 269.

61 *Ibid.*, p. 274.

62 See also the satiric verses in Bodleian Library, Locke MS e. 17, p. 81; Bodleian Library, Stowe MS 185, folio 85r; and Bodleian Library, Rawlinson MS Poet. 26, folio 153r.

63 British Library, Additional MS 28,758, folio 109v.

64 *Ibid.*, folio 109v-110r.

65 *Ibid.*, folio 110r.

66 George Wither, *Vaticinium Causuale. A Rapture Occasioned by the late Miraculous Deliverance.* Joad Raymond, "The Daily Muse," points out that Wither published part of these verses anonymously in *The Faithful Scout* in October 1654, and that the complete poem was likely published in early 1655, although Thomason gives it an earlier date. On Wither, also see Christopher Hill, "George Wither and John Milton"; David Norbrook, "'Safest in Storms': George Wither in the 1650s" and Norbrook, *Writing the English Republic*, pp. 353–54.

67 J. A. Mazzeo, "Cromwell as Davidic King," points to the biblical king David, while Steven Zwicker, "Models of Governance in Marvell's 'The First Anniversary,'" sees the figure of Old Testament judge as more central to the poem, and A. J. N. Wilson, "Andrew Marvell's 'The First Anniversary,'" focuses on Caesar Augustus. Derek Hirst, "'That Sober Liberty': Marvell's Cromwell in 1654," views the poem as unified in opposition to the fifth monarchists, while Gerald MacLean, *Time's Witness*, pp. 240–48, reads Cromwell as millennial hero. David Norbrook, *Writing the English Republic*, pp. 339–51, characterizes the poem as a synthesis of courtly and apocalyptic elements.

68 In readings informing my own, Annabel Patterson, *Marvell and the Civic Crown*, observes that the poem shows "functional indeterminacy" and seems "an exercise in how to avoid conventional definitions and postures" (p. 70); and M. L. Donnelly, "Marvell, Cromwell, and the Problem of Representation at Midcentury," argues that Marvell substitutes "for the repetitive types and icons of royalist *figura* the fiercely active images of chiliasm" (p. 159).

69 Joad Raymond, "The Daily Muse," p. 198.

70 Cited by line number from *The Poems and Letters of Andrew Marvell*, ed. H. M. Margoliouth, pp. 108–19.

71 See J. M. Wallace, "Marvell's 'lusty Mate' and the Ship of the Commonwealth" on the lineage of this metaphor.

72 Hence, while Derek Hirst, "That Sober Liberty," points out fifth-monarchist disaffection, the attacks on Cromwell at the time of the riding accident were more broadly based. Marvell's focus on the fifth monarchists seems strategic, perhaps a way of stigmatizing Cromwell's detractors as radical extremists. See also the discussion of "Marvell, the Saints, and the Protectorate," in David Loewenstein, *Representing Revolution in Milton and His Contemporaries.*

73 Nonetheless, Howard Erskine-Hill, *The Augustan Idea in English Literature*, p. 200, describes Waller's poem as a "poetic bid to close the narrowing gap between Protectorate and monarchy"; and David Norbrook, *Writing the English Republic*, pp. 299–325, assimilates Augustanism to monarchy in his discussion of Waller. Waller, of course, does move, in his later panegyric *Of a War with Spain, and a Fight at Sea*, to open advocacy of a crown for Cromwell. See *The Poems of Edmund Waller*, ed. G. Thorn Drury, vol. II, pp.23–27.

74 Warren Chernaik, *The Poetry of Limitation*, p. 15.

75 *A Panegyric to my Lord Protector*, lines 1–4. Cited by line from *The Poems of Edmund Waller*, ed. G. Thorn Drury, vol. II, pp. 10–17.

76 Richard Watson, *The Panegyrike and The Storme*, Sig. B1v. Published in 1659, the collection includes parodies that were apparently written earlier,

77 "Mrs. Hutchinsons Answer to Mr Wallers Panegyric to Cromwell." British Library Additional MS 17,018, folios 213–17. For a transcription of Hutchinson's parody and a discussion of authorship, see David Norbrook, "Lucy Hutchinson versus Edmund Waller." See also Norbrook, *Writing the English Republic*, pp. 313–16.

78 See N. H. Keeble's valuable discussion of the complexities of this text in "'The Colonel's Shadow': Lucy Hutchinson, Women's Writing and the Civil War."

79 Cited from David Norbrook's transcription, "Lucy Hutchinson versus Edmund Waller," pp. 72–85.

80 On the major-generals, see Anthony Fletcher, "Oliver Cromwell and the Localities: The Problem of Consent" and Austin Woolrych, "The Cromwellian Protectorate: A Military Dictatorship?" On Cromwellian foreign policy, see Steve Pincus, *Protestantism and Patriotism*; and Timothy Venning, *Cromwellian Foreign Policy*. Specifically on Cromwell's reaction to the failure of the Western Design, see Blair Worden, "Oliver Cromwell and the Sin of Achan."

81 George Wither, *The Protector* (1655) and John Moore, *Protection Proclaimed* (1655), for instance, represent Cromwell as Moses, while such texts as *The Protector (So Called) In Part Unvailed* (1655) continue the outspoken fifth-monarchist attacks in print.

4 Contesting Cromwell in the late Protectorate

1 Hence I take issue with Roy Sherwood's argument (*Oliver Cromwell: King in All But Name*) for assimilation of the Protectorate to kingship in 1657. Many of the texts to which Sherwood points, such as *The Unparalleld Monarch* which serves as subtitle to his book, are rhetorical arguments, rather than statements of fact. And a number of texts arguing against monarchy or non-monarchical images of Cromwell, not cited by Sherwood, show that representations of Cromwell in terms other than kingship remained viable.

2 On the history of coronations, see P. Schramm, *A History of the English Coronation*; L. G. Wickham Legg, *English Coronation Records*. On Charles's coronation, see David Bergeron, *English Civic Pageantry*, pp. 106–09; Ronald Lightbown, "The King's Regalia, Insignia and Jewellery"; Christopher Wordsworth, ed., *The Manner of the Coronation of King Charles the First*; and "The Coronation of the King and Queene of England As the same was Performed and Solemnized upon the most high & mighty Prince Charles," British Library, Harleian MS 5222, folios 1–31.

3 Richard McCoy, "The Wonderfull Spectacle" and "Thou Idol Ceremony," argues that Elizabeth, uncomfortable with her bishops and skilled at the theatrics of public

display, transformed ecclesiastical ritual into civic pageantry. On James's coronation and entry, see Malcolm Smuts, "Public Ceremony and Royal Charisma"; and Jonathan Goldberg, *James I and the Politics of Literature*, pp. 1–39.

4 David Bergeron, *English Civic Pageantry*, pp. 107–08. *Calendar of State Papers, Venetian, 1653–54*, p. 464.

5 John Chamberlain, *The Letters of John Chamberlain*, vol. II, p. 627.

6 Mr. Mead to Sir Martin Stuteville, in Henry Ellis, ed., *Original Letters*, vol. III, pp. 212–13.

7 See Jennifer Woodward, *The Theatre of Death*, p. 127, on the "symbiotic" relationship between Charles and Laud. In an important recent study, Achsah Guibbory, *Ceremony and Community from Herbert to Milton*, addresses contemporary ecclesiastical controversy in relation to literary texts.

8 Ellis, *Original Letters*, vol. III, pp. 218–19.

9 *Ibid.*, p. 218.

10 *Ibid.*, p. 218.

11 *Ibid.*, pp. 218–19.

12 *Ibid.*, p. 220.

13 Richard McCoy, "The Wonderfull Spectacle," p. 225.

14 Scholars have likewise traced similarities between Cromwell's court and monarchy, although (as I will argue below) there were also significant differences. See C. H. Firth, "The Court of Oliver Cromwell," and Roy Sherwood's important *The Court of Oliver Cromwell* and *Oliver Cromwell: King in All But Name*.

15 *The Faithful Scout* no. 158 (23–30 December 1653), p. 1264.

16 *Calendar of State Papers, Venetian, 1653–54*, p. 196.

17 Bodleian Library, Clarendon MS 48, folio 38r.

18 *Ibid.*, folio 186r.

19 *HMC Sixth Report*, Appendix, p. 438.

20 Whitmore to Colonel Herbert Price, *The Nicholas Papers*, vol. III, p. 295.

21 Michael Roberts, ed., *Swedish Diplomats at Cromwell's Court*, p. 75.

22 *Ibid.*

23 *Ibid.*, p. 270.

24 *Ibid.*, pp. 317–18.

25 *Ibid.*, p. 326.

26 Earlier printed satires represented Cromwell as embodying and going beyond all the abuses of Stuart kingship. See, for instance, [John Streater], *The Picture of a New Courtier drawn in a Conference* (April 1656).

27 J. G. A. Pocock first pointed out the significance of Nedham's republication in his important essay, "James Harrington and the Good Old Cause."

28 Blair Worden, "Marchamont Nedham and the Beginnings of English Republicanism."

29 Nedham, *The Excellencie of a Free-State*, p. 234.

30 Indeed, another contemporary republican tract audaciously argues for Cromwell's assassination. See Edmund Sexby (attrib.), *Killing Noe Murder* (May 1657), and Michael Hawke's (attrib.) response, *Killing is Murder* (September 1657). James Holstun, "Ehud's Dagger," discusses the tracts in detail.

31 On *Oceana*, see Blair Worden, "James Harrington and *The Commonwealth of Oceana*," Worden, "Harrington's *Oceana*: Origins and Aftermath, 1651–1660"; and David Armitage, "The Cromwellian Protectorate and the Languages of Empire."

32 Blair Worden, "Harrington's *Oceana*," pp. 114–24, compellingly makes this point.

33 Harrington, *The Commonwealth of Oceana, and A System of Politics*, p. 245.

34 Bodleian Library, Clarendon MS 45, folio 292v.

35 *Ibid.*

36 Abbott, *The Writings and Speeches*, vol. III, p. 453.

37 Stanley Fish, *Self-Consuming Artifacts*.

38 *The Unparalleld Monarch. Or, The Portraiture of a Matchless Prince*, Sig. A4v.

39 C. H. Firth, "Cromwell and the Crown," is an early classic study. Roy Sherwood, *Oliver Cromwell: King in All But Name*, argues that Cromwell refused the title only and not the office of king. Blair Worden, "Oliver Cromwell and the Sin of Achan," sees the defeat in Hispaniola as darkening Cromwell's view of providence and persuading him against the crown. Conversely, Barry Coward, *Oliver Cromwell*, rejects the view of the Protectorate as a progressively conservative reaction and sees deeper reasons than the army's hostility behind Cromwell's refusal of the crown.

40 See Blair Worden's cautionary "Review Article: *The 'Diary' of Bulstrode Whitelocke*." The report of the Swedish ambassador that Whitelocke was in favor of Cromwell's assuming the throne is further evidence of Whitelocke's later disingenuity. See Roberts, *Swedish Diplomats at Cromwell's Court*, p. 317.

41 Bodleian Library, Clarendon MS 53, folio 111r.

42 Evelyn, *Diary*, vol. III, pp. 190–91.

43 Bodleian Library, Clarendon MS 54, folio 105v.

44 *Ibid.*

45 *Ibid.*, folios 105v–106r.

46 Abbott, *The Writings and Speeches*, vol. IV, p. 470.

47 *Ibid.*, p. 470.

48 *Ibid.*, p. 417.

49 *Ibid.*, p. 473.

50 *Ibid.*

51 C. H. Firth, "Cromwell and the Crown," also attends to some of the correspondence with Henry Cromwell that I cite and discuss below.

52 British Library, Lansdowne MS 822, folio 57r.

53 *Ibid.*, folio 51r.

54 *Ibid.*

55 *Ibid.*, folio 69r.

56 *Ibid.*, folio 71r.

57 *Ibid.*, folio 75r.

58 Bodleian Library. Clarendon MS 54, folio 273r.

59 Bodleian Library, Clarendon MS 55, folio 12r.

60 Wither, *A Suddain Flash*, p. 1.

61 On this point, see David Norbrook, "'Safest in Storms'."

62 Sherwood, *Oliver Cromwell: King in All But Name*, pp. 91–107.

63 British Library, Lansdowne MS 822, folio 120r.

64 Account of Edmund Prestwich, in Thomas Burton, *Diary of Thomas Burton*, vol. II, Appendix, pp. 511–12.

65 *Ibid*, p. 513.

66 *Ibid.*, pp. 513–14.

67 *Ibid.*, p. 514.

68 *Mercurius Politicus* no. 369 (25 June – 2 July 1657), p. 7882.

69 Burton, *Diary of Thomas Burton*, vol. II, Appendix, p. 514.

70 *Mercurius Politicus* no. 369 (25 June – 2 July 1657), p. 7883.

71 *Ibid.*, pp. 7882–83.

72 *Ibid.*, p. 7884.

73 *HMC Sixth Report*, Appendix, pp. 441–42.

74 Bodleian Library, Clarendon MS 55, folio 127r.

75 *Ibid.*

76 Fraser, "Triennial Travels." Aberdeen University Library, MS 2538 / 1, folio 32v.

77 *Ibid.*

78 *Ibid.*, folio 34v.

79 *Ibid.*

80 *Anglia Rediviva: Or, England Revived. An Heroick Poem*, Sig. A1.

81 See C. H. Firth, "The Court of Oliver Cromwell," and Roy Sherwood, *The Court of Oliver Cromwell* and *Oliver Cromwell: King in All But Name*.

82 In his seminal presentation of Fraser, Joad Raymond, "An Eyewitness to King Cromwell," also points to the vitality of republican culture even in the late Protectorate.

83 Fraser, "Triennial Travels." Aberdeen University Library, MS 2538 / 1, folio 33r.

84 *Ibid.*

85 *Ibid.*, folio 34r.

5 "I saw him dead": Cromwell's death and funeral

1 For historical accounts of Cromwell's death and its aftermath, see Godfrey Davies, *The Restoration of Charles II, 1658–1660*; Ronald Hutton, *The Restoration*; C. H. Firth, *Oliver Cromwell and the Rule of the Puritans in England*, and Firth, *The Last Years of the Protectorate*; and biographers Antonia Fraser, *Cromwell, The Lord Protector*; Barry Coward, *Oliver Cromwell*; and Peter Gaunt, *Oliver Cromwell*. Specifically on the last year, see Frederick John Varley, *Oliver Cromwell's Latter End*.

2 Roy Sherwood, who has recently unearthed and discussed important new archival materials relating to the Cromwellian obsequies, argues that the protocol for the funeral of James I was followed for Oliver "because they were burying a king" (*The Court of Oliver Cromwell*, p. 166). On monarchical funerals, see Paul Fritz, "From 'Public' to 'Private': The Royal Funerals in England, 1500–1830"; Jennifer Woodward, *The Theatre of Death*; and Clare Gittings, *Death, Burial, and the Individual in Early Modern England*. Both Woodward and Gittings discuss Cromwell, albeit briefly.

3 For primary texts on the funeral of James I, see John Nichols, *The Progresses, Processions, and Magnificent Festivities of King James the First*. I discuss Cromwellian appropriations below pp. 139–45.

4 Jennifer Woodward, *The Theatre of Death*, pp. 183–84, perceptively makes this point.

5 *Calendar of State Papers, Venetian, 1625–26*, p. 53.

6 *Ibid.*, p. 55.

7 John Chamberlain describes the solemn procession of the body to Denmark House, "accompanied by all the nobilitie about the towne, the pensioners, officers, and houshold servants, besides the Lord Mayor and aldermen" but marred by "fowle weather, so that there was nothing to be seen but coaches and torch," "To Sir Dudley Carleton," *The Letters of John Chamberlain*, vol. II, p. 609.

8 Such an effigy on display imitated French rather than traditional English practices; see Jennifer Woodward, *The Theatre of Death*.

9 John Nichols, *The Progresses, Processions, and Magnificent Festivities of King James the First*, vol. IV, p. 1039.

10 *Calendar of State Papers, Venetian, 1625–26*, p. 22.

11 Chamberlain, *Letters*, vol. II, p. 616.

12 D'Ewes, *Autobiography*, vol. I, p. 267.

13 Chamberlain, *Letters*, vol. II, p. 616.

14 *Calendar of State Papers, Venetian, 1625–26*, p. 55.

15 Chamberlain, *Letters*, vol. II, p. 616.

16 *Ibid.*

17 John Williams, *Great Britain's Salomon*, p. 75.

18 John Taylor, *A Living Sadnes, In Duty consecrated to the Immortall memory of our late Deceased albe-loved Soveraigne Lord . . . James*, pp. 10–11.

19 Thomas Heywood, *A Funerall Elegie*, Sig. D3r.

20 *Mercurius Politicus* no. 432 (2–9 September 1658), p. 803.

21 *Calendar of State Papers, Venetian, 1657–59*, p. 242.

22 *Ibid.*

23 [Roger L'Estrange,] *A True Catalogue, or An Account of the Several Places and most Eminent Persons . . . where, and by whom Richard Cromwell was proclaimed Lord Protector* (September 1659). Although this is a hostile tract, written after the fall of Richard's Protectorate to expose these "blasphemous, flattering, and undue expressions," L'Estrange usefully reproduces a number of the addresses, as does *A Second Narrative of the Late Parliament* (April 1659).

24 Slater, *The Protectors Protection: Or, The Pious Prince guarded by a Praying People*, pp. 57–58.

25 See the similar use of biblical paradigms in Thomas Harrison, *Threni Hybernici*, and George Lawrence, *Peplum Olivarii. Or, A Good Prince Bewailed by a Good People*.

26 Evelyn, *Diary*, vol. III, p. 220.

27 Josselin, *Diary*, p. 430.

28 Bodleian Library, English Poetry MS* f. 24, folio 7r. See also the satiric manuscript verses on Cromwell's death in Bodleian Library, Rawlinson MS Poet. 26, folio 163r; Bodleian Library Rawlinson MS Poet. 84, folio 58 reverse; and the virulent "On Cromwell Sick," British Library, Additional MS 28,758, folio 109r.

29 Bodleian Library, Clarendon MS 58, folio 286r.

30 *HMC Fifth Report*, Appendix, pp. 143–44.

31 *Calendar of State Papers, Venetian, 1657–59*, p. 243.

32 *Ibid.*, p. 248.

33 Frances Verney and Margaret Verney, eds., *Memoirs of the Verney Family*, vol. III, p. 422. A correspondent of Hyde's also writes of the private burial, Bodleian Library, Clarendon MS 59, folio 190v.

34 *Calendar of State Papers, Venetian, 1657–59*, p. 248.

35 See Roy Sherwood, *The Court of Oliver Cromwell* and *Oliver Cromwell: King in All But Name*.

36 On funeral effigies, see W. H. St. John Hope, "On the Funeral Effigies of the Kings and Queens of England." Ernst Kantorowicz, *The King's Two Bodies*, writes that the king's two bodies, his natural body and the body politic, were united in the living king, but visibly segregated upon his death (p. 423). The triumphal state ceremonial

added to the sempiternal glory symbolized by the effigy (p. 429). Nigel Llewellyn, "The Royal Body: Monuments to the Dead, For the Living," follows Kantorowicz. But the applicability of the mystical, medieval view of kingship in early modern England has been recently challenged by David Norbrook, "The Emperor's New Body?" and by Jennifer Woodward, *The Theatre of Death*, pp. 177–80.

37 "Description of the adornments of the hearse or bed of state whearin lyes the effigies of his serene Highnes Oliver Lord Protector," British Library, Harleian MS 1438, folios 79–81. The same account appears in British Library, Harleian MS 1099, folios 108–09. See also the printed account in Prestwich, *Respublica*, pp. 174, 188. On Cromwell's lying-in-state and funeral, in addition to the sources cited below, see Thomas Burton, *Diary*, vol. II, Appendix, p. 7.

38 British Library, Harleian MS 1438, folio 79r.

39 *Mercurius Politicus* no. 438 (14–21 October 1658), p. 918.

40 *Ibid.*, p. 927.

41 *Ibid.*

42 *Ibid.*, pp. 927–28.

43 *Ibid.*, p. 928.

44 The engraving was included in *The Pourtraiture of His Royal Highness, Oliver, Late Lord Protector &c. in his Life and Death*, 1659.

45 In Frances Verney and Margaret Verney, eds., *Memoirs of the Verney Family*, vol. III, p. 422.

46 *The True Manner of the most Magnificent Conveyance of His Highnesse Effigies*, p. 11.

47 Westminster Abbey MS 6371. Cited with the kind permission of Dr. Richard Mortimer, Westminster Abbey Library.

48 *Ibid.*

49 In addition to the sources cited below, see two detailed manuscript accounts: "The particulars of the funeral procession of the Most Noble and Puissant Oliver Lord Protector by George Dethick," British Library, Lansdowne MS 95, folios 31–45, and the accounting and pricing of work done by Henry Parker, painter–stainer for the funeral of Oliver Cromwell, British Library, Harleian MS 1438, folios 74–77.

50 Mundy, *Travels*, p. 104.

51 Sir Edward Dering, *Ephemeris, 1656–1662*, Huntington Library MS 41536, folio 28r.

52 *Calendar of State Papers, Venetian, 1657–59*, p. 269.

53 Huntington Library MS 41536, folio 28r.

54 *Calendar of State Papers Venetian, 1657–59*, p. 268.

55 *Mercurius Politicus* no. 443 (18–25 November 1658), p. 32.

56 *Ibid.*

57 British Library, Harleian MS 1438, folios 77v–78r.

58 Prestwich, *Respublica*, pp. 178–79; Burton, *Diary*, vol. II, p. 529; and John Peacock, "Inigo Jones' Catafalque for James I."

59 Mundy, *Travels*, pp. 103–4.

60 *Calendar of State Papers Venetian, 1657–59*, p. 269.

61 Westminster Abbey MS 6372.

62 *Mercurius Politicus* no. 443 (18–25 November 1658), p. 32.

63 Ludlow, *Memoirs*, vol. II, p. 260.

64 Evelyn, *Diary*, vol. III, p. 224.

65 Bodleian Library, Clarendon MS 59, folio 238r.

66 *Ibid.*

67 *Ibid.*

68 *Ibid.*

69 *Ibid.*

70 Burrough, *A Testimony Against a Great Idolatry Committed*, pp. 3, 4.

71 Wither, *Salt upon Salt*, p. 19.

72 François Guizot, *History of Richard Cromwell*, vol. I, p. 270.

73 In addition to the elegies that I discuss below, see Thomas Davies, *The Tenth Worthy* (1658); Samuel Slater, *A Rhetorical Rapture* (1658); *Musarum Cantabrigiensium Luctus & Gratulatio: Ille in Funere Oliveri* (1658); and Payne Fisher, *Threnodia Triumphalis* (1659). See also "On Oliver Lord Protector Occasiond by ye many coppies of verses made after his death," Bodleian Library, Locke MS e. 17, pp. 82–86.

74 Roger Pooley, "The Poets' Cromwell," writes that "the consensus is that no one was on top form at Cromwell's death" (p. 223). Derek Hirst, "The Lord Protector, 1653–1658," sees the funeral elegies as marked by "uncertainty and a sense of dislocation" (p. 120). M. L. Donnelly, "Marvell, Cromwell, and the Problem of Representation at Midcentury," similarly points to "the impossibility of giving any kind of intellectual or emotional coherence or promise to the event of Cromwell's death in the generic terms available to funeral panegyric" (p. 167).

75 *Three Poems Upon the Death of his late Highnesse*, p. 22.

76 For convenience of reference, I am citing by line from *The Poems of Edmund Waller*, ed. G. Thorn Drury, vol. II, pp. 34–35.

77 See also the parodies of Waller in Richard Watson, *The Panegyrike and The Storme*.

78 Bodleian Library, Rawlinson MS B.35, folios 41r–40v.

79 Bodleian Library, MS Locke e.17, p. 75.

80 *Ibid.*

81 *Ibid.*

82 For convenience of reference, I am citing Dryden's poem by line number from *The Works of John Dryden*, ed. Edward Niles Hooker and H. T. Swedenberg, Jr., vol. I, pp. 11–16.

83 See "The Listing of Cromwell's Funeral Procession by George Dethick," British Library, Lansdowne MS 95, folios 31–75. Dryden ("Mr. Dradon") appears on folio 41v.

84 Derek Hirst, "The Lord Protector, 1653–1658," writes that "Dryden found it as difficult as did Marvell to comprehend Cromwell's character and career once the obvious tribute had been paid to military greatness" (p. 120). Paul Hammond, *John Dryden: A Literary Life*, views the praise of Cromwell as limited, commenting that "Dryden's silence on the future of the Protectorate is eloquent" (p. 20). Steven Zwicker, *Politics and Language in Dryden's Poetry*, finds "ironic qualification" in the exclusion of Scripture and "the failure of the elegy to turn from praise to apotheosis" (p. 73). James Winn, *John Dryden and his World*, sees Dryden as careful to avoid offending the royalists and cautiously detached in the face of the unsettled political situation (pp. 93–94).

85 See Winn, *John Dryden and his World*, p. 86.

86 Marvell's poem has received only limited scholarly attention, much of it critical. Annabel Patterson, *Marvell and the Civic Crown*, argues that the elegy "competes effectively neither with the strenuous mental activity of the earlier Cromwell poems nor with the voluptuous emotional activity of an elegy, like *Lycidas*, written to explore the meaning of grief" (p. 94). M. L. Donnelly, "Marvell, Cromwell, and the Problem of Representation at Midcentury," views the poem as "among Marvell's

works a comparatively unsuccessful piece, rising in only a few places to memorable weight and power" (p. 167). Derek Hirst, "The Lord Protector, 1653–1658," finds "perplexity" and even moments of "bathos, remarkable for this most controlled of poets" (p. 120). David Norbrook, *Writing the English Republic*, pp. 386–88, concurs in the scholarly consensus of inferiority, situating Marvell and the other elegists at the weary end of Cromwellian Augustanism.

87 Cited by line number from *The Poems and Letters of Andrew Marvell*, ed. H. M. Margoliouth, vol. I, pp. 129–37.

88 On this point see M. L. Donnelly, "Marvell, Cromwell, and the Problem of Representation," p. 167.

89 The engraving served as frontispiece, for instance, to Samuel Carrington, *The History of the Life and Death of his most Serene Highness, Oliver*, published in April 1659.

90 Biographies that attempted to make sense of the meaning of Cromwell in the months after his death sometimes evoked a Machiavellian paradigm: see, for instance, Henry Fletcher, *The Perfect Politician*.

91 Henry Dawbeny, *Historie and Policie Re-viewed*, Sig. a2r.

92 William Winstanley, *England's Worthies*, p. 560.

93 *Nicholas Papers*, vol. IV, p. 154.

94 *Ibid.*, p. 161.

95 *The Weekly Post* no. 5 (31 May–7 June 1659), p. 37.

96 *Ibid.*

97 See Westminster Abbey MSS 6374 and 6375A.

98 Some positive representations appeared as well, including Charles Harvey's account of Cromwell's last pious hours in *A Collection of Several Passages concerning his late Highnesse Oliver Cromwell* (June 1659).

99 *The World in a Maize, Or, Olivers Ghost*, p. 4.

100 *A Dialogue Betwixt the Ghosts of Charls the I, Late King of England: and Oliver, The late Usurping Protector*, p. 4.

101 *A New Conference Between the Ghosts of King Charles and Oliver Cromwell*, p. 2.

102 *The Court Career, Death Shaddow'd to life*, p. 3.

103 Austin Woolrych gives an excellent account of the final days of the republic and the return of the king in his Introduction to *Prose Works of John Milton*, ed. R. W. Ayres, vol. VII. See also Godfrey Davies, *The Restoration of Charles II, 1658–1660*.

6 Ceremony, print, and punishment in the early Restoration

1 See J. R. Jones, ed. *The Restored Monarchy, 1660–1688*; Ronald Hutton, *The Restoration*; and Tim Harris, *Politics under the Later Stuarts*.

2 Gerald MacLean, *Time's Witness*; M. L. Donnelly, "Caroline Royalist Panegyric and the Disintegration of a Symbolic Mode." Paul Hammond, "The King's Two Bodies: Representations of Charles II"; and Harold Weber, *Paper Bullets*.

3 While Christopher Hill, *Some Intellectual Consequences of the English Revolution*, pp. 3–6 and pp. 7–15, points to court records that capture disaffection, Richard Greaves, *Deliver Us From Evil* and *Enemies Under His Feet*, shows the continuance of radical voices and resistance to the restored monarchy and church. Tim Harris, *Politics under the Later Stuarts*, cogently argues that the ecclesiastical and political issues of the civil war continued to be debated in Restoration England. See also Mark Goldie, Tim Harris, and Paul Seaward, eds., *The Politics of Religion in Restoration England*; and Jonathan

Scott, *Algernon Sidney and the English Republic*. On continuities in the literary sphere, see N. H. Keeble, *The Literary Culture of Nonconformity*; Nigel Smith, *Perfection Proclaimed*; Thomas N. Corns, *Uncloistered Virtue*; Laura Knoppers, *Historicizing Milton*; David Norbrook, *Writing the English Republic*; and the essays in Gerald MacLean, ed., *Culture and Society in the Stuart Restoration*.

4 Paula Backscheider, *Spectacular Politics*, posits a fully theatrical monarchy in which Charles II turns London itself into a stage, while Harold Weber, *Paper Bullets*, argues that Charles II was the first monarch to seek legitimation through print. My own position draws upon both of these studies to argue that print is effective for Charles precisely because it reproduces and disseminates public ceremony and visual spectacle.

5 For instance, David Norbrook, *Writing the English Republic*, pp. 433–95, argues for the persistence of republican thought in a veiled critique of Cromwell in *Paradise Lost*; Paula Backscheider, *Spectacular Politics*, discusses royalist satire, but sees the new ceremonies as erasing the Interregnum: "As [Charles II] obliterated the fear, dishonor, and defeat of the early 1640s, he wrote the Interregnum out of the nation's history" (p. 21).

6 Evelyn, *Diary*, vol. III, p. 246.

7 *Ibid.*

8 *Ibid.*

9 *Ibid.*

10 *Calendar of State Papers, Venetian, 1659–61*, p. 155.

11 *Ibid.* See also the descriptions of Charles's entry in Peter Mundy, *Travels*, pp. 117–18; and Thomas Rugge, *Diurnal*, pp. 88–90.

12 In addition to the panegyrics discussed below, see such texts as Thomas Higgons, *A Panegyrick to the King* (June 1660); Samuel Willes, *To the Kings Most Sacred Majesty* (June 1660); S. W., *Epinicia Carolina, or an Essay Upon the Return of His Sacred Majesty* (June 1660); and the Oxford collection *Britannia Rediviva* (1660).

13 Rachel Devon, *Exultationis Carmen*, p. 1.

14 *To the King, upon his Majesties Happy Return*, p. 6.

15 Harold Weber, *Paper Bullets*, pp. 25–49, astutely traces similar obfuscations and tensions in the romance narratives on Charles's escape from Worcester.

16 Henry Beeston, *A Poem to His most Excellent Majesty*, p. 5.

17 Alex Brome, *A Congratulatory Poem*, p. 5.

18 William Walwyn, *God Save the King, or a Sermon of Thanksgiving for His Majesties Happy Return to his Throne*, frontispiece.

19 See also Harold Weber, *Paper Bullets*.

20 On this point, see Jonathan Sawday, "Re-Writing a Revolution."

21 Rugge, *Diurnal*, p. 90.

22 *Ibid.*

23 *Calendar of State Papers, Venetian, 1659–61*, p. 155.

24 *Mercurius Publicus* no. 21 (17–24 May 1660), p. 330.

25 *Ibid.*

26 *Ibid.*

27 Rugge, *Diurnal*, p. 92.

28 *Calendar of State Papers, Venetian, 1659–61*, p. 162.

29 Thomas Rugge, *Diurnal*, p. 114.

30 *Ibid.*

31 In addition to those texts discussed below, other printed satires from spring / summer
    1660 include: *O. Cromwells Thankes to the Lord Generall* (May 1660); *The Traytors Tragedy*
    (July 1660); *The English Devil* (July 1660); *Oliver Cromwell the late great Tirant his Life-
    Guard* (August 1660); and *The Blazing-Star: or, Nolls Nose Newly Revived* (August 1660).

32 *A Parly between the Ghosts of the Late Protector and the King of Sweden*, p. 5.

33 *A Third Conference between O. Cromwell and Hugh Peters*, pp. 6, 3.

34 *The Case is Altered; or, Dreadful news from Hell*, p. 6.

35 [John Gauden], *Cromwell's Bloody Slaughter-house*, p. 7.

36 *Calendar of State Papers, Venetian, 1659–61*, p. 245.

37 *Ibid.*

38 Rugge, *Diurnal*, p. 143.

39 *Calendar of State Papers, Venetian, 1659–61*, p. 246.

40 *Calendar of State Papers, Domestic, 1661*, p. 506.

41 Evelyn, *Diary*, vol. III, p. 269.

42 Cited in Frederick Varley, *Oliver Cromwell's Latter End*, pp. 55–56.

43 *Ibid.*

44 *Ibid.*

45 Pepys, *Diary*, vol. I, p. 309.

46 *The last Farewell of three bould Traytors*, broadsheet.

47 *A New Meeting of Ghosts at Tyburn*, p. 3.

48 Thomas Laqueur, "Crowds, Carnival and the State in English Executions, 1604–1868,"
    argues that the carnivalesque is always implicit in these displays.

49 See J. A. Sharpe, "'Last Dying Speeches.'"

50 *The Speeches of Oliver Cromwell, Henry Ireton, and John Bradshaw*, p. 1. The tract is
    satirically attributed to Payne Fisher and Marchamont Nedham.

51 *Justa Sive Inferiæ Regicidarum*, broadsheet.

52 J. D. Durnovariae, *Short Meditations on . . . the Life and Death of Oliver Cromwell*, p. 7.

53 Heath, *Flagellum: or, The Life and Death, Birth and Burial of Oliver Cromwell*,
    frontispiece.

54 See the discussion in Barbara Levick, *Tiberius the Politician*, ch. 10, pp. 148–79.

55 See discussion in Knoppers, *Historicizing Milton*, pp. 96–105; and Paula Backscheider,
    Spectacular Politics, pp. 3–31. Backscheider, however, sees the denigration as (at least
    initially) wholly successful, part of the "consolidation of power."

56 See also *Hell's Higher Court of Justice* (1661); *The Court & Kitchin of Elizabeth, Commonly
    Called Joan Cromwell* (1664); Abraham Cowley, *A Vision*, in *Essays, Plays, and Sundry
    Verses*, ed. A. R. Waller.

57 See Nancy Klein Maguire's valuable discussion of the drama in *Regicide and
    Restoration*.

58 See Roger Howell, "'That Imp of Satan': The Restoration Image of Cromwell," p. 43.

59 Lucy Hutchinson, *Memoirs of the Life of Colonel Hutchinson*.

60 Raine, *Depositions from the Castle of York*, p. 84.

61 *Ibid.* p. 94.

62 *Ibid.* pp. 115–16.

63 *Ibid.* p. 94.

64 Pepys, *Diary*, vol. VIII, p. 50.

65 *Ibid.*, p. 332.

Works cited

MANUSCRIPT SOURCES

Aberdeen University Library, Special Collections and Archives
MS 2538 / 1

Bodleian Library, University of Oxford
Ashmole MSS 36 – 37
Clarendon MSS 45 – 59
Don. MS e.6
English Poetry MS* f.4
Locke MS e.17
Rawlinson MS b.35
Rawlinson MSS Poet. 26, 84, 173, 246
Stowe MS 185
Tanner MSS 52, 56

British Library
Additional MS 17,018
Additional MS 22,590
Additional MS 23,069
Additional MS 28,758
Additional MS 37,719
Harleian MS 991
Harleian MS 1099
Harleian MS 1438
Harleian MS 5222
Lansdowne MS 95
Lansdowne MS 822
Sloane MS 3243

Huntington Library, San Marino
MS 41536

Westminster Abbey
MS 6371, 6372, 6373, 6374, 6375A

PRINTED PRIMARY SOURCES

Place of publication for early modern texts is London unless otherwise noted. Months of publication are taken from George Thomason's dates of acquisition.

Abbott, Wilbur Cortez, ed. *The Writings and Speeches of Oliver Cromwell.* 4 vols. Cambridge, Mass.: Harvard University Press, 1937–47.

Anglia Rediviva: Or, England Revived. An Heroick Poem. 1658.

Another Victory in Lancashire Obtained against the Scots by Major General Harrison and Collonel Lilburn . . . Together with the Manner of my Lord General Cromwels comming up and noble Reception by the City of London. September 1651.

Balaams Asse, or, the City-Fast for Cursing the King and Blessing Oliver. July 1649.

Beeston, Henry. *A Poem to His most Excellent Majesty Charles the Second.* September 1660.

The Blazing-Star: or, Nolls Nose Newly Revived and taken out of his Tomb. By Collonel Baker. August 1660.

Bond, John. *King Charles his welcome home, or, a Congratulation of all his loving Subjects in thankefulnesse to God for his Majesties safe and happie returne from Scotland.* 1641.

Britannia Rediviva. Oxford, 1660.

Brome, Alex. *A Congratulatory Poem, on the Miraculous, and Glorious Return of that unparalleld King Charls the II.* June 1660.

Bruce, J. and D. Masson, eds. *The Quarrel between the Earl of Manchester and Oliver Cromwell.* Camden Society, Second Series, vol. xii. London: The Royal Historical Society, 1875.

B[urrough], E[dward]. *A Testimony Against a Great Idolatry Committed and a true Mourning of the Lords Servant upon the many Considerations of his heart.* 1658.

Burton, Thomas. *Diary of Thomas Burton.* 4 vols. Ed. John Towill Rutt. London: Henry Colburn, 1828.

Calendar of State Papers and Manuscripts Relating to English Affairs, Existing in the Archives and Collections of Venice. 1625–26; 1653–54; 1657–59; 1659–61. Ed. Allen B. Hinds. Vols. xix, xxix–xxxii. London: Longmans & Green, 1913–31.

Calendar of State Papers, Domestic Series, 1653–1654; 1661. Ed. Mary Anne Everett Green. Vol. lxii. London: Longman & Co., 1879.

Carrington, Samuel. *The History of the Life and Death of his most Serene Highness, Oliver, Late Lord Protector.* April 1659.

A Case for Nol Cromwells Nose, and the Cure of Tom Fairfax's Gout. Both which Rebells are dead, and their deaths kept close, by the policy of our new States. June 1648.

The Case is Altered; or, Dreadful news from Hell. In a discourse between the Ghost of this grand Traytor and Tyrant Oliver Cromwel and Sir reverence my Lady Joan his wife. August 1660.

Chamberlain, John. *The Letters of John Chamberlain.* Ed. Norman Egbert McClure. 2 vols. Philadelphia: The American Philosophical Society, 1939.

"The Character of a Protector." June 1654.

The Clarke Papers. Ed. C. H. Firth. 4 vols. London: Longmans, Green, and Co, 1891–1901.

Cleveland, John. *The Character of a London Diurnall.* Oxford. February 1645.

A Coffin for King Charles, A Crowne for Cromwell, A Pit for the People. April 1649.

Comparatio Inter Claudium Tiberium Principem et Olivarium Cromwellium Protectorem In qua Utriusque simulationes, dissimulationes, & scelerata arcana dominandi inquiruntur. 1656.

A Conference Held between the Old Lord Protector And the New Lord General, Truly Reported by Hugh Peters. March 1660.

The Court & Kitchin of Elizabeth, Commonly called Joan Cromwel, the Wife of the late Usurper, Truly Described and Represented, And now Made Publick for general Satisfaction. 1664.

The Court Career, Death Shaddow'd to life. Or Shadowes of Life and Death. A Pasquil Dialogue. July 1659.

Cowley, Abraham. *Essays, Plays, and Sundry Verses.* Ed. A. R. Waller. Cambridge University Press, 1906.

Craftie Cromwell: or, Oliver ordering our New State. A Tragi-Comedie. Wherein is discovered the Trayterous undertakings of the said Nol, and his Levelling Crew. Written by Mercurius Melancholicus. February 1648.

Cromwelliana. A Chronological Detail of Events in which Oliver Cromwell was engaged from the Year 1642 to his Death 1658: With a Continuation of other Transactions to the Restoration. Ed. J. Caulfield. Westminster: Machel Stace, 1810.

Cromwell's Conspiracy. A Tragy-Comedy Relating to our latter Times. Beginning at the Death of King Charles the First, and ending with the happy Restauration of King Charles the Second. August 1660.

Cromwell's Recall: or, The Petition of the zealous Fraternity, convented iniquity, at the House of John Goodwin, Arch-flamin of England, To the Supreme Authority of the Nation, the House of Common-Traytors assembled in Parliament, With A Declaration of the said House, for the recall of Cromwell. August 1649.

Crouch, John, *A Tragi-Comedy called New-Market-Fayre.* June 1649. Ed. Paul Werstine. *Analytical and Enumerative Bibliography* 6.2 (1982), 71–101.

The Second Part of New-Market-Fayre. July 1649. Ed. Paul Werstine. *Analytical and Enumerative Bibliography* 6.4 (1982), 209–39.

A Curse Against Parliament-Ale. With a Blessing to the Juncto; a Thanksgiving to the Councel of State; and a Psalm to Oliver. October 1649.

Davies, Thomas. *The Tenth Worthy; or, Several Anagrams in Latine, Welsh and English, upon the Name of that most highly Renowned Worthy of Worthies, Oliver, Late Lord Protector. Together with some Elegeical Verses upon his much lamented Death.* September 1658.

D[awbeny], H[enry]. *Historie & Policie Re-viewed, in the Heroick Transactions of his Most Serene Highnesse, Oliver, Late Lord Protector . . . as they are drawn in lively Parallels to the Ascents of the Great Patriarch Moses.* April 1659.

The Devils Cabinet Councell Discovered. July 1660.

Devon, Rachel. *Exultationis Carmen to the Kings Most Excellent Majesty upon his most Desired Return.* (August 1660).

D'Ewes, Sir Simonds. *The Autobiography and Correspondence of Sir Simonds D'Ewes,*

Bart., *During the Reigns of James I and Charles I*. Ed. James Orchard Halliwell. 2
vols. London: Richard Bentley, 1845.

*A Dialogue Betwixt the Ghosts of Charls the I, Late King of England: and Oliver, the late
Usurping Protector.* June 1659.

*The Divine Right of Government Naturall and Politique. More Particularly of Monarchie the
onely Legitimate and Natural spece of Politique Government.* September 1647.

Dryden, John. *The Works of John Dryden*. Ed. Edward Niles Hooker and H. T.
Swedenberg, Jr. Vol 1. Berkeley and Los Angeles: University of California, Press,
1956.

Durnovariae, J. D. *Short Meditations on, with a briefe Description of the Life and Death of
Oliver Cromwell.* February 1661.

*The Earl of Pembrookes Speech to Nol-Cromwell, Lord Deputy of Ireland. With his Royall
Entertainment of him at his Mannor of Ramsbury in Wiltshire on his Journey to Ireland.*
July 1649.

Ellis, Henry, ed. *Original Letters, Illustrative of English History*. 3 vols. 2nd ed. London:
Harding, Triphook, and Lepard, 1925.

The English Devil: or, Cromwel and his Monstrous Witch discover'd at White-Hall. July 1660.

Evelyn, John. *The Diary of John Evelyn*. Ed. E. S. de Beer. Vol. III. Oxford: Clarendon
Press, 1955.

The Faithful Scout. 1653.

The Famous Tragedie of King Charles I Basely Butchered. 1649.

Fisher, Payne. *Irenodia Gratulatoria, Sive Illustrissimi amplissimiq: Viri Oliveri Cromwelli,
&c Epinicion.* August 1652.

  Inauguratio Olivariana, Sive Pro Præfectura Serenissimi Principis. 1655.

  Oratio Anniversaria in diem Inaugurationis Serenissimi nostri Principis Olivari. 1655.

  *Threnodia Triumphalis, a triumphal funeral-ode: being a compendious and succinct series
  of his late most invincible highness stupendious successes at home and abroad.* 1659.

[Fletcher, Henry]. *The Perfect Politician; or, A Full View of the Life and Actions of O.
Cromwel.* February 1660.

A Full Answer to a Scandalous Pamphlet Intitled A Character of a London Diurnall. 1645.

*A Full Relation of the late Victory Obtained (Through Gods Providence) . . . on Marston-
Moor.* July 1644.

A Further Narrative of the Passages of the Times in the Commonwealth of England, 1657.

[Gauden, John]. *Eikon Basilike: The Portraiture of His Sacred Majesty in His Solitudes and
Sufferings* (1649). Ed. Philip Knachel. Ithaca, N.Y.: Cornell University Press for the
Folger Shakespeare Library, 1966.

[Gauden, John]. *Cromwell's Bloody Slaughter-house; or, His Damnable Designes . . . in
Contriving the Murther of his Sacred Majesty King Charles I Discovered.* July 1660.

Great Brittain's Post. 1653.

Guerdon, Aaron. *A Most Learned, Conscientious and Devout-Exercise held forth the last
Lords-day at Sir Peter Temples in Lincolnes-Inne-Fields by Lieut-Generall Crumwell.*
June 1649.

Guizot, François. *History of Richard Cromwell and the Restoration of Charles II,* trans.
Andrew R. Scoble. 2 vols. London: Richard Bentley, 1856.

Harrington, James. *The Commonwealth of Oceana, and A System of Politics*. Ed. J. G. A.
Pocock. Cambridge University Press, 1992.

Harrison, Thomas. *Threni Hybernici: or, Ireland Sympathizing with England and Scotland, In a Sad Lamentation for the Loss of their Josiah.* 1658.

[Harvey, Charles.] *A Collection of Several Passages concerning his late Highnesse Oliver Cromwell, In the time of his Sickness.* June 1659.

[Hawke, Michael.] *Killing is Murder: or, An Answer to a Treasonous Pamphlet Entituled Killing is no Murder.* September 1657.

Heath, James. *Flagellum: or, The Life and Death, Birth and Burial of Oliver Cromwell Faithfully described in an Exact Account of his Policies and Successes.* 1663.

Hell's Higher Court of Justice: or, The Triall of the three Politick Ghosts, viz. Oliver Cromwell, King of Sweden, and Cardinal Mazarine. April 1661.

Henfrey, Henry. *Numismata Cromwelliana, or, The Medallic History of Oliver Cromwell.* London: J. R. Smith, 1877.

Heywood, Thomas. *A Funerall Elegie Upon the Much Lamented Death of the Trespuissant and unmatchable King, King James, King of Great Brittaine, France and Ireland, defender of the Faith.* London, 1625.

Higgons, Thomas. *A Panegyrick to the King.* June 1660.

Historical Manuscripts Commission, Fifth Report. London: Her Majesty's Stationery Office, 1876, Appendix. Manuscripts of His Grace the Duke of Sutherland, pp. 135–214.

Historical Manuscripts Commission, Sixth Report. London: Her Majesty's Stationery Office, 1882, Appendix. The Manuscripts of Miss Ffarington, of Worden Hall, Co. Lancaster, pp. 426–48.

A Hue and Crie after Cromwell: or, The Cities Lamentation for the losse of their Coyne and Conscience. July 1649.

Hutchinson, Lucy. *Memoirs of the Life of Colonel Hutchinson.* Ed. James Sutherland. London and New York: Oxford University Press, 1973.

Josselin, Ralph. *The Diary of Ralph Josselin 1616–1683.* Ed. Alan Macfarlane. London: Oxford University Press, 1976.

Justa Sive Inferiæ Regicidarum: or, Tyburns Revels, Presented before Protector Cromwel, Lord President Bradshaw, Lord Deputy Ireton. February 1661.

The Kingdomes Weekly Intelligencer. 1644.

The last Farewell of three bould Traytors. 1661.

The last Newes from the King of Scots. September 1651.

Lawrence, George. *Peplum Olivarii. Or, a Good Prince Bewailed by a Good People. Represented in a Sermon October 13.1658 Upon the death of Oliver, Late Lord Protector.* November 1658.

[L'Estrange, Roger.] *A True Catalogue, or An Account of the several Places, and most Eminent Persons, in the three Nations and elsewhere, where, and by whom Richard Cromwell was Proclaimed Lord Protector.* September 1659.

Lilburne, John. *The Juglers Discovered. In two letters writ by Lieut. Col. John Lilburne . . . discovering the turn-coat Machiavell practises and under-hand dealings of Lieut. Gen Cromwell and his sonne in law Commissary Generall Ireton and the rest of their Hocus-Pocus faction.* September 1647.

Litsfield, Edmund. *Triambeisis Celsissimi Domini Oliverii Cromwelli.* February 1655.

The Loyall Subjects Jubilee, or Cromwels Farewell to England, being a Poem on his advancing to Ireland. July 1649.

Ludlow, Edmund. *The Memoirs of Edmund Ludlow, 1625–72.* Ed. C. H. Firth. 2 vols. Oxford: Clarendon Press, 1894.

Machiavelli, Nicholas. *Machiavels Discourses upon the First Decade of T. Livius.* Trans. E[dward] D[acres]. 1636.

   Nicholas Machiavel's Prince. Trans. E[dward] D[acres]. 1640.

The Machivilian Cromwellist and Hypocritical, perfidious New Statist: Discovering the most detestable Falshood, Dissimulation and Machivilian Practises of L.G. Cromwel and his Confederates. January 1648.

M[anley], T[homas]. *Veni, Vidi, Vici. The Triumphs of the Most Excellent & Illustrious Oliver Cromwell, &c. Set forth in a Panegyricke. Written Originally in Latine and faithfully done into English Heroicall Verse by T. M.* February 1653.

The Man in the Moon. 1649.

Marvell, Andrew. *The Poems and Letters of Andrew Marvell.* Vol. 1. Ed. H. M. Margoliouth. 3rd ed. Revised by Pierre Legouis with E. E. Duncan-Jones. Oxford: Clarendon Press, 1971.

Mercurius Civicus. 1644.

Mercurius Elencticus. 1648–49.

Mercurius Politicus. 1653–58.

Mercurius Publicus. 1660.

Military Orders, and Articles Established by his Majestie. 1643.

Milton, John. *The Works of John Milton.* Ed. Frank Allen Patterson, *et al.* 18 vols. New York: Columbia University Press, 1931–38.

   Complete Prose Works of John Milton. Ed. Don M. Wolfe, et al. 8 vols. New Haven: Yale University Press, 1953–82.

   John Milton: Complete Poems and Major Prose. Ed. Merritt Hughes. 1957. New York: Macmillan, 1985.

The Moderate Intelligencer. 1649.

A Modest Narrative of Intelligence. 1649.

Moore, John. *Protection Proclaimed . . . Wherein the Government Established, in the Lord Protector and his Council, Is proved to be of Divine Institution.* November 1655.

A More Exact Relation of the late Battell Neer York; Fought by the English and Scotch Forces, Against Prince Rupert. July 1644.

Mr. Recorders Speech to the Lord Protector, Upon Wednesday the eight of Febru. 1653, Being the day of His Highnesse Entertainment in London. February 1654.

Mundy, Peter. *The Travels of Peter Mundy in Europe and Asia, Vol.* v. Ed. Richard C. Temple and Lavinia Mary Anstey. London: The Hakluyt Society, 1936.

Musarum Cantabrigiensium Luctus & Gratulatio: Ille in Funere Oliveri Angliae, Scotiae, & Hiberniae Protectoris. 1658.

Nedham, Marchamont. *The Case of the Commonwealth of England, Stated.* Ed. Philip A. Knachel. Charlottesville: The University of Virginia Press, 1969.

   The Excellencie of a Free-State: or The Right Constitution of a Common- wealth. 1656.

A New Conference Between the Ghosts of King Charles and Oliver Cromwell. June 1659.

A New Meeting of Ghosts at Tyburn. Being a Discourse of Oliver Cromwell, John Bradshaw, Henry Ireton. March 1661.

The Nicholas Papers: Correspondence of Sir Edward Nicholas. Ed. George F. Warner. Vols. III, IV. London: Camden Society, 1892, 1920.

Nichols, John. *The Progresses, Processions, and Magnificent Festivities of King James the First.* 4 vols. London, 1828.

Oliver Cromwell the late great Tirant his Life-Guard; or, the Names of those who complied and conspired with him all along in his Horrid Designs. August 1660.

O. Cromwells Thankes to the Lord Generall, Faithfully presented by Hugh Peters in another Conference. May 1660.

On the Death of that Grand Imposter Oliver Cromwell. February 1661.

Ovatio Carolina. The Triumph of King Charles, or The Triumphant Manner and Order of Receiving His Majesty into His City of London . . . upon his safe and happy Return from Scotland. 1641.

The Oxford Character of the London Diurnall Examined and Answered. March 1645.

A Parly between the Ghosts of the Late Protector and the King of Sweden at their meeting in Hell. May 1660.

The Parliament Scout. 1644.

Pepys, Samuel. *The Diary of Samuel Pepys.* Ed. Robert Latham and William Matthews. 11 vols. Berkeley and Los Angeles: University of California Press, 1970–83.

The Perfect Diurnall. 1654.

A Perfect List of all the Victories Obtained by the Lord General Cromwell from the time that his Excellency was made Cap. Gen. and Commander in Chief . . . to this present time. October 1651.

A Perfect Table of One Hundred Forty and Five Victories Obtained by the Lord Lieutenant of Ireland and Parliaments Forces under his Command. August 1650.

Perrinchief, Richard. *The Syracusan Tyrant or the Life of Agathocles.* 1661.

Philipps, Fabian. *Veritas Inconcussa, Or, A most certain Truth asserted, That King Charles the First, Was no Man of Blood, But a Martyr For His People.* 1660.

Pocock, J. G. A. "James Harrington and the Good Old Cause: A Study of the Ideological Context of his Writings." *Journal of British Studies* 10 (1970).

The Pourtraiture of His Royal Highness, Oliver, Late Lord Protector &c in his Life and Death . . . As also a Description of his standing and lying in State at Sommerset-house, 1659.

Prestwich, Sir John. *Respublica.* London, 1787.

Price, Lawrence. *Great Britaines Time of Triumph; or, the Solid Subjects Observation Shewing in what a magnificent manner the Citizens of London entertained the Kings most excellent majestie.* 1641.

The Protector (So Called) In Part Unvailed: By whom the Mystery of Iniquity is now Working. October 1655.

Raine, J. R. *Depositions from the Castle of York.* London: Surtees Society, 1861.

The Right Picture of King Oliver from top to toe: That all the World may a false Rebell know. January 1650.

Roberts, Michael, ed. *Swedish Diplomats at Cromwell's Court, 1655–1656.* London: Camden Society, 1988.

Rogers, John. *Mene, Tekel, Perez: Or, A little Appearance of the Hand-Writing (In a Glance of Light) Against the Powers and Apostates of the Times. By a Letter written to, and lamenting over Oliver Lord Cromwel.* June 1654.

Rugge, Thomas. *The Diurnal of Thomas Rugg, 1659–1661.* Ed. William L. Sachse. Camden Third Series, Vol. 91. London, 1961.

Ryves, Bruno. *Mercurius Rusticus: or The Countries Complaint of the barbarous Outrages Committed by the Sectaries of this late flourishing Kingdome.* April 1646.

A Sad Sigh, with some Heart-Cracking Groanes sent after the Lord Governour and his whole Hoast of Mirmidons. 16 July 1649.

[Sadler, Anthony]. *The Subjects Joy for the Kings Restoration, Cheerfully made known in a Sacred Masque.* 1660.

A Second Narrative of the Late Parliament (so called). 1659.

The Second Part of Crafty Crumwell, or, Oliver in his Glory as King. A Trage Commedie. 1648.

Severall Proceedings of State Affaires. 1653.

[Sexby, Edmund, attrib.]. *Killing Noe Murder. Briefly Discoursed in Three Questions. By William Allen.* May 1657.

Slater, Samuel. *The Protectors Protection: Or, The Pious Prince guarded by a Praying People.* October 1658.

  A Rhetorical Rapture as Composed Into a Funeral Oration at the Mournfull Moving of His Highnes Stately Effigies from Somerset-House. 1658.

Some Farther Intelligence of the Affairs of England. 1658.

A Speech or Declaration of the Declared King of Scots . . . Also some Excellent Passages concerning the Lord Generall Cromwell, his Entertainment at Windsor Castle, and the Manner of his coming hence to London, the first of June 1650. June 1650.

The Speeches of Oliver Cromwell, Henry Ireton and John Bradshaw. Intended to have been spoken at their Execution at Tyburne, Jan. 30. 1660. But for many weightie Reasons omitted. February 1661.

Sprigge, Joshua. *Anglia Rediviva. Englands Recovery.* 1647. Ed. Harry T. Moore. Gainesville, Florida: Scholars' Facsimiles & Reprints, 1960.

[Streater, John.] *A Politick Commentary On the Life of Caius July Caesar, Written by Caius Suetonius Tranquilius.* May 1654.

[Streater, John.] *The Picture of a New Courtier drawn in a Conference between Mr. Timeserver and Mr. Plain-heart. In which is discovered the abhominable Practises and horrid Hypocrisies of the Usurper and his time-serving Parasites. By J. S.* April 1656.

Taylor, John. *A Living Sadnes, In Duty consecrated to the Immortal memory of our late Deceased albe-loved Soveraigne Lord . . . James.* 1625.

A Third Conference between O. Cromwell and Hugh Peters in Saint James's Park; Wherein the horrible Plot is Discovered about the barbarous Murder of our late Soveraign Lord King Charls the I. May 1660.

Three Poems Upon the Death of his late Highnesse Oliver Lord Protector of England, Scotland, and Ireland. Written by Mr. Edm. Waller, Mr. Jo. Dryden, Mr. Sprat, of Oxford. 1659.

Thurloe, John. *A Collection of the State Papers of John Thurloe . . . containing Authentic Memorials of the English Affairs from the year 1638, to the Restoration of King Charles II.* 7 vols. Ed. Thomas Birch. London, 1742.

To the King, upon his Majesties Happy Return. By a Person of honour. June 1660.

Trapnel, Anna. *The Cry of a Stone; or, A Relation of Something Spoken in Whitehall by Anna Trapnel, being in the Visions of God.* February 1654.

  Strange and Wonderful Newes from Whitehall, or The Mighty Visions Proceeding from Mistris Anna Trapnel. March 1654.

The Traytors Tragedy: or, Their great Plot and Treasonable Design Discovered. July 1660.

The True Manner of the most Magnificent Conveyance of his Highnesse Effigies from Sommerset House to Westminster. November 1658.

A True Relation of the Late Fight Between the Parliament Forces and Prince Rupert, Within Four Miles of Yorke. July 1644.

The Unparalleld Monarch. Or, The Portraiture of a Matchless Prince, exprest in some shadows of His Highness my Lord Protector. September 1656.

Verney, Frances Parthenope and Margaret Verney, eds. *Memoirs of the Verney Family During the Seventeenth Century*. 3 vols. London: Longmans, Green, & Co., 1892.

A Vindication of King Charles: Or, A Loyal Subjects Duty . . . Whereunto is added A True Parallel betwixt the sufferings of our Saviour and our Soveraign. November 1647.

W. S. *Epinicia Carolina, or an Essay Upon the Return of His Sacred Majesty Charles the Second*. June 1660.

Walker, Clement. *Anarchia Anglicana. The Second Part of The History of Independency*. 1649.

[Waller] *The Poems of Edmund Waller*. Ed. G. Thorn Drury. 2 vols. London: George Routledge & Sons, 1893.

Walpole, Horace, ed. *Anecdotes of Painting in England Collected by Mr. George Vertue*. 3 vols. London, 1743.

Walwyn, William. *God Save the King, or a Sermon of Thanksgiving For His Majesties Happy Return to his Throne. Together with a Character of His Sacred Person*. July 1660.

Watson, Richard. *The Panegyrike and The Storme. Two Poetike Libells by Ed. Waller Vassall To the Usurper Answered*. 1659.

[Waller] *The Weekly Post*. 1659.

Whitelocke, Bulstrode. *Memorials of the English Affairs*. 4 vols. Oxford, 1853.

Willes, Samuel. *To the Kings Most Sacred Majesty, Upon his Happy and Glorious Return*. June 1660.

Williams, Bishop John. *Great Britain's Salomon: A Sermon Preached at the Magnificent Funerall of the most high and mighty King, James*. London, 1625.

Winstanley, William. *England's Worthies. Select Lives of the most Eminent Persons from Constantine the Great, to the death of Oliver Cromwel, late Protector*. February 1660.

Wither, George. *Vaticinium Causuale. A Rapture Occasioned by the late Miraculous Deliverance of His Highness, the Lord Protector from a Desperate Danger*. October 1654.

   The Protector. A Poem Briefly illustrating the Supereminency of that Dignity. July 1655.

   A Suddain Flash Timely Discovering Some Reasons wherefore the stile of Protector should not be deserted by these Nations. October 1657.

   Salt upon Salt: Made out of certain Ingenious Verses Upon the Late Storm and the Death of his Highness Ensuing. 1658.

A Word to Lieut. Gen. Cromwel and Two Words For the Setling of the King, Parliament and Kingdom. December 1647.

Wordsworth, Christopher, ed., *The Manner of the Coronation of King Charles the First*. London: Harrison and Sons for the Henry Bradshaw Society, 1892.

The World in a Maize, Or, Olivers Ghost. May 1659.

SECONDARY SOURCES

Achinstein, Sharon. "Audiences and Authors: Ballads and the Making of English Renaissance Literary Culture." *Journal of Medieval and Renaissance Studies* 22.3 (1992), 311–26.

Milton and the Revolutionary Reader. Princeton University Press, 1994.

Adamson, J. S. A. "Oliver Cromwell and the Long Parliament." In *Oliver Cromwell and the English Revolution*, ed. John Morrill. London and New York: Longman, 1990, pp. 49–92.

Amussen, Susan D. and Mark A. Kishlansky, eds. *Political Culture and Cultural Politics in Early Modern England.* Manchester University Press, 1995.

Archer, Ian. *The Pursuit of Stability: Social Relations in Elizabethan London.* Cambridge University Press, 1991.

Armitage, David. "The Cromwellian Protectorate and the Languages of Empire." *The Historical Journal* 35.3 (1992), 531–55.

Armitage, David, Armand Himy, and Quentin Skinner, eds. *Milton and Republicanism.* Cambridge University Press, 1995.

Ashton, Robert. "Insurgency, Counter-Insurgency and Inaction: Three Phases in the Role of the City in the Great Rebellion." In *London and the Civil War*, ed. Stephen Porter. Basingstoke: Macmillan Press, 1996, pp. 45–64.

Aston, Margaret. *England's Iconoclasts: Volume I, Laws Against Images.* Oxford: Clarendon Press, 1988.

Aylmer, G. E. *The Levellers in the English Revolution.* London, 1975.

Rebellion or Revolution? England 1640–1660. New York: Oxford University Press, 1986.

Backscheider, Paula R. *Spectacular Politics: Theatrical Power and Mass Culture in Early Modern England.* Baltimore: The Johns Hopkins University Press, 1993.

Baker, C. H. Collins. *Lely and the Stuart Portrait Painters. A Study of English Portraiture Before and After Van Dyck.* 2 vols. London: Philip Lee Warner, 1912.

Bakhtin, Mikhail. *Rabelais and His World.* Trans. Helene Iswolsky. Cambridge, Mass.: MIT Press, 1968.

Barber, Sarah. *Regicide and Republicanism: Politics and Ethics in the English Revolution, 1646–1659.* Edinburgh University Press, 1998.

Barnard, Toby. *Cromwellian Ireland. English Government and Reform in Ireland, 1649–1660.* New York: Oxford University Press, 1975.

"Irish Images of Cromwell." In *Images of Oliver Cromwell: Essays for and by Roger Howell, Jr*, ed. R.C. Richardson. Manchester University Press, 1993, pp. 180–206.

Beaven, Alfred B. *The Aldermen of the City of London.* 2 vols. London: E. Fisher, 1908, 1913.

Belsey, Andrew and Catherine Belsey. "Icons of Divinity: Portraits of Elizabeth I." In *Renaissance Bodies: The Human Figure in English Culture c.1540–1660*, ed. Lucy Gent and Nigel Llewellyn. London: Reaktion Books, 1990, pp. 11–35.

Bergeron, David. *English Civic Pageantry, 1558–1642.* Columbia: University of South Carolina Press, 1971.

Breitenberg, Mark. "'. . . the hole matter opened': Iconic Representation and Interpretation in 'The Quenes Majesties Passage.'" *Criticism* 28 (1986), 1–25.

Brooks, Cleanth. "Marvell's *Horatian Ode*," *English Institute Essays 1946* (New York, 1947), pp. 127–58.

Brown, Christopher. *Van Dyck*. Oxford: Phaidon, 1982.

Burke, Peter. *The Fabrication of Louis XIV*. New Haven and London: Yale University Press, 1992.

Butler, Martin. *Theatre and Crisis 1632–1642*. Cambridge University Press, 1984.

    "Politics and the Masque: *Salmacida Spolia*." In *Literature and the English Civil War*, ed. Thomas Healy and Jonathan Sawday. Cambridge University Press, 1990, pp. 59–74.

    "Reform or Reverence? The Politics of the Caroline Masque." In *Theatre and Government Under the Early Stuarts*, ed. J. R. Mulryne and Margaret Shewring. Cambridge University Press, 1993, pp. 118–56.

Capp, Bernard S. *The Fifth Monarchy Men: A Study in Seventeenth-Century English Millenarianism*. Totowa, N.J.: Rowman and Littlefield, 1972.

Chartier, Roger. *The Cultural Uses of Print in Early Modern France*. Trans. Lydia G. Cochrane. Princeton University Press, 1987.

    ed. *The Culture of Print. Power and the Uses of Print in Early Modern Europe*. Trans. Lydia G. Cochrane. Princeton University Press, 1989.

    The Cultural Origins of the French Revolution. Trans. Lydia G. Cochrane. Durham, N.C.: Duke University Press, 1991.

Chernaik, Warren L. *The Poetry of Limitation: A Study of Edmund Waller*. New Haven: Yale University Press, 1968.

    The Poet's Time: Politics and Religion in the Work of Andrew Marvell. Cambridge University Press, 1983.

Clyde, William M. *The Struggle for the Freedom of the Press from Caxton to Cromwell*. London and New York: Oxford University Press, 1934.

Coiro, Ann Baynes. "Milton and Class Identity: The Publication of *Areopagitica* and the 1645 Poems." *Journal of Medieval and Renaissance Studies* 22.2 (1992), 261–89.

Corish, Patrick. "The Cromwellian Conquest, 1649–1653." In *A New History of Ireland*, ed. T. W. Moody, F. X. Martin, and F. J. Byrne. Vol. III, *Early Modern Ireland, 1534–1691*. New York: Oxford University Press, 1976, pp. 336–52.

    "The Cromwellian Regime, 1650–1660." In *A New History of Ireland*, ed. T. W. Moody, F. X. Martin, and F. J. Byrne. Vol. III, *Early Modern Ireland, 1534–1691*. New York: Oxford University Press, 1976, pp. 353–86.

Corns, Thomas N. *Uncloistered Virtue: English Political Literature, 1640–1660*. Oxford: Clarendon Press, 1992.

    ed. *The Royal Image: Representations of Charles I*. Cambridge University Press, 1999.

    "Duke, Prince and King." In *The Royal Image: Representations of Charles I*, ed. Corns. Cambridge University Press, 1999, pp. 1–25.

Cotton, A. N. B. "Cromwell and the Self-Denying Ordinance." *History* 62 (1977), 211–31.

Coward, Barry. "Was there an English Revolution in the Middle of the Seventeenth Century?" In *Politics and People in Revolutionary England: Essays in Honour of Ivan Roots*, ed. Colin Jones, Malyn Newitt, and Stephen Roberts. Oxford: Basil Blackwell, 1985, pp. 9–39.

    Oliver Cromwell. London and New York: Longman, 1991.

Cressy, David. *Literacy and the Social Order: Reading and Writing in Tudor and Stuart England.* Cambridge University Press, 1980.

  Bonfires and Bells: National Memory and the Protestant Calendar in Elizabethan and Stuart England. Berkeley and Los Angeles: University of California, 1989.

Cumming, Valerie. "'Great vanity and excesse in Apparell': Some Clothing and Furs of Tudor and Stuart Royalty." In *The Late King's Goods: Collections, Possessions and Patronage of Charles I in the Light of the Commonwealth Sale Inventories,* ed. Arthur MacGregor. London and Oxford: Alistair McAlpine in association with Oxford University Press, 1989, pp. 322–50.

Cust, Richard. "News and Politics in Early Seventeenth-Century England." *Past and Present* 112 (1986), 60–90.

Cust, Richard and Ann Hughes, eds. *Conflict in Early Stuart England: Studies in Religion and Politics, 1603–1642.* London and New York: Longman, 1989.

Darnton, Robert. "History of Reading." In *New Perspectives on Historical Writing,* ed. Peter Burke. Cambridge University Press, 1991, pp. 140–67.

Davies, Godfrey. *The Restoration of Charles II, 1658–1660.* San Marino: Huntington Library, 1955.

Davis, J. C. "Cromwell's Religion." In *Oliver Cromwell and the English Revolution,* ed. John Morrill. London and New York: Longman, 1990, pp. 181–208.

Davis, Natalie Zemon. *Society and Culture in Early Modern France.* Stanford University Press, 1975.

Donnelly, M. L. "Caroline Royalist Panegyric and the Disintegration of a Symbolic Mode." In *"The Muses Common-Weale": Poetry and Politics in the Seventeenth Century,* ed. Claude J. Summers and Ted-Larry Pebworth. Columbia: University of Missouri Press, 1988, pp. 163–76.

  "'And still new stopps to various time apply'd': Marvell, Cromwell, and the Problem of Representation at Midcentury." In *On the Celebrated and Neglected Poems of Andrew Marvell,* ed. Claude J. Summers and Ted-Larry Pebworth. Columbia: University of Missouri Press, 1992, pp. 154–68.

Dow, F. D. *Cromwellian Scotland, 1651–1660.* Edinburgh: John Donald Publishers, 1979.

Dunbabin, J. P. D. "Oliver Cromwell's Popular Image in Nineteenth-Century England." In *Britain and the Netherlands,* ed. J. S. Bromley and E. H. Kossman. The Hague: Martinus Nijhoff, 1975, pp. 141–63.

Dzelzainis, Martin. "Milton's Classical Republicanism." In *Milton and Republicanism,* ed. David Armitage, Armand Himy, and Quentin Skinner. Cambridge University Press, 1995, pp. 3–24.

Eimer, Christopher. *An Introduction to Commemorative Medals.* London: B. A. Seaby, 1989.

Eisenstein, Elizabeth L. *The Printing Press as an Agent of Change: Communications and Cultural Transformations in Early-Modern Europe.* 2 vols. Cambridge University Press, 1979.

Erskine-Hill, Howard. *The Augustan Idea in English Literature.* London: Edward Arnold, 1983.

Everett, Barbara. "The Shooting of the Bears: Poetry and Politics in Andrew Marvell." In *Andrew Marvell: Essays on the Tercentenary of his Death,* ed. R. L. Brett. New York: Oxford University Press, 1979, pp. 62–103.

Fallon, Robert. *Milton in Government*. University Park: The Pennsylvania State University Press, 1993.

Feather, John. *A History of British Publishing*. London and New York: Croom Helm, 1988.

Febvre, Lucien and Henri-Jean Martin. *The Coming of the Book: The Impact of Printing 1450–1800*. 1958. Trans. David Gerard. London: Verso, 1976.

Firth, C. H. "The Court of Oliver Cromwell." *The Cornhill Magazine* n.s. Vol. III (September 1897), 349–64.

"Marston Moor," *Transactions of the Royal Historical Society*, n.s. VI (1899).

Oliver Cromwell and the Rule of the Puritans in England. London: Putnam, 1901.

"Cromwell and the Crown." *The English Historical Review* 17 (1902), 429–42 and 18 (1903), 52–80.

The Last Years of the Protectorate. 2 vols. 1909. New York: Russell & Russell, Inc., 1964.

Fish, Stanley. *Self-Consuming Artifacts: The Experience of Seventeenth-Century Literature*. Berkeley and Los Angeles: University of California Press, 1972.

Fletcher, Anthony. *The Outbreak of the English Civil War*. New York and London: New York University Press, 1981.

"Oliver Cromwell and the Localities: The Problem of Consent." In *Politics and People in Revolutionary England*, ed. C. Jones, M. Newitt, and S. Roberts. Oxford: Basil Blackwell, 1986, pp. 187–204.

"Oliver Cromwell and the Godly Nation." In *Oliver Cromwell and the English Revolution*, ed. John Morrill. London and New York: Longman, 1990, pp. 209–33.

Ford, Wyn. "The Problem of Literacy in Early Modern England." *History* 78 (1993), 22–37.

Foskett, Daphne. *Samuel Cooper, 1609–1672*. London: Faber & Faber, 1974.

Frank, Joseph. *The Beginnings of the English Newspaper, 1620–1660*. Cambridge, Mass.: Harvard University Press, 1961.

Fraser, Antonia. *Cromwell, The Lord Protector*. New York: Knopf, 1973.

Freist, Dagmar. *Governed by Opinion: Politics, Religion and the Dynamics of Communication in Stuart London, 1637–1645*. London and New York: Tauris Academic Studies, 1997.

Fritz, Paul S. "From 'Public' to 'Private': The Royal Funerals in England, 1500–1830." In *Mirrors of Mortality: Studies in the Social History of Death*, ed. Joachim Whaley. London: Europa Publications, 1981, pp. 61–79.

Frye, Susan. *Elizabeth I: The Competition for Representation*. New York: Oxford University Press, 1993.

Gaunt, Peter. *Oliver Cromwell*. Oxford: Blackwell, 1996.

Gaunt, William. *Court Painting in England from Tudor to Victorian Times*. London: Constable, 1980.

Geertz, Clifford. "Centers, Kings, and Charisma: Reflections on the Symbolics of Power." In Geertz, *Local Knowledge: Further Essays in Interpretive Anthropology*. New York: Basic Books, 1983, pp. 121–46.

Gentles, Ian. *The New Model Army in England, Ireland and Scotland, 1645–1653*. Oxford: Blackwell, 1992.

Gittings, Clare. *Death, Burial, and the Individual in Early Modern England*. London and Sydney: Croom Helm, 1984.

Globe, Alexander. *Peter Stent: London Printseller circa 1642–1665*. Vancouver: University of British Columbia Press, 1985.

Goldberg, Jonathan. *James I and the Politics of Literature*. Baltimore and London: The Johns Hopkins University Press, 1983.

Goldie, Mark, Tim Harris, and Paul Seaward, eds. *The Politics of Religion in Restoration England*. Oxford: Clarendon Press, 1990.

Greaves, Richard L. *Deliver Us From Evil: The Radical Underground in Britain, 1660–1663*. New York: Oxford University Press, 1986.

　Enemies Under his Feet: Radicals and Nonconformists in Britain, 1664–1677. Stanford University Press, 1990.

Greenberg, Stephen J. "Dating Civil War Pamphlets, 1641–1644." *Albion* 20.3 (1988), 387–401.

　"The Thomason Collection: Rebuttal to Michael Mendle." *Albion* 22.1 (1990), 95–98.

Guibbory, Achsah. *Ceremony and Community from Herbert to Milton: Literature, Religion and Cultural Conflict in Seventeenth-Century England*. Cambridge University Press, 1998.

Habermas, Jürgen. *The Structural Transformation of the Public Sphere: An Inquiry into a Category of Bourgeois Society*. Trans. Thomas Burger. Cambridge, Mass.: The MIT Press, 1989.

Hammond, Paul. *John Dryden: A Literary Life*. Basingstoke: Macmillan, 1991.

　"The King's Two Bodies: Representations of Charles II." In *Culture, Politics, and Society in Britain, 1660–1800*, ed. Jeremy Black and Jeremy Gregory. Manchester and New York: Manchester University Press, 1991, pp. 13–48.

Harpham, Geoffrey Galt. *On the Grotesque: Strategies of Contradiction in Art and Literature*. Princeton University Press, 1982.

Harris, Tim. *Politics under the Later Stuarts: Party Conflict in a Divided Society 1660–1715*. London and New York: Longman, 1993.

Healy, Thomas and Jonathan Sawday, eds. *Literature and the English Civil War*. Cambridge University Press, 1990.

Helgerson, Richard. "Milton Reads the King's Book: Print, Performance, and the Making of a Bourgeois Idol." *Criticism* 29.1 (1987), 1–26.

Hill, Christopher. *God's Englishman: Oliver Cromwell and the English Revolution*. Harmondsworth: Penguin, 1970.

　Some Intellectual Consequences of the English Revolution. Madison: University of Wisconsin Press, 1980.

　"Censorship and English Literature." In *The Collected Essays of Christopher Hill, Vol. I: Writing and Revolution in Seventeenth-Century England*. Brighton: Harvester Press, Ltd., 1985, pp. 32–71.

　"George Wither and John Milton." In *The Collected Essays of Christopher Hill, Vol. I: Writing and Revolution in Seventeenth-Century England*. Brighton: Harvester Press, Ltd., 1985, pp. 135–56.

Hirst, Derek. "'That Sober Liberty': Marvell's Cromwell in 1654." In *The Golden & the Brazen World: Papers in Literature and History*, ed. John M. Wallace. Berkeley and Los Angeles: University of California Press, 1985, pp. 17–53.

　Authority and Conflict: England 1603–1658. London: Edward Arnold, 1986.

"The Lord Protector, 1653–1658." In *Oliver Cromwell and the English Revolution*, ed. John Morrill. London and New York: Longman, 1990, pp. 119–48.

"Locating the 1650s in England's Seventeenth Century." *History* 81 (1996), 359–83.

Holmes, Clive. *The Eastern Association in the English Civil War*. Cambridge University Press, 1974.

Holstun, James. "Ehud's Dagger: Patronage, Tyrannicide, and *Killing No Murder*," *Cultural Critique* 22 (1992), 99–142.

Honigmann, E. A. J. *Milton's Sonnets*. London: Macmillan, 1966.

Hope, W. H. St. John. "On the Funeral Effigies of the Kings and Queens of England, with special reference to those in the Abbey Church of Westminster." *Archaeologia*, vol. LX (1907), 517–70.

Howarth, David, ed. *Art and Patronage in the Caroline Courts: Essays in Honour of Sir Oliver Millar*. Cambridge University Press, 1993.

Images of Rule: Art and Politics in the English Renaissance, 1485–1649. Berkeley and Los Angeles: University of California Press, 1997.

Howell, Roger, Jr. "'That Imp of Satan': The Restoration Image of Cromwell." In *Images of Oliver Cromwell: Essays for and by Roger Howell, Jr.*, ed. R. C. Richardson. Manchester University Press, 1993, pp. 33–47.

Huemer, Frances. *Corpus Rubenianum Ludwig Burchard*. Part XIX, I, Portraits. London: Harvey Miller, 1977.

Hughes, Ann. *The Causes of the English Civil War*. New York: St. Martin's Press, 1991.

Hutton, Ronald. *The Restoration: A Political and Religious History of England and Wales, 1658–1667*. Oxford: Clarendon Press, 1985.

The British Republic, 1649–1660. New York: St. Martin's Press, 1990.

Jaffé, Michael. "*The Standard Bearer*: Van Dyck's Portrayal of Sir Edmund Verney." In *Art and Patronage in the Caroline Courts: Essays in Honour of Sir Oliver Millar*, ed. David Howarth, pp. 90–106. Cambridge University Press, 1993.

Johnson, Vivienne Stevens. "Images of Power: Oliver Cromwell in Seventeenth Century Writings." Duke University D. Phil thesis, 1990.

Jones, J. R., ed. *The Restored Monarchy, 1660–1688*. London: Macmillan, 1979.

Kahn, Victoria. *Machiavellian Rhetoric: From the Counter-Reformation to Milton*. Princeton University Press, 1994.

Kantorowicz, Ernst H. *The King's Two Bodies: A Study in Mediaeval Political Theology*. Princeton University Press, 1957.

Kayser, Wolfgang. *The Grotesque in Art and Literature*. Trans. Ulrich Weisstein. Bloomington: Indiana University Press, 1963.

Keeble, N. H. *The Literary Culture of Nonconformity in Later Seventeenth-Century England*. Leicester University Press, 1987.

"'The Colonel's Shadow': Lucy Hutchinson, Women's Writing and the Civil War." In *Literature and the English Civil War*, ed. Thomas Healy and Jonathan Sawday. Cambridge University Press, 1990, pp. 227–47.

Kelsey, Sean. *Inventing a Republic: The Political Culture of the English Commonwealth, 1649–1653*. Manchester University Press, 1997.

King, John. *Tudor Royal Iconography: Literature and Art in an Age of Religious Crisis*. Princeton University Press, 1989.

Knoppers, Laura Lunger. *Historicizing Milton: Spectacle, Power, and Poetry in Restoration England*. Athens, Georgia: University of Georgia Press, 1994.

"The Politics of Portraiture: Oliver Cromwell and the Plain Style." *Renaissance Quarterly* 51.4 (1998), 1283–1319.

"Noll's Nose or Body Politics in Cromwellian England." In *Form and Reform in Renaissance England: Essays in Honor of Barbara Kiefer Lewalski*, ed. Amy Boesky and Mary Crane. Newark: University of Delaware Press.

"'Sing old Noll the Brewer': Royalist Satire and Social Inversion," *The Seventeenth Century*, forthcoming.

Lambert, Sheila. "The Beginning of Printing for the House of Commons, 1640–42." *The Library* 3 (1981), 43–61.

Laqueur, Thomas W. "Crowds, Carnival and the State in English Executions, 1604–1868." In *The First Modern Society: Essays in English History in Honour of Lawrence Stone*, ed. A. L. Beier, David Cannadine and James M. Rosenheim. Cambridge University Press, 1989, pp. 305–55.

Lawson, Bruce. "'A King He Seems, and Something More': Providentialism and Machiavellianism in the Poetry, Prose, and Pulpit Oratory about Oliver Cromwell." University of Southern California D. Phil. Thesis, 1988.

"Fortuna as Political Image in Three Poems on Cromwell." *American Notes & Queries* 7 (1994), 68–71.

Legg, L. G. Wickham. *English Coronation Records*. New York: E. P. Dutton & Company, 1901.

Levick, Barbara. *Tiberius the Politician*. London: Thames and Hudson, 1976.

Lewalski, Barbara K. "Milton: Political Beliefs and Polemical Methods." *PMLA* 74 (1959), 191–202.

Lightbown, Ronald. "Charles I and the Tradition of European Princely Collecting." In *The Late King's Goods: Collections, Possessions and Patronage of Charles I in the Light of the Commonwealth Sale Inventories*, ed. Arthur MacGregor. London and Oxford: Alistair McAlpine in association with Oxford University Press, 1989, pp. 53–72.

"The King's Regalia, Insignia and Jewellery." In *The Late King's Goods: Collections, Possessions and Patronage of Charles I in the Light of the Commonwealth Sale Inventories*, ed. Arthur MacGregor. London and Oxford: Alistair McAlpine in association with Oxford University Press, 1989, pp. 257–73.

Llewellyn, Nigel. "The Royal Body: Monuments to the Dead, For the Living." In *Renaissance Bodies: The Human Figure in English Culture c.1540–1660*, ed. Lucy Gent and Nigel Llewellyn. London: Reaktion Books, 1990, pp. 218–40.

Loewenstein, David. *Milton and the Drama of History: Historical Vision, Iconoclasm, and the Literary Imagination*. Cambridge University Press, 1990.

"Milton and the Poetics of Defense." In *Politics, Poetics, and Hermeneutics in Milton's Prose*, ed. David Loewenstein and James Grantham Turner. Cambridge University Press, 1990, pp. 171–92.

Representing Revolution in Milton and his Contemporaries; Literature, Rebellion, and the Politics of Radical Puritanism. Cambridge University Press, forthcoming.

Loewenstein, Joseph. "The Script in the Marketplace." *Representations* 12 (1985), 101–14.

Love, Harold. *Scribal Publication in Seventeenth-Century England*. Oxford: Clarendon Press, 1993.

Loxley, James. *Royalism and Poetry in the English Civil Wars*. Basingstoke and London: Macmillan Press, 1997.

MacCormack, Sabine G. *Art and Ceremony in Late Antiquity*. Berkeley and Los Angeles: University of California Press, 1981.

McCoy, Richard C. "'Thou Idol Ceremony': Elizabeth I, *The Henriad*, and the Rites of the English Monarchy." In *Urban Life in the Renaissance*, ed. Susan Zimmerman and Ronald F. E. Weissman. Newark: University of Delaware Press, 1989, pp. 240–66.

 "'The Wonderfull Spectacle': The Civic Progress of Elizabeth I and the Troublesome Coronation." In *Coronations: Medieval and Early Modern Monarchic Ritual*, ed. Janos M. Bak. Berkeley and Los Angeles: University of California Press, 1990, pp. 217–27.

MacGregor, Arthur. "King Charles I: A Renaissance Collector?" *The Seventeenth Century* 11.2 (1996), 141–60.

McKnight, Laura Blair. "Crucifixion or Apocalypse? Refiguring the *Eikon Basilike*." In *Religion, Literature, and Politics in Post-Reformation England, 1540–1688*, ed. Donna B. Hamilton and Richard Strier. Cambridge University Press, 1996, pp. 138–60.

MacLean, Gerald M. *Time's Witness: Historical Representation in English Poetry, 1603–1660*. Madison: University of Wisconsin Press, 1990.

 ed. *Culture and Society in the Stuart Restoration: Literature, Drama, History*. Cambridge University Press, 1995.

Maguire, Nancy Klein. "The Theatrical Mask / Masque of Politics: The Case of Charles I." *Journal of British Studies* 28 (1989), 1–22.

 Regicide and Restoration: English Tragicomedy, 1660–1671. Cambridge University Press, 1992.

Marotti, Arthur F. *Manuscript, Print, and the English Renaissance Lyric*. Ithaca, N.Y.: Cornell University Press, 1995.

Mazzeo, Joseph Anthony. "Cromwell as Davidic King." In his *Renaissance and Seventeenth- Century Studies*. New York: Columbia University Press, 1964, pp. 183–208.

 "Cromwell as Machiavellian Prince in Marvell's 'Horatian Ode.'" In his *Renaissance and Seventeenth-Century Studies*. New York: Columbia University Press, 1964, pp. 166–82.

Mendle, Michael. "The Thomason Collection: A Reply to Stephen J. Greenberg." *Albion* 22.1 (1990), 85–93.

Merritt, J. F., ed. *The Political World of Thomas Wentworth, Earl of Strafford, 1621–1641*. Cambridge University Press, 1996.

Metcalfe, Jean LeDrew. "The Politics of Panegyric: Poetic Representations of Oliver Cromwell." *Restoration* 18 (1994), 1–16.

Millar, Sir Oliver. *Sir Peter Lely 1618–80*. London: National Portrait Gallery, 1978.

 Van Dyck in England. London: National Portrait Gallery, 1982.

Moretti, Franco. "'A Huge Eclipse': Tragic Form and the Deconsecration of Sovereignty." In *The Power of Forms in the English Renaissance*, ed. Stephen Greenblatt. Norman, Okla.: Pilgrim Books, 1982, pp. 7–40.

Morrill, John. "Cromwell and his Contemporaries." In *Oliver Cromwell and the English Revolution*, ed. John Morrill. London and New York, Longman, 1990, pp. 259–81.

"The Making of Oliver Cromwell." In *Oliver Cromwell and the English Revolution*, ed. John Morrill. London and New York, Longman, 1990, pp. 19–48.

ed. *Oliver Cromwell and the English Revolution*. London and New York: Longman, 1990.

"Textualizing and Contextualizing Cromwell" *The Historical Journal* 33.3 (1990), 629–39.

ed. *Revolution and Restoration: England in the 1650s*. London: Collins & Brown, 1992.

The Nature of the English Revolution. London and New York: Longman, 1993.

Mowl, Timothy and Brian Earnshaw. *Architecture without Kings: The Rise of Puritan Classicism Under Cromwell*. Manchester University Press, 1995.

Mullaney, Steven. *The Place of the Stage: License, Play, and Power in Renaissance England*. University of Chicago Press, 1988.

Nardo, Anna K. *Milton's Sonnets and the Ideal Community*. Lincoln: University of Nebraska Press, 1979.

Nevo, Ruth. *The Dial of Virtue: A Study of Poems on Affairs of State in the Seventeenth Century*. Princeton University Press, 1963.

Norbrook, David. "Marvell's 'Horatian Ode' and the Politics of Genre." In *Literature and the English Civil War*, ed. Thomas Healy and Jonathan Sawday. Cambridge University Press, 1990, pp. 147–69.

"*Areopagitica*, Censorship, and the Early Modern Public Sphere." In *The Administration of Aesthetics: Censorship, Political Criticism, and the Public Sphere*, ed. Richard Burt. Minneapolis and London: University of Minnesota Press, 1994, pp. 3–33.

"Lucan, Thomas May, and the Creation of a Republican Literary Culture." In *Culture and Politics in Early Stuart England*, ed. Kevin Sharpe and Peter Lake. Stanford University Press, 1994, pp. 45–66.

"'Safest in Storms': George Wither in the 1650s." In *Heart of the Heartless World: Essays in Cultural Resistance in Memory of Margot Heinemann*, ed. David Margolies and Maroula Joannou. London and Boulder: Pluto Press, 1995, pp. 19–32.

"Lucy Hutchinson versus Edmund Waller; An Unpublished Reply to Waller's *A Panegyrick to my Lord Protector*." *The Seventeenth Century*, 11.1 (1996), 61–86.

"The Emperor's New Body?: *Richard II*, Ernst Kantorowicz, and the Politics of Shakespeare Criticism." *Textual Practice* 10.2 (1996), 329–57.

Writing the English Republic: Poetry, Rhetoric and Politics, 1627–1660. Cambridge University Press, 1998.

Nuttall, Geoffrey. "Was Cromwell an Iconoclast?" *Transactions of the Congregational Historical Society*, ed. Albert Peel, 12 (1933–36), 51–66.

Ogg, David. *England in the Reign of Charles II*. 2nd ed. 2 vols. London: Oxford University Press, 1963.

Orgel, Stephen. *The Illusion of Power: Political Theater in the English Renaissance*. Berkeley and Los Angeles: University of California Press, 1975.

Parry, Graham. *The Golden Age Restor'd: the Culture of the Stuart Court, 1603–1642*. Manchester University Press, 1981.

Patterson, Annabel M. *Marvell and the Civic Crown*. Princeton University Press, 1978.

Censorship and Interpretation: The Conditions of Writing and Reading in Early Modern England. Madison: University of Wisconsin Press, 1984.

Peacock, John. "Inigo Jones' Catafalque for James I." *Architectural History* 25 (1982), 1–5.
   "The Visual Image of Charles I." In *The Royal Image: Representations of Charles I*, ed. Thomas Corns, Cambridge University Press, 1999, pp. 176–239.

Pearl, Valerie. *London and the Outbreak of the Puritan Revolution*. London: Oxford University Press, 1961.

Pincus, Steven. "'Coffee Politicians Does Create': Coffeehouses and Restoration Political Culture." *The Journal of Modern History* 67 (1995), 807–34.
   Protestantism and Patriotism: Ideologies and the Making of English Foreign Policy, 1650–1668. Cambridge University Press, 1996.

Piper, David. "The Contemporary Portraits of Oliver Cromwell." *Walpole Society* 34 (1958), 27–41.

Pocock, J. G. A. *The Machiavellian Moment: Florentine Political Thought and the Atlantic Republican Tradition*. Princeton University Press, 1975.
   "James Harrington and the Good Old Cause: a Study of the Ideological Context of his Writings." *Journal of British Studies* 10 (1970), 30–48.

Pooley, Roger. "The Poets' Cromwell." *Critical Survey* 5.3 (1993), 222–34.

Potter, Lois. *Secret Rites and Secret Writing: Royalist Literature, 1641–1660*. Cambridge University Press, 1989.

Raab, Felix. *The English Face of Machiavelli: A Changing Interpretation, 1500–1700*. London: Routledge & Kegan Paul, 1964.

Randall, Dale B. J. *Winter Fruit: English Drama 1642–1660*. Lexington: The University Press of Kentucky, 1995.

Raven, James, Helen Small, and Naomi Tadmor, eds. *The Practice and Representation of Reading in England*. Cambridge University Press, 1990.

Raymond, Joad, ed. *Making the News: An Anthology of the Newsbooks of Revolutionary England, 1641–1660*. New York: St. Martin's Press, 1993.
   "The Daily Muse; Or, Seventeenth-Century Poets Read the News." *The Seventeenth Century* 10.2 (1995), 189–218.
   The Invention of the Newspaper: English Newsbooks, 1641–1649. Oxford: Clarendon Press, 1996.
   "An Eyewitness to King Cromwell." *History Today* 47 (1997): 35–41.
   "John Streater and *The Grand Politick Informer*." *The Historical Journal* 41.2 (1998), 567–74.
   "Popular Representations of Charles I." In *The Royal Image: Representations of Charles I*, ed. Thomas Corns, Cambridge University Press, 1999, pp. 47–73.

Richards, Judith. "'His Nowe Majestie' and the English Monarchy: The Kingship of Charles I Before 1640." *Past and Present* 113 (1986), 70–96.

Richardson, R. C., ed. *Images of Oliver Cromwell: Essays for and by Roger Howell, Jr.* Manchester University Press, 1993.

Robertson, J. C. "Caroline Culture: Bridging Court and Country?" *History* 75 (1990), 388–416.

Rogers, P. G. *The Fifth Monarchy Men*. London and New York: Oxford University Press, 1966.

Rollins, Hyder. "The Black-letter Broadside Ballad." *PMLA* 34 (1919), 258–339.

Roots, Ivan. *Commonwealth and Protectorate: The English Civil War and its Aftermath*. New York: Schocken Books, 1966.

Russell, Conrad, ed. *The Origins of the English Civil War*. New York: Barnes & Noble, 1973.

    The Causes of the English Civil War. Oxford: Clarendon Press, 1990.

Sawday, Jonathan. "Re-Writing a Revolution: History, Symbol, and Text in the Restoration." *The Seventeenth Century*. 7.2 (1992), 171–99.

Schramm, Percy Ernst. *A History of the English Coronation*. Trans. L. G. W. Legg. Oxford: Clarendon Press, 1937.

Scott, Jonathan. *Algernon Sidney and the English Republic*. Cambridge University Press, 1988.

Seymour, Michael. "Pro-Government Propaganda in Interregnum England, 1649–1660." University of Cambridge D. Phil. Thesis, 1986.

Sharpe, J. A. "'Last Dying Speeches': Religion, Ideology and Public Execution in Seventeenth-Century England." *Past and Present* 107 (1985), 144–67.

Sharpe, Kevin. *Criticism and Compliment: The Politics of Literature in the England of Charles I*. Cambridge University Press, 1987.

    Politics and Ideas in Early Stuart England: Essays and Studies. London and New York: Pinter Publishers, 1989.

    The Personal Rule of Charles I. New Haven and London: Yale University Press, 1992.

    "'An Image Doting Rabble': The Failure of Republican Culture in Seventeenth-Century England." In *Refiguring Revolutions: Aesthetics and Politics from the English Revolution to the Romantic Revolution*, ed. Kevin Sharpe and Steven N. Zwicker. Berkeley and Los Angeles: University of California Press, 1998, pp. 25–56.

Sharpe, Kevin and Peter Lake, eds. *Culture and Politics in Early Stuart England*. Stanford University Press, 1994.

Sherwood, Roy. *The Court of Oliver Cromwell*. London: Croom Helm Ltd, 1977.

    Oliver Cromwell: King In All But Name, 1653–1658. New York: St. Martin's Press, 1997.

Siebert, Frederick S. *Freedom of the Press in England, 1476–1776*. Urbana: University of Illinois Press, 1952.

Skerpan, Elizabeth. *The Rhetoric of Politics in the English Revolution, 1642–1660*. Columbia: University of Missouri Press, 1992.

Skerpan Wheeler, Elizabeth. "*Eikon Basilike* and the Rhetoric of Self-Representation." In *The Royal Image: Representations of Charles I*, ed. Thomas Corns, Cambridge University Press, 1999, pp. 122–140.

Smith, Alan. "The Image of Cromwell in Folklore and Tradition." *Folklore* 79 (1968), 17–39.

Smith, David. *Oliver Cromwell: Politics and Religion in the English Revolution, 1640–1658*. Cambridge University Press, 1991.

Smith, Nigel. *Perfection Proclaimed: Language and Literature in English Radical Religion, 1640–1660*. Oxford: Clarendon Press, 1989.

    Literature and Revolution in England, 1640–1660. New Haven and London: Yale University Press, 1994.

    "Popular Republicanism in the 1650s: John Streater's 'Heroic Mechanicks.'" In *Milton and Republicanism*, ed. David Armitage, Armand Himy, and Quentin Skinner. Cambridge University Press, 1995, pp. 137–55.

Smuts, Malcolm. *Court Culture and the Origins of a Royalist Tradition in Early Stuart England*. Philadelphia: University of Pennsylvania Press, 1987.

"Public Ceremony and Royal Charisma: The English Royal Entry in London, 1485–1642." In *The First Modern Society: Essays in English History in Honour of Lawrence Stone*, ed. A. L. Beier, David Cannadine, and James M. Rosenheim. Cambridge University Press, 1989, pp. 65–94.

Sommerville, C. John. *The News Revolution in England: Cultural Dynamics of Daily Information*. New York: Oxford University Press, 1996.

Spalding, Ruth, ed. *The Diary of Bulstrode Whitelocke, 1605–1675*. Oxford University Press for British Academy, 1990.

Spencer, Lois. "The Professional and Literary Connections of George Thomason." *The Library* 13 (1958), 102–18.

"The Politics of George Thomason." *The Library* 14 (1959), 11–27.

Spufford, Margaret. *Small Books and Pleasant Histories: Popular Fiction and its Readership in Seventeenth-Century England*. London: Methuen, 1981.

Stallybrass, Peter and Allon White. *The Politics and Poetics of Transgression*. Ithaca: Cornell University Press, 1986.

Stevenson, David. "Cromwell, Scotland and Ireland." In *Oliver Cromwell and the English Revolution*, ed. John Morrill. London and New York, Longman, 1990, pp. 149–80.

Strong, Roy. *The English Icon: Elizabethan and Jacobean Portraiture*. London: Routledge & Kegan Paul, 1969.

Van Dyck: Charles I on Horseback. New York: Viking Press, 1972.

Thomas, Keith. "The Meaning of Literacy in Early Modern England." In *The Written Word: Literacy in Transition*, ed. G. Baumann. Oxford: Clarendon Press, 1986, pp. 97–131.

Unwin, George. *The Gilds and Companies of London*. London: Frank Cass & Company, Ltd, 1963.

Varley, Frederick John. *Oliver Cromwell's Latter End*. London: Chapman & Hall, 1939.

Venning, Timothy. *Cromwellian Foreign Policy*. New York: St. Martin's Press, 1995.

Versnel, H. S. *Triumphus*. Leiden: Brill, 1970.

Wall, Wendy. *The Imprint of Gender: Authorship and Publication in the English Renaissance*. Ithaca: Cornell University Press, 1993.

Wallace, John. "Marvell's 'lusty Mate' and the Ship of the Commonwealth." *Modern Language Notes* 76 (1961), 106–10.

Waterhouse, Ellis. *Painting in Britain, 1530–1790*. Harmondsworth: Penguin, 1964.

Watt, Tessa. *Cheap Print and Popular Piety, 1550–1640*. Cambridge University Press, 1991.

Weber, Harold M. *Paper Bullets: Print and Kingship under Charles II*. Lexington: University Press of Kentucky, 1996.

Wedgwood, C. V. *The Trial of Charles I*. London, Collins, 1964.

Wethey, Harold. *The Paintings of Titian*. 3 vols. London: Phaidon, 1969–75.

Wheelock, Arthur, Jr., Susan J. Barnes, and Julius Held, eds. *Anthony van Dyck*. New York: Harry N. Abrams, 1990.

Whinney, Margaret and Oliver Millar. *English Art, 1625–1714*. In *Oxford History of English Art*, ed. T. S. P. Boase. Oxford: Clarendon Press, 1957.

Whitelocke, Bulstore. *Diary of Bulstrode Whitelocke, 1605–1671*. Ed. Ruth Spalding. Oxford University Press, 1990.

Wilding, Michael. *Dragon's Teeth: Literature in the English Revolution*. Oxford: Clarendon Press, 1987.

Wilson, A. J. N. "Andrew Marvell's 'The First Anniversary of the Government under Oliver Cromwell': The Poem and its Frame of Reference," *The Modern Language Review* 69 (1974), 254–73.

Winn, James Anderson. *John Dryden and his World*. New Haven: Yale University Press, 1987.

Wiseman, Susan. *Drama and Politics in the English Civil War*. Cambridge University Press, 1998.

Woodward, Jennifer. *The Theatre of Death: The Ritual Management of Royal Funerals in Renaissance England 1570–1625*. Woodbridge, Suffolk: Boydell Press, 1997.

Woolrych, Austin. "Milton and Cromwell: 'A Short but Scandalous Night of Interruption?'" In *Achievements of the Left Hand: Essays on the Prose of John Milton*, ed. Michael Lieb and John Shawcross, pp. 185–218. Amherst: University of Massachusetts Press, 1974.

"Introduction." *Prose Works of John Milton*, vol. VII. Ed. R. W. Ayres, gen. ed. Don Wolfe. New Haven: Yale University Press, 1982.

Commonwealth to Protectorate. Oxford: Clarendon Press, 1982.

"The Cromwellian Protectorate: A Military Dictatorship?" *History* 75 (1990), 207–31.

England Without a King, 1649–1660. London and New York: Routledge, 1983.

Worden, Blair. *The Rump Parliament, 1648–1653*. Cambridge University Press, 1974.

"Toleration and the Cromwellian Protectorate." In *Persecution and Toleration: Studies in Church History 21*, ed. W. J. Sheils. Oxford: Basil Blackwell, 1984, pp. 199–233.

"Oliver Cromwell and the Sin of Achan." In *History, Society and the Churches: Essays in Honour of Owen Chadwick*, ed. Derek Beales and Geoffrey Best. Cambridge University Press, 1985, pp. 125–45.

"Providence and Politics in Cromwellian England." *Past and Present* 109 (1985), 55–99.

"Andrew Marvell, Oliver Cromwell, and the Horatian Ode." In *Politics of Discourse: The Literature and History of Seventeenth-Century England*, ed. Kevin Sharpe and Steven N. Zwicker. Berkeley and Los Angeles: University of California Press, 1987, pp. 147–80.

"Literature and Political Censorship in Early Modern England." In *Too Mighty to be Free: Censorship and the Press in Britain and the Netherlands*, ed. A. C. Duke and C. A. Tamse. Zutphen: De Walburg Pers, 1987, pp. 45–62.

"Review Article: The 'Diary' of Bulstrode Whitelocke." *English Historical Review* 108 (1993), 122–34.

"Harrington's *Oceana*: Origins and Aftermath, 1651–1660." In *Republicanism, Liberty, and Commercial Society, 1649–1776*, ed. David Wootton. Stanford University Press, 1994, pp. 11–38.

"James Harrington and *The Commonwealth of Oceana*, 1656." In *Republicanism, Liberty, and Commercial Society, 1649–1776*, ed. David Wootton. Stanford University Press, 1994, pp. 82–110.

"Marchamont Nedham and the Beginnings of English Republicanism, 1649–1656." In *Republicanism, Liberty, and Commercial Society, 1649–1776*, ed. David Wootton. Stanford University Press, 1994, pp. 45–81.

"Milton and Marchamont Nedham." In *Milton and Republicanism*, ed. David Armitage, Armand Himy, and Quentin Skinner. Cambridge University Press, 1995, pp. 156–80.

"John Milton and Oliver Cromwell." In *Soldiers, Writers, and Statesmen of the English Revolution*, ed. Ian Gentles, John Morrill, and Blair Worden. Cambridge University Press, 1998, pp. 243–64.

Zaret, David. "Religion, Science, and Printing in the Public Spheres in Seventeenth-Century England." In *Habermas and the Public Sphere.*, ed. Craig Calhoun. Cambridge, Mass.: The MIT Press, 1992, pp. 212–35.

Zwicker, Steven. "Models of Governance in Marvell's 'The First Anniversary,'" *Criticism* 16 (1974), 1–12.

Politics and Language in Dryden's Poetry: The Arts of Disguise. Princeton University Press, 1984.

Lines of Authority: Politics and English Literary Culture, 1649–1689. Ithaca: Cornell University Press, 1993.

Index

Illustrations appear in **bold**

NIGERIA

COUNTRY EXPLORERS

Mary N Oluonye

Lerner

Lerner Books • London • New York • Minneapolis

First published in the United Kingdom in 2009 by
Lerner Books,
Dalton House,
60 Windsor Avenue,
London SW19 2RR

Website address: www.lernerbooks.co.uk

This edition was updated and edited for UK publication by Discovery Books Ltd.,
Unit 3, 37 Watling Street, Leintwardine, Shropshire SY7 0LW

Words in **bold** type are explained in the glossary on page 46.

British Library Cataloguing in Publication Data

Oluonye, Mary N.
Nigeria. - (Country explorers)
1. Nigeria - Juvenile literature
 I. Title
966.9'054

 ISBN-13: 978 1 58013 490 3

Printed in Singapore

Table of Contents

Welcome!

Nigeria is a big country on the west coast of the **continent** of Africa. Nigeria is shaped a bit like a square. The countries of Niger and Chad lie at the top, or north, of the square. Benin sits to Nigeria's left, or west. To the right, or east, is Cameroon. The **Gulf** of Guinea forms Nigeria's bottom, or southern side. The gulf is part of the Atlantic Ocean.

Nigerians enjoy a sunny day at a sandy beach along the Gulf of Guinea.

ATLANTIC OCEAN

NIGER

CHAD

Argungu

RIVER SOKOTO

Kano

LAKE
CHAD

NIGERIA

BENIN

LAKE
KAINJI

Abuja ★

RIVER NIGER

RIVER BENUE

CAMEROON

Lokoja

KILOMETRES
200

RIVER NIGER

200
MILES

Lagos

NIGER DELTA

GULF OF
GUINEA

rainforest

coastal zone

savannah

plateau

mountains

★ country's capital

• city

5

The Land

Children from southern Nigeria can play on the beaches along the coast. Some children might take a trip to the **tropical rainforests** in the south. These wet, green forests provide homes for gorillas, chimpanzees, forest elephants and more.

Thick, green rainforests cover parts of southern Nigeria.

In the middle of the country, children can run through big, grassy fields called **savannahs**. Children in the dry and dusty north have fun too. This area is not far from the Sahara. People in that desert still travel around on camels!

Camels reach for leaves growing on trees in the dry north.

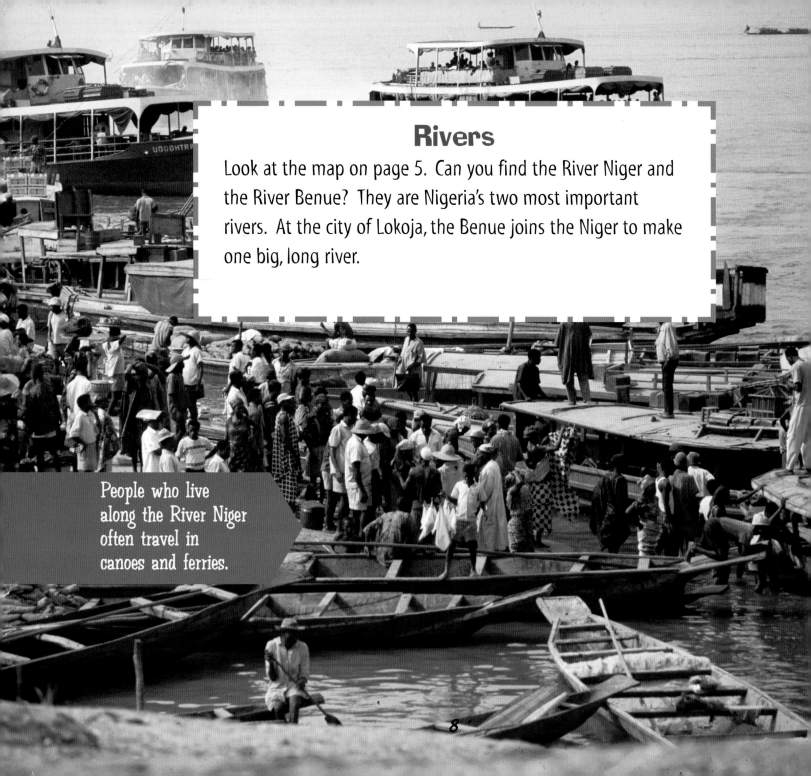

Rivers

Look at the map on page 5. Can you find the River Niger and the River Benue? They are Nigeria's two most important rivers. At the city of Lokoja, the Benue joins the Niger to make one big, long river.

People who live along the River Niger often travel in canoes and ferries.

During the rainy season, lots of rain falls on the Niger. The river floods. The water washes away roads and picks up soil. What happens to all that swirling mud? The river dumps it into the Niger **Delta**. This piece of land sits near the Gulf of Guinea.

Map Whiz Quiz

Take a look at the map on page 5. Trace the outline of Nigeria onto a piece of paper. Can you find the Gulf of Guinea? Mark this end of the map with an *S* for south. Do you see Benin? Mark it with a *W* for west. How about Niger? Mark this with an *N* for north. Then look for Cameroon. Mark it with an *E* for east. Use a blue crayon to trace the path of the Niger and Benue rivers. Colour the land of Nigeria green.

A large village sits along swamplands of the Niger Delta. The delta has huge amounts of the world's oil.

People

A long time ago, different groups of people ruled parts of Nigeria. Each group had its own language, religion and history. Two major groups, the Hausa and the Fulani, lived in the north. The Yoruba lived in the south-west. The Igbo lived in the south-east.

A Fulani girl carries a decorated pot on her head.

In the 1800s, Great Britain took over all of the land. The British named the area Nigeria, after the big river. In 1960, the British left and the people of Nigeria again ruled the country.

Students celebrate Nigeria's independence on 1 October 1960.

Hausa often decorate their homes with colourful patterns and shapes. This house is in the city of Kano.

Up North

Both the Hausa and the Fulani live north of the Niger and Benue rivers. The Hausa have farmed and traded in northern Nigeria for a long time. They grow rice, fruits and vegetables.

A Fulani man moves his zebus across the savannah.

Many Fulani move from place to place. They look for water and food for the animals they raise. Other Fulani live in Nigeria's cities.

13

Down South

Most Yoruba live in south-western Nigeria. Many fish or farm for a living. Some Yoruba farmers grow cacao beans. The beans are used to make chocolate.

This Yoruba woman and her daughter live in the city of Lagos.

14

The Igbo make their homes in the south-east. When the British first came to Nigeria, they hired the Igbo for important jobs. The Igbo started to live like the British. These days, many Igbo are doctors, lawyers or traders.

Three Igbo women in traditional dress pose for a photo.

Stay Cool!

Do you put on shorts when it is hot outside? Nigerian kids do too. But they also wear traditional clothes. Nigerian men and boys wear caps and long robes over loose trousers. The clothes are made of a thin cloth that keeps people cool.

These Yoruba men are wearing long, wide robes called *agbadas*.

Village girls show off their brightly coloured clothing.

Each group wears different colours. Hausa men like white. Fulani men like light yellow or blue. Yoruba men like patterns, and Igbo men like dark red.

Northern women wear robes and head coverings. Yoruba and Igbo women and girls wear long, colourful skirts, shirts and head scarves.

Villages and Cities

Where do you live? Most Nigerians live in villages and towns. Their houses are made of wood or mud. There is usually no electricity and there are no indoor toilets.

People in this Yoruba village built their homes out of wood.

Nigeria's cities are crowded. Many city dwellers live in high-rise blocks of flats. Lagos, in southern Nigeria, is the biggest city. Traffic jams are so bad they are called go-slows.

Kano is a northern city. It has a new section and an old section. Most Hausa live in the Old City. Its huge mud walls were built long ago to protect the Hausa from attackers.

Cars and buses make their way through the centre of Lagos.

19

Family Life

In Nigeria, mothers, fathers, brothers, sisters, grandparents, aunts, uncles and cousins are all part of one, big extended family. In small towns and villages, an extended family shares a group of houses called a compound. There are always other children around to play with! All grown-ups take turns watching the kids.

This is a Hausa compound.

All in the Family

Here are some Hausa words for family members.

grandfather	kaka
grandmother	kakani
uncle	kawu
aunt	iya
father	uba
mother	uwa
son	yaro
daughter	yarinya
brother	dan'uwa
sister	'yar'uwa

A family in Lagos poses for a photograph.

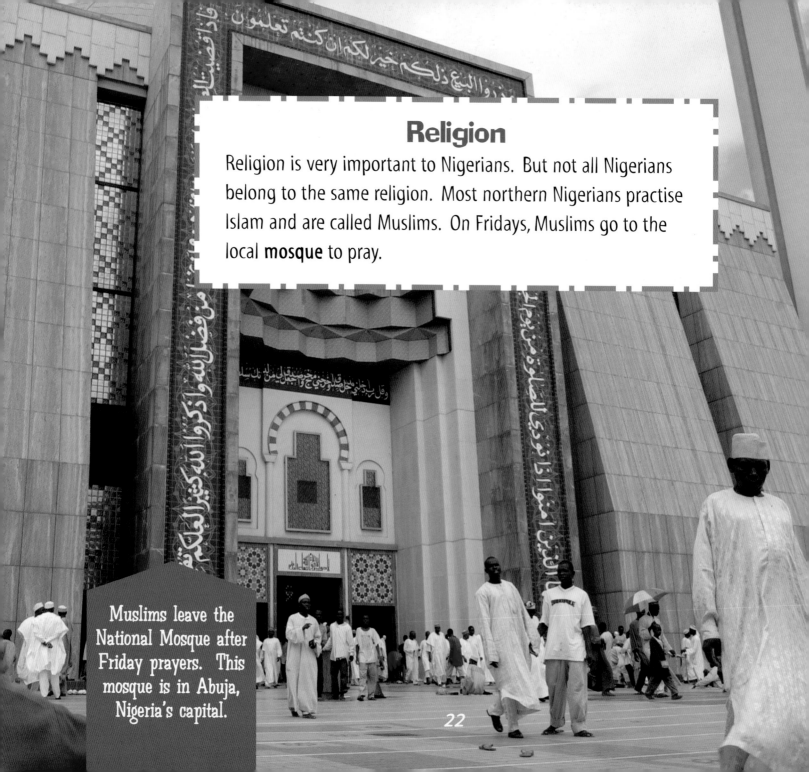

Religion

Religion is very important to Nigerians. But not all Nigerians belong to the same religion. Most northern Nigerians practise Islam and are called Muslims. On Fridays, Muslims go to the local **mosque** to pray.

Muslims leave the National Mosque after Friday prayers. This mosque is in Abuja, Nigeria's capital.

22

Most Christians live in the south. In Nigerian churches, the prayer leader says the Sunday service in English. Then another person says it in a local Nigerian language.

Many Nigerians also practise traditional African religions. They pray to many different gods. Sometimes, they ask dead relatives for help with problems.

Nigerian men sing, shout and chant during a Sunday service at a Christian church.

Names

After a baby is born, family and friends have a naming party. In Yoruba families, the oldest family member prays for the new baby and sprinkles the child's mouth with honey, water and salt. The honey is for the good times in the child's life. The water is supposed to bring greatness. The salt is for the hard times in life.

A Nigerian man holds his newborn child.

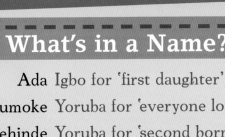

What's in a Name?

Ada Igbo for 'first daughter'

Jumoke Yoruba for 'everyone loves the child'

Kehinde Yoruba for 'second born of twins'

Taiye Yoruba for 'first born of twins'

Uzoamaka Igbo for 'the way is good'

All the guests put the mixture on their tongues too. The oldest family member calls out the baby's name. Everyone repeats the name. The ceremony ends with a big party. How did you get your name?

Twins in Nigeria are celebrated. Many Nigerians think twins are special gifts from God.

Celebrate!

Nigerians celebrate many events throughout the year. Some festivals happen when Nigerians gather food.

In Igbo towns and villages, people have a yam party. When the yams are ready to be harvested, villagers get together to celebrate. Cooks boil, roast or fry yams to make tasty Nigerian dishes. Everyone eats lots of yams, dances and plays games.

A farmer pulls yams out of the ground. Yams look like long potatoes.

The town of Argungu holds a fishing festival once a year. Thousands of men and boys wade into the River Sokoto carrying nets. They use the nets to try to scoop up the biggest fish.

Nigeria

Hi Mum & Dad!

I'm having fun here in Nigeria. Today, Granddad and I went to watch the Argungu Fishing Festival. It's the only time when people are allowed to fish in the river. That's a shame because some people were catching really big fish! Later, we watched dancing and wrestling. The wrestling matches are a pretty big deal. Boys come from other villages to compete. The winners get prizes.

See you soon!

Your

Your

Anywh

27

School

Nigerian children start school at six years old. In Nigeria, students wear school uniform. The school day lasts from 8.00 to 1.00. School is fun, but it is also hard work. After school, children must do their homework before they can play.

A Nigerian girl and boy study together at school.

Every few years, students have to take a big exam. If they pass, they can go to the next level of school.

The Market

Bananas here! Red-hot peppers for sale! Most Nigerians buy their food at outdoor markets. Markets are great places to buy fresh fruits and vegetables, meat, fish, cloth, pottery and almost everything else. Everyone tries to get the best price. Even children learn to **bargain**. The market is also a fun place to chat with friends.

Food sits out at a market in the north-eastern city of Bauchi.

Bargaining

Buyer: How much is that bunch of bananas?

Seller: 40 naira

Buyer: No, I'm sorry, but I can't pay 40 naira for them. (The buyer starts to walk away.)

Seller: Okay, customer, come back. How much do you want to pay for them?

Buyer: 10 naira.

Seller: 15 naira.

Buyer: How about 12? That's all I can pay.

Seller: Okay, okay.

A man sells carrots at a Nigerian street market.

Time for lunch! These Nigerian women prepare food over fires.

Food

Yeow! Drink plenty of milk during a Nigerian dinner because the food is hot! A popular dish is pepper soup. This thick, spicy soup is eaten with boiled cassava or yams.

After the cassava or yams are pounded, they look and taste a little like mashed potatoes. Nigerians roll a bit of the mashed cassava or yam into a ball. Then, they dip it into the soup and pop it into their mouths.

This Nigerian meal includes goat stew, peanuts, yams and cooking bananas called plantains.

Artwork

Long ago, Nigerian artists made **sculptures** out of metal, wood or ivory. Carving and sculpting are still popular. These days, artists **carve** wood to make the masks that dancers wear at festivals. Some artists carve pictures to tell stories. Artists sell their work at the market, in shops or even by the roadside.

Women use hot pieces of iron to carve designs onto calabash gourds.

34

In Kano, artists colour cloth in dye pits. They take white cloth and soak it in dyes made from indigo plants. The cloth becomes a shade of deep blue.

Artists use long sticks to stir cloth in dye pits.

Music and Dance

Do you like to beat on a drum? Then Nigeria might be just the place for you. The country has drums in all shapes and sizes. Drummers use their hands or sticks to beat to the music. Drum beats make people want to dance, clap or tap their feet.

A group of children perform a dance to juju music.

Different groups have their own music, dances and costumes.
Many dancers put on masks or wear bells around their ankles.
Some even walk on stilts!

Nigerian girls dance in Lagos.

A dancer wears a costume for a village festival.

Story Time

Long before there were books in Nigeria, grandparents taught children by telling stories. Most of these stories were folk tales. They explained where a group of people came from or how the world began.

A nursery school teacher tells children a story.

Storytelling is still alive in Nigeria. These days, many Nigerians write down their stories. Ifeoma Onyefulu writes books that are read by children all over the world. In *A Is for Africa,* she takes each letter of the alphabet and matches it to something in her homeland of Nigeria. What musical instrument do you think goes with *D*?

Chinua Achebe is a famous Nigerian writer.

Football Rules!

Nigerians love football! As soon as children start school, they begin to play football. School and club football teams meet every week or month to play games.

Nigerian boys play football in a field. Some famous footballers are Nigerian.

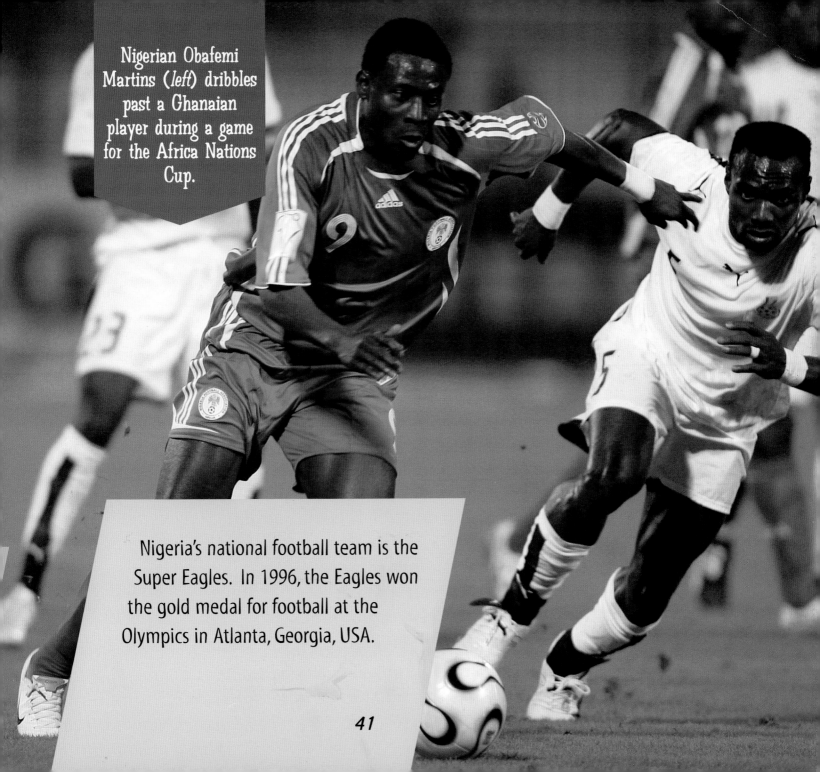

Nigerian Obafemi Martins (*left*) dribbles past a Ghanaian player during a game for the Africa Nations Cup.

Nigeria's national football team is the Super Eagles. In 1996, the Eagles won the gold medal for football at the Olympics in Atlanta, Georgia, USA.

Films and Games

Boom! Pow! Hiss! Splat! Nigerians are big film fans. They enjoy love stories, adventure movies and action films. When something sad happens on the screen, the people watching make crying or hissing sounds. During exciting scenes, the audience claps and shouts. Sometimes, people even act as if they are in the movie. They dodge fists or bullets.

A student walks by a wall covered with posters for Nigerian films.

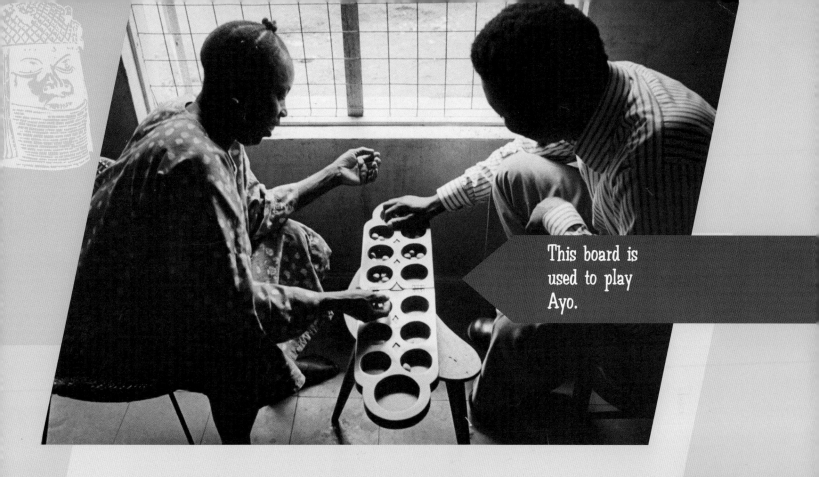

This board is used to play Ayo.

Nigerians like to play games too. Ayo is popular. It is a traditional Yoruba game. People have played it for many years. Two players move seeds or pebbles around a wooden board. Whoever ends up with the most seeds wins.

THE FLAG OF NIGERIA

Nigeria's flag is green and white. The green stripes stand for the country's agriculture, or farming. The white stripe in the centre is for peace and togetherness. Nigerians started using this flag in 1960. That is the year Nigeria became an independent country.

FAST FACTS

FULL COUNTRY NAME: Federal Republic of Nigeria

AREA: 923,768 square kilometres (356,669 square miles), about four times the size of the United Kingdom.

CAPITAL CITY: Abuja

OFFICIAL LANGUAGE: English

POPULATION: about 135,000,000

SOME MAJOR LANDFORMS:

MOUNTAIN RANGES: Shebshi, Mandara and Gotel

RIVERS: River Niger, River Benue

HIGHLANDS: Jos Plateau

LAKES: Kainji and Chad

SAVANNAHS: Guinea Savannah, Sudan Savannah and the Sahel

ANIMALS AND THEIR HABITATS:

SWAMPS AND RIVERS: Nile crocodiles, pygmy hippopotamuses, hairy mangrove crabs

FORESTS: drill monkeys, chimpanzees, hornbills

SAVANNAHS: African elephants roan antelopes, lions

GLOSSARY

bargain: a talk between a buyer and a seller about the cost of an item. Bargaining ends when both sides agree on a price.

carve: to shape an object from wood or stone

continent: any one of seven large areas of land. The continents are Africa, Antarctica, Asia, Australia, North America and South America.

delta: a triangle of land that forms where a river enters an ocean

folk tale: a story told by word of mouth

gulf: a part of an ocean or sea that reaches into land

mosque: a building where Muslims go to pray

savannah: a tropical grassland with some trees

sculpture: a work of art carved from wood or stone

tropical rainforest: a thick, green forest that gets lots of rain every year

TO LEARN MORE

Graham, Ian. *Nigeria* (Country Files) Franklin Watts Ltd, 2004.

Brownlie Bojang, Ali. *Nigeria* (We Come From) Hodder Wayland, 2002.

Onyefulu, Ifeoma. *Ikenna Goes to Nigeria* (Children Return to Their Roots) Frances Lincoln Children's Books, 2007.

Cooke, Tim. *Nigeria* (Fiesta) Franklin Watts Ltd, 2001.

WEBSITES

Motherland Nigeria: Kid Zone
http://www.motherlandnigeria.com/kidzone.html
Check out Boomie O's page of stories, games, pictures, music, jokes and more.

INDEX

The photographs in this book are used with the permission of: © Andrew Holt/Alamy, pp 4, 31; © Victor Englebert, pp 6, 7, 12, 13, 18, 25, 35; © Paul Almasy/CORBIS, pp 8, 36; © Jacob Silberberg/Getty Images, p 9; © Kerstin Geier; Gallo Images/CORBIS, p 10; © William Vanderson/Getty Images, p 11; © SuperStock, Inc./SuperStock, p 14; © Eye Ubiquitous/Alamy, p 15; © Juliet Highet/Art Directors, p 16; © John Cole/Alamy, p 17; © Betty Press/Panos Pictures, pp 19, 26; © Werner Forman/CORBIS, p 20; © Picture Contact/Alamy, p 21; © Jacob Silberberg/Panos Pictures, p 22; © Sven Torfinn/Panos Pictures, p 23; © Giacomo Pirozzi/Panos Pictures, pp 24, 29, 38; © Giles Moberly/Panos Pictures, p 27; © powderkeg stock/Alamy, p 28; © Gary Cook/Alamy, p 30; © Liba Taylor/CORBIS, p 32; © Envision/CORBIS, p 33; © Margaret Courtney-Clarke/CORBIS, p 34; © TIM GRAHAM/Alamy, p 37 (left); © David Levenson/Alamy, p 37 (right); © Ralph Orlowski/CORBIS, p 39; © Martin Adler/Panos Pictures, p 40; © Neil Marchand/Liewig Media Sports/CORBIS, p 41; © FINBARR O'REILLY/Reuters/CORBIS, p 42; © Owen Franken/CORBIS, p 43. Illustrations by © Bill Hauser/Independent Picture Service.

Cover: AP Photo/George Osodi

This book was first published in the United States of America in 2008.